Behind the Bedroom Door

getting it, giving it, loving it, missing it

EDITED BY

PAULA DERROW

Delacorte Press

BEHIND THE BEDROOM DOOR
A Delacorte Press Book / January 2009

Published by Bantam Dell
A Division of Random House, Inc.
New York, New York

Book design by Catherine Leonardo

Delacorte Press is a registered trademark of Random House, Inc., and the
colophon is a trademark of Random House, Inc.

Library of Congress Cataloging in Publication Data

Behind the bedroom door : getting it, giving it, loving it, missing it /
edited by Paula Derrow.
p. cm.
ISBN 978-0-385-34154-7 (hardcover)
1. Man-woman relationships—Anecdotes 2. Sex—Anecdotes. 3. Sex customs—
Anecdotes. I. Derrow, Paula.
HQ801.B365   2008
306.77082—dc22
2008031414

Printed in the United States of America
Published simultaneously in Canada

www.bantamdell.com

10 9 8 7 6 5 4 3 2 1

BVG

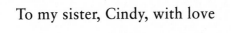

To my sister, Cindy, with love

CONTENTS

ACKNOWLEDGMENTS   xi

Introduction: Reflections from a Late Bloomer   1

1. IN PRAISE OF ONE-NIGHT STANDS
   Susan Cheever   15

2. TOMCATS IN LOVE
   Cheryl Strayed   21

3. TURN ME ON, TURN ME OFF
   Bella Pollen   35

4. OVERCOME
   Lauren Slater   48

5. OUCH, YOU'RE LYING ON MY HAIR!
   Valerie Frankel   57

6. TURNING THE OTHER CHEEK
   Deanna Kizis   64

7. PREGNANT PAUSE
   Pari Chang   76

8. UNDER THE INFLUENCE
    Anna Marrian   90

9. THE SWEETEST SEX I NEVER HAD
    Hope Edelman   104

10. SEXERCISE
    Abby Sher   126

11. LOOK BOTH WAYS BEFORE CROSSING
    Meredith Maran   137

12. LOST IN SPACE
    Julie Powell   151

13. OUT OF REACH
    Martha Southgate   167

14. TOYS IN THE BEDROOM
    Suzanne Paola   177

15. THE OVERNIGHT
    Susanna Sonnenberg   188

16. CONFESSIONS OF A FORMER SEX GEEK
    Abiola Abrams   200

17. MOMMY LUST
    Lori Gottlieb   211

18. LOOKING FOR MR. SNICKERS
    Jenny Lee   224

19. PROCREATIONAL SEX
    Brett Paesel   236

20. DO NOT ENTER
    Betsy Stephens   246

21. MY NOT-SO-KINKY SEX LIFE
    M. P. Dunleavey   261

22. FANTASY MAN
    Susan Shapiro   269

23. KISS POKER
    Stephanie Dolgoff   278

24. THE GREAT PRETENDER
    Jane Juska   292

25. IN THE BEGINNING
    Ali Liebegott   305

26. SEX WITH A (MUCH) YOUNGER MAN
    Elizabeth Cohen   315

ABOUT THE CONTRIBUTORS   329
ABOUT THE EDITOR   335

ACKNOWLEDGMENTS

This book was conceived with the help and support of so many people, far more than I can name here, not least of all the writers in these pages; I am deeply grateful for their willingness to write about sex truthfully. I would also like to thank my sister, Cindy Derrow, brother-in-law and legal maven Roy Kaufman, and nephews Jordan and Caleb for their boundless love and encouragement, as well as my parents, Joyce and Alfred Derrow, for tolerating my working on an admittedly risqué topic with grace and good humor. A heartfelt thanks to my second family at *Self* magazine—Lucy Danziger, Dana Points, Liz Egan, Kate Lewis, Cristina Tudino, Jean Cabacungan-Jarvis, Wendy Marcus, Stephanie Dolgoff, Laura Brounstein, Catherine Ryan, and Lauren Theodore, among others—for doing more than I could have dared hope to nurture me along the way. Thanks, too, to all my wonderful friends on both sides of the Atlantic and Pacific; this book would not have come to fruition without you all, especially the Off-Road Girls M. P. Dunleavey and Caroline Hwang, as well as Pam Kaufman, Nancy Wartik, Dennis Overbye, Toby Axelrod, Millicent Cooley, Diana Willensky Thompson (for teaching me about Rome), Gayle Forman, Andrzej Janerka, Hope Edelman, Lauren Slater,

Valerie Frankel, Susan Cheever, Bettina Elias Siegel, Meredith Maran, Glenn Gordon, Elizabeth DeVita-Raeburn, Paul Raeburn, and Ellen Seidman. Thanks also to my sharp-eyed editor at Bantam Dell, Danielle Perez, as well as to Nita Taublib and Marisa Vigilante. And a special *grazie* to Alexis Hurley, my wonderful and whip-smart agent, friend, and mentor in all things book-related.

Behind the Bedroom Door

INTRODUCTION: REFLECTIONS FROM A LATE BLOOMER

There's one in every crowd, the person who can always be counted on to slyly, subtly bring the conversation around to sex. I'll admit, it's usually me. I could blame that on the fact that I've spent the better part of the past twenty years working as an editor at various women's magazines, mining friends' sexual adventures (or lack thereof) for story ideas and splashy cover lines. Yet despite my journalist training, teasing forth honest conversations about sex isn't always easy, even when the subject arises spontaneously. I still recall a dinner with two close friends a few years ago: As the hour grew late, one woman, newly engaged and spurred by several vodka tonics, wondered aloud if either of us had ever tried "you know, back-door sex." There was a pause, I felt myself smiling stupidly, and before I could speak, I could tell from the sheepish expression on her face that she was sorry she'd ever mentioned it. We did get around to swapping experiences that night, but all of us, as close as we were, felt awkward about our attempts to open up.

Afterward, I found myself wondering why three sophisticated, been-around-the-block, liberal-minded types had gotten so embarrassed by the mere mention of a sexual taboo, and a relatively tame one at that. It's not that I'd never had frank sex talks with friends: Several times a year we'd dish over a new lover or snipe about a lackluster ex, and there had certainly been more than one drinks-fueled discussion over dinner about vibrators and blow-job techniques. But as we got older and many of us occupied ourselves with husbands and households and jobs and new babies, these exchanges happened less and less. When they did, they mostly served to remind me how much remained unsaid, how little the women I know talked about the awkward couplings and surprising urges, the long dry spells or messy, mind-blowing encounters that make up a person's sexual history.

Partly, I think, this silence stems from fear—fear of being exposed as inadequate or worse, of being boring. Living in an all-sex-all-the-time culture may be liberating in many ways, but it can also breed shame—shame for not keeping up, for not being invited to the party. When most of what women read, see, and hear about sex has little to do with their own everyday, perhaps less-than-HBO-worthy experiences, there's a disconnect, which breeds anxiety: How can any one of us know that what we feel and do is normal, that we're good in bed, that our desires are kinky, tame, or somewhere in between?

The twenty-six brave, funny, ballsy, smart, searching writers in *Behind the Bedroom Door* explore the sexual territory it's so tough to talk about, telling the not-so-ordinary stories of women in their twenties through their seventies, black and white, gay and straight, in love or embittered or perpetually hooked up. Because though we live in a time when strangers' intimate dealings are available on TV and online for everyone to see, when it's possible to peer directly into bedrooms across the country via Web cam, getting to the truth about sex hasn't necessarily gotten easier. With few exceptions, what's portrayed in the media is as inauthentic as

Lucy and Ricky Ricardo throwing each other good-night kisses from their separate twin beds.

On Nerve.com, for instance, a dating and "literary erotica" Web site, I came upon this typical blog from a twenty-one-year-old waitress:

> *I headed over to a bar...the bartender was a sexual conquest from a few months back who didn't return my calls. Free drinks, easy chatter, knowing smiles all around . . . My new guy [showed] up . . . about an hour later and the bartender jokes, "What, you're bringing boys around here to make me jealous?" Later, when I share a line with him, he kisses my forehead and grins and I wonder whether I've really chosen the evening's most enviable penis.... In the bathroom, a blue-eyed blonde waif walks in [and] asks me if I'd like company in my stall. Um. Yes? Yes, please? She closes the door behind her and all of a sudden I'm inspecting her tattoos and putting my hands all over her.*

Are most women really so nonchalant about sex in real (as opposed to virtual) life? Certainly, in the mostly female memoir-writing workshops I teach in New York City, the students in their early twenties, especially, seem almost bored by sex, though they write about it incessantly. There's a toughness to many of these women: One student described herself in an essay as an "alpha female," switching off between her men and women best friends on a whim.

Yet one thing I've learned from delving into women's intimate stories is that appearances aside, for many—maybe even most—of us, it's tough to have sex "like a man," to completely divorce emotion from the coming together of two bodies. I've certainly never been good at it. Then again, I was a late bloomer, sexually speaking—no switch-hitting or wandering hands in bathroom stalls for me. I got my first kiss at age seven from a nine-year-old boy at a Jewish sleep-away camp in the Catskills. It was all downhill from there. When puberty hit, I morphed from cute girl to gal pal—a slightly awkward, moderately overweight teen who was half proud, half horrified by the appearance of my ample breasts, hips, and pubic hair.

By the summer after my senior year of high school, all my decidedly nice-girl friends were intent on "doing it" before heading off to college. My best friend lost her virginity to the twenty-four-year-old manager of a car wash where she worked on weekends. "How was it? Did it hurt?" I asked, eager for the details I knew were coming. "It was okay," she said, her lack of enthusiasm more shocking to me than any act she could have described. I wanted to know what she was feeling, whether she'd been scared, if the experience had changed her somehow. I wanted us to talk the way we'd talked a week earlier, when both of us had still been virgins. But my friend's new, grown-up-seeming coolness left me intimidated. Somehow, I knew not to press her for details.

I'd hoped sex would come more easily to me once I got to college. By sophomore year, I'd even acquired a "hometown honey," as we called them, a tall, lanky, fiercely introverted boy I'd known slightly in high school. He was as sexually inexperienced as I, and his existence at a small-town campus six hours away gave me an excuse to skip the hot, beery-smelling parties to which we Harvard underclassmen traveled in packs. I had romantic crushes, but the objects of my affection invariably ended up spending late nights in my dorm room talking about the girls (or guys) they were truly interested in, while I dispensed sage advice. It was only during the occasional visit from that long-distance boyfriend and our hours spent groping and grappling on my single bed that I realized I was missing something I badly wanted. Though I had the opportunity to have sex (which, like Bill Clinton did twenty-odd years later, I defined strictly as intercourse), I felt too self-protective to go through with it on those infrequent visits from my beau. What if I did, then felt bereft when he left? What if sex caused me to fall inappropriately in love, when I knew the two of us would not be together forever? But when I mentioned my agonized back-and-forthing to a friend, she only laughed and told me to "go for it."

It was no coincidence that I chose to do my senior-year thesis on D. H. Lawrence, notorious breaker of class and sexual barriers and author of the once-scandalous *Lady Chatterley's Lover*. If I had to spend an entire year writing one paper, I reasoned, I could at least make it about sex. After all, my college roommates and I lived so close together that it was impossible to escape the muffled sounds (and sometimes, when I couldn't avoid it, sights) of the couplings going on around me. There were diaphragms on the mantelpiece above the wood-burning fireplace and birth control pills spilling messily off bathroom shelves, casually displayed badges of honor. But my friends and I weren't exactly talking about sex, at least not in the way I needed to. I felt fuzzy on the specifics of what, exactly, was happening behind all those closed doors: Was everyone having orgasms? Did my friends always have sex with the guys (or "men," as we so self-consciously called them) they brought back to their beds? My questions felt too prying and naive to ask.

I graduated in 1985 with a bachelor's degree in British history and literature and the dawning of the AIDS crisis, as innocent as any twenty-one-year-old with a taste for D. H. Lawrence could be. I wasn't a virgin anymore, technically at least, but I still felt like a raw beginner in the intercourse department. My shy guy and I had both "lost it" on the night of my twentieth birthday on a summer evening when my parents were out of town. Much of our foreplay consisted of giggling, alternating with instruction giving; mechanics didn't seem to be a strong point for either one of us. Physically, the experience was anticlimactic in both senses of the word. I'd felt far more aroused, been far more satisfied, during our hours-long make-out sessions on the lime-green vinyl sofa in my family room, even with one ear perpetually straining for my mother's footsteps padding down the hall.

After our mutual deflowering, my boyfriend sprawled across my parents' bed with a dreamy smile on his face. He wanted to cuddle, but I was preoccupied with getting rid of the "evidence." ("What if my mother spotted the used condom in the kitchen trash?") I was a good girl, after all, unskilled at deception. So I wrapped the condom in a layer of aluminum foil, then another and another, until there was a wad the size of a baseball lying at the bottom of the can. Inconspicuous it wasn't.

Not until I was out on my own, living in New York City, rubbing shoulders and bodies with business-suited men on the subway, flirting hesitantly with the sexily professorial editors at work, did I begin to revel in the very new feeling of being a single woman in Manhattan with no one watching me. I'd landed a job as an editorial assistant at an old-school book publishing house and moved into a barely affordable apartment with two women I didn't know. Maybe it was the exhilarating freedom or the cigarettes I'd surreptitiously smoke now and then while perched on the window seat in my living room, but my extra pounds—padding that had helped me to effectively keep most men away—started melting. I began going on dates with guys who slipped me their numbers at parties, flirted with me in bars. For the first time in my life, I felt a little bit sexy.

One night, I had dinner with a man I'd known slightly years before. I'd always had a crush on him; he'd always had a steady girlfriend. Now he was single and a mutual friend had helpfully fixed us up. Back at my place, as we settled on my couch for a glass of wine, he ran a finger along my newly revealed collarbone, and I realized I had no idea what was expected of me—and no one I could ask. It would be fun to be in bed with this man, to have him touch me. But though he might eagerly embrace me, what would he think of me? Would he smirk to himself that I was a slut, ready to jump into bed at the first opportunity? What, I wondered, did people do, sexually, on a first date in New York City? So I plunged ahead and took the middle ground: "I want to fool around, but I'm not going to have sex with you," I announced. If he was taken aback, he didn't show it. We went straight to my bedroom.

Eventually, I moved to another editorial assistant position, this time at a glossy, now-defunct women's magazine. For $17,500 a year, a big bump up from my first job, I answered phones and typed manuscripts in triplicate on an IBM Selectric. I quickly discovered that story ideas about sex were much in demand, which put me at a distinct disadvantage. In recent months, I'd started to gain weight again, the appreciative glances and dinner invitations dwindling with each added pound. Truthfully, I hadn't felt quite comfortable with the slender-but-curvy version of myself and the attention it garnered. "I'm the same person," I'd grumble to myself. "So why didn't anyone want me before?" I could only conclude, sorrowfully, that men were as superficial as I'd feared.

So I trained my focus away from men and toward my new job and the five other overeducated assistants who shared the drab, gray-carpeted space that made up the articles department. At first, I assumed my colleagues were like the women in our magazine's often semifictional articles: always confident at parties, bold in the bedroom, fit, forward, and polished. In story meetings, everyone talked knowledgeably of G-spots and multiple orgasms and expressed strong opinions on boxers versus briefs. When one of our writers pitched an article on how she survived a single year without sex—which, from what I could see, was exactly where I was headed—not only did we immediately draw her up a contract, but we deemed her tale of woe freakish enough to merit a plug on the cover.

Yet despite my coworkers' high heels, good haircuts, and impossibly short skirts, I eventually figured out that most were less self-confident about sex, or at least love, than they appeared, ping-ponging between bad boyfriends and occasionally crying quietly into their salads after a particularly nasty breakup. As for the friends I socialized with after work, most, like me, weren't getting enough sex for an ongoing conversation. Instead, we talked of our budding careers, downing bottles of cheap red wine while deeply probing each other's psyches. I took comfort in the fact that most women my age seemed a bit lonely and lost, too, yet it felt too painful to address my biggest concern directly: Would I ever participate in the sexual plenitude that by all rights should be mine? I was, after all, in my early twenties, supposedly at my most physically desirable and free. If sex wasn't feeling like a possibility for me now, would it ever?

A year of celibacy stretched into six, punctuated by several job changes, steady progress up the masthead, and, in those pre-Internet-dating days, the very occasional, utterly unmemorable blind date. Then friends set me up with a short, smart, bespectacled journalist who was easy to talk to and seemed quirky in a nice way. On our second date, after a dinner filled with talk about writing, the city, and our families, this man and I spent several hours sitting on my stoop, kissing, laughing, talking. "You beguile me," he told me, kissing me some more, his little round glasses glinting in the moonlight. At the relatively ripe age of twenty-eight, I fell in love. Soon after that night, I found myself in his bed, a pristine oasis in the middle of the messiest apartment I'd ever seen.

I had gone six years without sex, and I was nervous. Or, at least, my body was. "It's like trying to fit a round peg in a square hole," my new beau remarked after several minutes of fruitless maneuvering. Seeing my stricken face, he kissed me and said, "Don't worry. There's always tomorrow."

And there was. The more we practiced, the better sex became. The better it became, the more I wanted. I felt like a sixteen-year-old boy trapped in a twenty-eight-year-old woman's body—I couldn't get enough. How did people accomplish anything in the world? Why did anyone bother getting out of bed at all? I wanted to talk about what I was feeling, shout about it from the tops of New York City's fire escapes, to anyone who'd listen.

Except I soon realized that it was unseemly to crow about how much fun I was having in bed. Apparently, not all couples had sex several times a night and lolled in rumpled, warm sheets all weekend. Even with my closest friends, I felt constrained when it came to owning up to my desire. What if, as I suspected, I loved sex too much?

*   *   *

Now, some fifteen years later, still single and dating, with countless crushes, a few great loves, and a lone, unsatisfying one-night stand in my wake, I'm once again looking for an-swers about sex. I read about threesomes and couple-swapping parties and swings attached to ceilings. (Don't the upstairs neighbors complain?) And I continue to wonder, as I did in my college days, what other women think, feel, and do in bed, how I measure up.

And so, the idea for this anthology. When I started men-tioning to friends and acquaintances that I was putting to-gether a collection of essays about the sexual feelings and experiences women are afraid to talk about, the stories spilled out. I was working on a book. I am a professional ed-itor at *Self,* a national magazine for women. Friends and strangers of both genders suddenly seemed to feel as if it was okay to talk openly to me about sex.

At a party one evening, a Texan woman with frosted hair and sparkly eye shadow told me she felt guilty about rejecting her husband's sexual advances the night before. "I needed to catch a plane early," she explained. "Besides, all he wanted was a quickie. Why should I bother taking off my clothes or messing up my hair?" Another night, at dinner with a recently married couple, the wife—a dark, serious intellectual in her late thirties—leaned toward me as soon as her husband slipped outside to take a call on his cell. "I'm only telling you this be-cause you're doing a book," she began. "But I'd be interested in having a threesome, with another woman." Another day, while hiking with a group of women during a vacation in Utah, our guide, a bright-eyed seventy-three-year-old former Mormon, told me she'd been married six times, had seven children—and had never had an orgasm. "But I'm done with men," she said with a laugh, stepping nimbly over the rocks in our path. "I wouldn't want anyone to see me naked now." Then there was the forty-one-year-old writer and mom who told me matter-of-factly, "I don't think married women with kids are interested in sex at all. My husband and I don't even sleep in the same bed anymore."

Not everyone was equally forthcoming. "It's fine to talk about sex when you're single and it doesn't mean as much," one financial editor said. "But if you're married, it seems too personal." A forty-nine-year-old declared, "Talking about sex is a betrayal of my husband." And a willowy, soft-spoken thirty-nine-year-old, who'd had long dry spells of her own, said, "For all the sex out there, I think we still feel embarrassed about admitting that it's not always so great for us."

Yet however circumspect, nearly everyone confessed to a yearning for other women's stories. "I wonder if my friends have sex more or less or better than I do, or have more fun. I want to know if there are any secrets my girlfriends have discovered" is the way a newly pregnant writer put it in an e-mail.

These conversations convinced me that women are hungry for a book that tells the truth about sex in real life. *Behind the Bedroom Door* is that book, its twenty-six original essays meant to open a window into the libidos and longings of women of every age and in every life phase. In so doing, it blasts away the assumptions we make about what exactly is going on in other people's bedrooms.

In her essay "In Praise of One-Night Stands," Susan

Cheever's paean to the joys, adventures, and risks that accompany casual sex, the author upends conventional notions about women, coupling up, and sentiment. In the harrowing "Sexercise," Abby Sher comes clean about her view of sex as a means of burning calories, of making herself disappear. In "Overcome," Lauren Slater contemplates the hurt, anger, and, sometimes, unexpected pleasures of a virtually sexless marriage, while Valerie Frankel takes a decidedly lighter view of things in "Ouch, You're Lying on My Hair!" Hope Edelman makes a case for innocence in "The Sweetest Sex I Never Had," Cheryl Strayed for fidelity in "Tomcats in Love." And in "Lost in Space," Julie Powell gives an unflinchingly honest account of the tempestuous affair that rocked her marriage and worldview.

As for my own story, it wasn't until my forties that I experienced the best of what sex could be: an ever-evolving adventure, the chance to finally let myself fall away from judgments (especially my own) and see how much pleasure I could stand. My weight still goes up and down depending on how sexual I'm feeling, and I inevitably experience the occasional dry spell and spate of loneliness. But I also know that good sex and deep love are possible no matter what I weigh, that there are men who love my curves, the pleasure I take in pleasure. At forty-five, I feel sexier, more confident, and freer than I ever have, in part because I've immersed myself in the tales of the women who have contributed to this collection. Because if talking about sex honestly is difficult, writing about it—committing words to paper—requires a double dose of courage. These stories, all so different, make it clear that for women, sex changes all the time, along with our hormones, our psyches, our partners. It swoops, soars, and occasionally stalls, always evolving, happily often for the better, as we learn what we love and what we won't tolerate, what we can give and allow ourselves to get in return.

I might have discovered this sooner had I been able to talk frankly with other women early on. Talking about sex is necessary—it allows us to acquire the confidence that it's okay to go at our own pace, to appreciate the joy we're capable of experiencing, not virtually, not vicariously or voyeuristically, but face-to-face. Let the conversation begin.

In Praise of One-Night Stands

SUSAN CHEEVER

Growing up in the fifties, I heard many stern warnings about one-night stands. Men don't respect you afterward. They won't buy the cow if they can get the milk for free. Personally, I don't like being compared to a cow. Maybe that's why I've always loved one-night stands.

I never was one for picking up men in bars or in the next seat on an airplane. I usually met them at parties—New York is a city of parties. The two of us would start to chat, and the chat became something more serious. We talked about work and our ambitions. We'd find a common interest in Edith Wharton, or Fellini, or the Boston Red Sox. Soon we were sitting somewhere private. We would have another scotch or another glass of wine.

Then we would begin to touch each other—a hand on a shoulder to make a point, a light squeeze of the knee if a joke was particularly funny. I felt that familiar hot and cold feeling, that soaring and sinking, which I knew was my mind being overwhelmed by my physical excitement. I let it happen. Sometimes we would leave for a drink at a neighborhood bar; sometimes we simply took a taxi back to my apartment. In the cab, we kissed. I wondered about the condition of my apartment—had I made the bed? We kissed again and I forgot about housekeeping. Soon, we would be in my unmade bed, embracing each other and experiencing the awkward, thrilling moments of sex with a stranger.

If you are looking for love, sexual intimacy can be a shortcut. It is among the fastest ways to get to know another person. During sex, we show physical parts of ourselves that are usually kept covered; we display our private likes and dislikes. In its moments of unconscious response to physical pleasure, the body reveals a great deal of involuntary information: a need to dominate or a difficulty following orders, whether we are good at letting go or are uncomfortable with how we look. All this is revealed in the two-person drama of the sex act.

It's scary to do something that lets another person in on so much private information, but it's also ruthlessly efficient. Dinner in a fancy restaurant or even a long conversation in a dimly lit bar can be completely misleading. In e-mails and letters and telephone calls, people can act their way into being someone different. It's easy to fool someone with a turn of phrase. Sex tells the truth.

Most erotic fantasies are about one-night stands. In my own, I imagine having sex with someone I've started dancing with at a party; we end up in a bedroom on a pile of coats left there by the other partygoers. I smell the scent of someone's perfumed lining and feel the softness of mink against my naked legs.

Somehow, I never fantasize about sex with my husband in a marital double bed that I've neatly made with hospital corners, or with a man who has just changed our baby's diapers or emptied the dishwasher. Marriage can be sexy, too, but in my experience, it is never the stuff of fantasy. I think this is nature's way of telling us that sexual intimacy is distinct from emotional and financial and domestic intimacy. What's wonderful in bed can be disastrous in the nursery or the kitchen.

My deepest connections to men have often been at times when sex seemed like an impossibility, or at least an unpleasant afterthought. Two weeks after the birth of my beloved son, his father went to my favorite lingerie store and bought me a fabulous black lace teddy. I oohed and aahed politely as I unwrapped the layers of pink tissue, but the truth was that the skimpy fabric looked like an artifact from another life. Childbirth and its aftermath had given me enough discomfort for a lifetime; I could no longer imagine why a woman would ever wear such an uncomfortable thing.

When my husband and I finally did have sex after the baby was born, it was without the seductions of black lace. It was clumsy. Tentative. It felt like sex between two people who had just had their first conversation. It was, in many ways, like a one-night stand.

*   *   *

When I was a young woman in the sixties, I knew my life wouldn't really start until I was married. In a world without legal abortion, one-night stands were both dangerous and prohibited by parents, teachers, and everyone else in authority. So I planned to sleep only with men who were willing to marry me. The trouble is, my sexual enthusiasm far outweighed my desire to be a twenty-year-old housewife. Still, I managed to restrain myself: By the time I did get married at what I thought was the ripe old age of twenty-three, I'd been sexually intimate with only a few men I'd assumed I would be with for the long haul. It wasn't until the sad end of my first marriage eight years later that I was released into the wild, fevered atmosphere of the 1970s.

I discovered that a one-night stand is the erotic manifestation of carpe diem—only we are seizing the night instead of the day. Though sex with a long-term partner is many things, it is not that. With a husband or a boyfriend, there is the delicious certainty that pleasure will be both given and received. Sex feels like a series of shared secrets, a passage through a maze leading to the most wonderful feelings available to human beings. With a long-term partner, I can relax. He is not surprised by the moles on my back, nor is he self-conscious about the hair on his shoulders. There's a kind of transcendence to married sex, a connection that is more than the sum of body parts linked and flesh responding, as if this most physical of acts was also the threshold to spiritual intimacy.

One-night stands are spiritual in another way: They are sex without expectations. They are a leap of faith because you never know quite where they will lead. My one-night stands were never planned, and they were always, in their own ways, mysterious. Occasionally they took place in the afternoon in a hotel. Once, there was a dazzling ten-minute interlude bent over a washing machine with a fellow Sunday luncheon guest in someone else's suburban laundry room. When I was an editor at *Newsweek*, they sometimes happened early in the morning in the little infirmary room next to the copy machine. At the time, staying at the office until the next morning and editing in the same clothes was a rite of passage for anyone with ambition. One night, a writer I admired was also working late, and we ended up walking out of the lobby together and into the romantic early-morning streets. Remember Marlon Brando singing about that time of day in *Guys and Dolls*? "The street belonged to the cop, and the janitor with the mop..." The writer offered to see me home.

When we got there, I opened a bottle of wine. "Let's drink this in bed," he said. Afterward, we both fell asleep for a few hours, and I woke up thinking how much happier I'd be if he wasn't there. I admired his work, not his body. He snored. He took up a lot of space in my bed. When he finally roused himself, he halfheartedly asked if I wanted to go out for breakfast, and I pleaded a headache. After that, we went back to being friendly officemates. We had tried out a different kind of relationship and found that it didn't work.

Most of my one-night stands have taken place in the conventional precincts of a bedroom, preceded by a few coincidences and some conversation. That didn't make them any less surprising. One-night stands can be nothing more than a few hours of pleasure, or they can be the beginning of something much more important, and it's impossible to tell until it's too late. Another man I slept with never intending anything serious was married to an acquaintance of mine, but she was far away. It was summer in New York City, when wives and children stayed in the country and all domestic rules seemed breakable. It was too hot to feel guilty. Slowly, with a lot of laughter and in the kind of emotionally woozy state that results from staying up too long, we repaired to my bedroom. The sex wasn't particularly memorable; we were both tired and quite drunk. I fell into a fitful sleep and woke to find myself sheltered in his arms. His flesh was pleasantly warm; he smelled good. I drifted off again, feeling buoyant and safe. When we officially woke up a few hours later we tried to pretend that everything was normal. I made coffee and changed the sheets. He got on the telephone with an editor, then called his wife and checked on his children. It was no use. By the time we wandered out to lunch we both knew something huge had happened. Our connection felt capricious, as if there had been a potion in my nightcap, or as if a rascally little boy had aimed an arrow in our direction. We sat in a bar holding hands, reveling in our exhilaration at having found each other and in our suffering at having to part. It was as if we had been together forever; I felt an uncanny sense of destiny fulfilled. The world, however, didn't care. I had to be in Boston for dinner. He had a plane to catch.

That one-night stand led to a thirty-five-year love affair—the most enduring love of my life. Some kind of deep intimacy between us had been released, an intimacy that remains decades later. After more than fifteen years of obstacles—my guilt, his guilt and pain, limited resources, our own confusion—we eventually married and had a wonderful son. We are now separated. I had no idea what was going to happen when I casually invited him up to my apartment. If I had known, would I have gone home alone?

That is the real danger of a one-night stand. Not that it will lead to nothing, but that it will lead to everything. In this way, casual sex is excruciatingly hazardous. Those who are not ready to have their life changed should probably abstain.

Tomcats in Love

CHERYL STRAYED

The night I met my husband he drove me home in a car that he'd inherited from his recently deceased stepfather. It was a strange car, big and dark and posh and not at all indicative of the person my future husband was, though I didn't know that then. Before my husband owned this car, he didn't have a car at all. He had a bike and a bus pass and a very bad reputation for being what my mother used to call a tomcat. But I didn't know this either. And had I known the part about him being a tomcat on that first night, as we exchanged scraps of paper with our respective names and phone numbers written on them, I wouldn't have cared. I was a tomcat, too. I didn't know it then, but at last I'd met my match.

We hadn't been on a date that first night. We'd met among a small group of mutual friends who'd gathered for dinner at a place called Esparza's in Portland, Oregon. It was late September, a week after my twenty-seventh birthday. I was new to the city, scrambling for a job, fresh off a summer-long solitary adventure hiking the Pacific Crest Trail. He was thirty-four, an independent filmmaker, and so truly handsome that even other men, I'd later learn, couldn't help but comment on his mighty good looks—straight men, men who did not usually feel compelled to speak about such things. Driving to the restaurant, my housemate had prepared me for my future husband's unspeakable, indisputable beauty, so much so that once I finally laid eyes on him, I reacted the way I do when someone raves too much about a movie or a book: with a mild sense of disappointment, not entirely convinced he was worthy of all the acclaim.

He wasn't convinced either, it quickly became apparent, which of course won me over. Plus, it was true that he was not only a very good-looking guy, but funny and smart and genuinely kind. He asked questions that he actually wanted to hear the answers to. As the night passed, the group of us migrated from the restaurant to a nearby bar to hear a band. There, perched together on a pair of stools wedged in between the doorway to the women's room and the crowd, we chatted about things large and small—relationships we'd both had that had ended in the recent past, movies we loved, whether or not it was ridiculous or cool that the lead singer of the band on the stage was dressed in drag, the death of my young mother from cancer five years before. I wasn't so much smitten as drawn in, curious about his own evident curiosity, lit up by the way his mind seemed to move along similar currents as mine, and charmed by his total lack of pretense.

Still, I wasn't looking for a boyfriend. That he drove me home that night was less about a spark of romance between us than it was that I needed a ride. As we drove, we talked about the possibility of going for a run together sometime. When he parked in front of my house, we exchanged numbers and said a platonic goodbye.

His name was Brian Lindstrom, I saw once I went inside and inspected the scrap of paper he'd given me. A good Minnesota name, I thought immediately, having grown up there among a gaggle of Finns and Danes and Norwegians and Swedes. There's even a town in Minnesota called Lindstrom. I'd bought a lamp in an antique store there once. I remember thinking of all of that then—of the town and the old lamp and of how much his name was like the names of all the boys and men I'd known growing up—and then I put the scrap of paper down and went on with things, which is to say, my life without Brian Lindstrom.

I was intrigued by him but not driven to do much about it, focused as I was on carving out a place in a new city, desperate for a job that would support my real work as a writer. I was living what I now know was the last year of an era in my life that I have witnessed others pass through, sometimes at nineteen, sometimes at forty-one, usually in the middle to late twenties. It's neither childhood nor adolescence nor adulthood, but a horrible, glorious, gut-wrenching, soul-searching, hilarious, and painful mash of all three. A phase of life when you're a free agent yet not actually grown-up, still pinned entirely by the weight of all the crazy, sad, sweet, absurd, inexplicable, wondrous, and heartbreaking things that your family and your first love or two did or didn't do. A time in which you're trying desperately to toss it off or make sense of it, and in the course of doing so you either repress it all completely, blow it entirely out of proportion, or both. You do things like get a Celtic tattoo across the upper rim of your ass or constantly wear a beat-up cowboy hat even though your parents were math professors in New York City. Or you develop a wild affinity for bowling or Virgin Mary figurines and claim that you are doing these things not because they are incredibly hip things to do but, rather, because they are an original and fierce expression of the original and fierce person you actually are. It's a time when, in fact, you don't have a clue who you are. Or you do have a clue, you have a whole pile of accumulating clues, but you're lost in that era that I will go ahead and call the wilderness of self, finding your way amidst a lovely mounting shit pile of clues, each of them telling a true story about you. You're in the deep, dark, mythic business of piecing all those clues together while attempting to look like you're merely hanging out and having the time of your life.

That's the era I'm talking about.

That's where I was the night I met Brian Lindstrom, not exactly in that time, but rather departing it. I was halfway out across the bridge from one era to the next, and it turns out that's where Brian Lindstrom was, too. We weren't conscious of this. What we were—separately—conscious of is that we'd each reached the end of a certain kind of living and wanted to find another, which in huge part meant coming to terms with our relationships with past lovers. We'd both had plenty. Lovers we'd loved, lovers we didn't love, lovers we didn't even entirely recall the names of, lovers we'd hoped to forget as soon as possible. It meant coming to terms with our inner tomcat.

We were different kinds of tomcat. I'd earned my stripes by committing to, then cheating on, my first—now ex—husband. Brian, on the other hand, was the noncommittal, keep-things-vague-so-no-one-gets-hurt, the road's-my-middle-name kind of tomcat. By the time I met him he'd slept with so many women he couldn't possibly count them. He'd been serious enough about only three to promise sexual fidelity, and he'd never kept his word.

"Why?" I'd asked him in the early months of our relationship, equal parts outraged on behalf of his ex-girlfriends and confounded by the behavior of this man who I knew was deeply loath to hurt anyone. Brian, I'd come to know, was not simply a nice guy. He was actually a very good man, considerate and compassionate, the kind of person who opens doors for people and gives thoughtful, handmade gifts. He brings his kindness into his work as well. He makes documentaries about drug addicts and ex-cons, people with AIDS and mental illness. He teaches filmmaking to kids who are on probation and out of luck. And he pours himself into these things without caring how long they will take or how little he's paid, believing always that what matters is doing work that does.

"He's so kind," all my friends said after they met him. They could see it immediately, the gentle light in his eyes. They didn't know he'd duped each and every one of the women he'd professed to love. He couldn't explain why. He said he was horny and scared and young. He wasn't proud of his actions; he didn't swagger or brag. He was discreet about his many affairs, a tomcat in disguise.

Plus, he reminded me when we talked of such things, he'd never actually been married to any of his exes. He hadn't vowed a thing. I was the one who had done that. I'd made a vow, married at barely twenty, tied myself down. Too, too young, I quickly realized. But instead of simply backing out as lovingly as I could, I betrayed my husband by embarking on a string of one-night stands until finally I couldn't live with myself any longer and confessed the whole ugly truth.

I'd divorced the year before I moved to Portland, a year during which I struggled to understand how I'd managed to unravel a relationship that had once been so sweet and strong; why I'd betrayed my best friend for something as absurd as sex. How little sex meant to me and yet how large it loomed. The sex I'd had while cheating hadn't been revelatory or meaningful. It was interesting. It was mildly hot. But it didn't come anywhere close to the actual intimacy I'd shared with my then-husband. I didn't need it to. I needed it to feel like an adventure, an exploration, a way of experiencing a mysterious part of human nature. It was my small cry of *yes!* in a world that often insisted on no. Sprung free of my marriage, I thought that perhaps I didn't believe in monogamy. How else to explain how choked I felt as a wife, even though I genuinely loved my husband? Monogamy was a farce, a trap, and impossible to honestly maintain, I argued to myself and to anyone who would listen. I had facts to prove it, both scientific and anecdotal. I was a tomcat in theory.

And in practice, too. In the year after my divorce, I continued what I'd started at the end of my marriage, having casual sex with a menagerie of men. Monogamy was easy to relinquish then, though occasionally I'd wonder what I'd think of monogamy once I met someone who made more than a fleeting appearance in my bed. Perhaps I'd be faithful to him for a while, I'd think abstractly. But in the end, it wasn't a man who changed my ways.

As the months passed, that heady time gave way to a slow but sure realization that I came to all on my own: Sex with one recently made acquaintance was not all that differ-

ent from sex with another recently made acquaintance. It
didn't leave me filled up with the excitement of adventure, I
came to understand. It left me feeling grim and alone.

I didn't want to be grim and alone. I wanted true love
and inward serenity and a fresh start. So I went west, seeking
those things. I got my first taste of inward serenity during
that summer before I moved to Portland, while hiking more
than one thousand miles by myself. The fresh start quickly
followed when I settled into my new hometown. Finding true
love, I knew, would be more complicated. It was the one
thing on my list that I was ready to be patient for, the one
thing I didn't expect anytime soon. Certainly, I wasn't going
to actually look for it. I knew only that my sex life was going
to be different than it had been. That, on the brink of meeting
Brian Lindstrom, on the cusp of twenty-seven, as I ambled
across that bridge between the wilderness of self and real
adult life, I wouldn't have sex with a near stranger just for the
hell of it again.

Until, of course, a near stranger named Brian Lindstrom
came along.

A week had passed since I'd met him, or maybe two—I
wasn't keeping track. I hadn't called him; he hadn't called
me. Then, one evening as I was sitting in my room with a candle burning, a sudden breeze blew the scrap of paper with
Brian Lindstrom's name and phone number on it directly into
the flame of the candle. The paper ignited and burned to
nothing within an instant.

I took it as a sign. Of what, I didn't know. But at least a
sign that I should call him, so I looked up his name in the
phone book and did.

We met for dinner and talked and flirted and then returned to my house. Again, I found him compelling. I was

entertained by his razor-sharp sense of humor, impressed by his passion for his work, warmed by his gentle nature, which overlaid his clearly fierce spirit. But again, I didn't feel any real compulsion to take things further. I'd been celibate for a good stretch, alone but not lonely. We talked about that as our date wound down, sitting together in my room on my futon on the floor, cups of hot tea on the shelf beside us. Brian explained very earnestly that he wasn't looking for a commitment right now, that he wanted to stay clear of getting into a relationship.

"That's what I want, too," I told him. "Let's just be friends." At that, he lurched over and kissed me with such vigor that I toppled onto my back, taking him with me, onto me, and in pretty short order, into me.

We woke up near dawn and looked at each other. I'd been stone cold sober the night before and I'd done it again. Fucked a guy I barely knew. I did with him what I'd done with all the other guys I'd fucked who I barely knew. I acted blasé and jovial, as if all of this was nothing to me, as if I wouldn't feel hollowed out for hours afterward, sunk with the weight of my very own weightlessness. He left by seven in the morning, claiming to have a meeting of some sort, and I was glad when he was gone.

I saw him next a week later and we had sex again, though again there was nothing special between us, no sense that this was the beginning of what it would come to be. We weren't dating. He didn't call me with any regularity and neither did I call him. We saw each other again a couple of weeks after the second time we'd slept together. We'd both been invited to a party and had decided to go together in a loose way, along with a few of our now-mutual friends. I drove myself to the party. I was not with Brian, and yet I was.

I had done intimate things to his body, and he to mine, and yet there was so little between us. We were like two pops of popcorn in the same big bowl. We met up and talked pleasantly for a while and then drifted apart. I was in the kitchen and he was on the porch, each of us talking to separate clusters of people. After a while I went out to the porch, where Brian stood talking to a woman. He introduced me to her and explained they'd worked together on a shoot all that day. It had been he, she chimed in, who'd invited her to the party. I chatted with them amiably, but inside I felt something crack. I left the party soon after, giving Brian a quick, falsely cheerful hug. I drove home with a sickness in my gut, a sorrow that felt rooted in nothing. I was sad not because what I had with Brian mattered so much to me, but because it mattered so very little. I felt small and stingy and sorry for having taken him into me without having taken him in at all. It was like nothing less than a betrayal of the person I was striving to be.

Once home, I burned candles and thought about everything. Sometimes it takes two times to make a vow and have it stick. That's what happened to me then, after I attended a party in a half-assed way with a guy I halfway liked, then met a woman he was half hitting on in my presence.

It occurred to me then that sex was not casual, or if it was, I wasn't. It was serious and I was serious. I would never take sex casually again, I knew with a sudden feverish zeal. I wasn't going to be a tomcat anymore, and I wasn't going to sleep with any tomcats either. I felt not angry at Brian but instead grateful to him for helping deliver me to this new place. By sleeping with him and seeing it for the deep mistake it was, I had finally crossed the bridge into real life. I was simply, deeply, joyfully done with tomcatting around. I decided I would call Brian first thing in the morning to tell him, in the nicest possible way, that I never wanted to see him again.

I slept restlessly and woke just past dawn, lying in bed waiting for the time to pass. It was a Sunday and I thought I should wait until at least nine to make the call. At eight-thirty my phone rang. I let the answering machine take it. It was Brian. His voice sounded tentative over the tiny speaker of my answering machine. I reached out and picked up the phone.

He wanted to talk to me, he said. He hadn't slept well, thinking about me all night. He felt bad about the party, about how I'd perhaps gotten the wrong impression of the woman on the porch, about how he and I had started off the wrong way—too quickly. He wanted something different in his life, he said, wanted to start over again, with me, strictly as friends.

I listened, stunned. Everything he said disarmed me and reversed everything I had planned to say to him.

"Okay," I said when he'd finished talking. "I'll be your friend."

And so we were. Friends for six exquisite, sexually fraught but entirely platonic weeks. We took long walks and short road trips. We read books out loud to each other and ate pie. We told each other our life stories and painted a cabinet we'd found on the street. We fell silently, madly, honestly in love with each other but didn't say that was what was happening. Most of all, we didn't touch each other beyond a friendly hug at the end of our visits.

I thought I would become ill from unacted-upon sexual desire. Once, in the midst of this time, he poked a finger into a tiny hole that was midthigh on my jeans.

"You've got a hole," he said, and took his finger away.

I almost came. Or fainted. Or came so hard I'd have fainted. It makes me feel faint to remember it still.

At last we got on with it. We'd made a date to meet at his house and take a walk. When I arrived, he was on the phone. He waved me inside as he continued talking, welcoming me with silent gestures. I sat down with my coat still on, waiting for him to finish his conversation. He was standing near me and I couldn't help it—I reached out and took his hand. By this point, each of us had imagined in great detail the things we'd like to do with each other's naked body, but on this, our first genuine leap into intimacy, we took our time. I grasped his hand with the force of everything that was behind it, all of my affection and desire and fear and hope and blossoming love, and I felt him grasping my hand back in the same way. A few minutes later, he hung up the phone and he looked at me without speaking, still holding my hand. We laughed together then, at the same unspoken joke. The joke was us, we knew without saying. Two tomcats falling in love.

We didn't on that day fall into bed—a first for both of us. We went for our walk and held hands. We kissed deeply as we said goodbye. "Are you going to be okay?" he asked me as I staggered out his door, wanting him so much I could barely walk.

"No," I said, feeling honestly that I wouldn't be, but I went home alone anyway.

Over the next months we progressed from kisses to the hottest sex of either of our lives. There were whole days we literally did not leave his bed. Countless dinners that went uneaten, movies that were not viewed, dance performances of friends that we missed, plays we'd already purchased tickets to that went on without us in the audience because we were gloriously pounding and sucking and rubbing and licking each other's body into absolute smithereens.

Sex with Brian this time around wasn't casual. It wasn't disconnected from the rest of my life. It didn't leave me hollowed out or grim. Instead, it filled me up. I'd loved and been loved before, but I'd never felt the way I did with him, which is to say content.

Content had once been a bad word to me—a thing to avoid, a state that only miserable, bored sell-outs achieved. To be content meant to be satisfied with the status quo, to literally *be in a container.* And yet here I was, happily contained by Brian Lindstrom, feeling absolutely no impulse to seek adventure elsewhere.

A year after I met him, I moved into his house. A couple of years after that, we decided to get married.

Which is when this reformed tomcat began to have her doubts.

"Really?" I'd ask Brian, studying his face for the slightest hesitation. "Only me? You want to have sex with me and only me for the rest of your life?"

"Yeah," he'd say with a knowing smirk, as if there was not a doubt in his mind.

I wasn't so sure and I told him so. I was sure I loved him. I was sure he was my best friend in the world. I was sure that, at least so far, I hadn't wanted to sleep with anyone else. I was happily monogamous with him—no flirtations on the side, no secret crushes or barely suppressed affairs. But I wasn't so sure that marriage wouldn't ruin all that, given what had happened to me the first time around. What if marriage itself had been to blame for my infidelities? What if the act of marrying Brian broke the spell? After I publicly and legally committed to wanting to be with him and only him, would it stop being true?

I didn't worry only about myself. Despite his assurances, I also worried that Brian wasn't ultimately up to the vow. I was dreaming about it and talking about it and asking myself and him the same question over and over again: How could two people who'd failed at monogamy so miserably build a monogamous marriage that was meant to last?

It was the question I carried with me even as I put on my fabulous dress and stood in front of all our friends and vowed to love Brian Lindstrom forever, to be faithful and true. A wedding is a day, an hour, an event that marks a passage that takes place in an instant. You walk up the aisle a bride or groom and down the aisle a wife or husband. But for me, it took some time to understand, really, what my marriage meant. The big surprise was how much it did mean. It wasn't until after Brian and I got married that I understood something had actually happened that day, something above and beyond and beside the festive fun of the wedding itself. Before we married, Brian and I were deeply committed to each other. We shared a house and a garden and two cats and a car. I thought our life after marriage would only be a continuation, that marriage was simply a piece of paper that gave our relationship legal standing. For some people, I'm sure it is, but in our case, something shifted in both of us after we married. Our gazes, perhaps. The clasp of our hands. I can't exactly put my finger on it, but the shift felt centered around the very thing I was initially so suspicious of: our wedding vows.

I'd recited wedding vows before. The promises I'd made to my first husband didn't much differ from what I promised Brian, but the intent behind them did. In my first marriage,

I'd vowed to be faithful with a casual certainty, without much thought. Of course I would be monogamous with the man I loved, I believed at the time. The second time around, with Brian, I promised fidelity with more trepidation and doubt. That skepticism, I've come to believe, has made being faithful to my husband over the long haul possible. To say that you will have sex with one and only one person for the rest of your life is a very big deal, and with Brian, I didn't enter into that commitment blindly. I did it with all of my intelligence and fear, my honesty, and, it turns out, my intention. I'd promised fidelity to Brian not because I was expected to, or because he or the institution of marriage demanded it of me, but because I wanted to. In vowing to be true to him, I had vowed, at last, to be true to myself.

With that realization, my doubts fell away. I've been monogamous with Brian for more than thirteen years now—almost ten of them as his wife. We no longer miss many dance performances or readings because we're too busy making love. The demands of caring for our two small children keep us celibate for long stretches of time. But with Brian, I'm still madly in love, still content and happily contained. And when we do get around to it, he's still perfectly capable of doing all those things that turn my body into absolute smithereens. We're still two tomcats at heart, curious about what's around the next bend, only now we do all our tomcatting with each other, searching deep instead of wide.

Turn Me On, Turn Me Off

BELLA POLLEN

It's a gray, blowy afternoon in the far north of Scotland, where I'm on holiday with my husband and an old friend of his, who, quite coincidentally, was a boyfriend of mine for about a minute and a half when I was seventeen. Rain has fallen incessantly for days now and my traveling partners are restless.

"What are you writing?" one asks moodily.

"An essay on sex."

"Really?" They immediately perk up. "Can we help?"

I consider this. Since I've slept with both, this might not be the wisest of exercises. On the other hand, I figure, why not? Frankly, I'm going to need all the help I can get.

"Great!" They sit on the sofa expectantly. "So, what are the specifics?"

"The usual," I say airily. "Girl on girl, three in a bed, anal sex."

"Really?" There's an almost religious light shining from their eyes.

"No, not really," I admit. "I'm writing about what turns men and women on and off."

"Ah." Their disappointment is palpable. "Interesting."

"So, shoot!" I tell them. "What do you guys consider a turn-on?"

"Oh, everything," they say, without the slightest hesitation.

"Okay, fine, what turns you off then?"

They look at each other, then at me, then at each other again.

"Well, er . . . nothing."

There's a short silence.

"That's it?'" I say. "That's the sum total of your contribution?" They nod apologetically and lumber off looking faintly abashed. Bewildered, I look at my notebook. I love sex and will take it in almost any form. Nevertheless, I've already managed to list not only a dozen turn-offs but an astonishing number of perfectly decent boyfriends I cast aside because of them. Take, for example, the cricket player who didn't laugh once during *Strictly Ballroom*, and the date who turned out to be a horribly sloppy kisser. And let's not forget the guitar player who, whenever he got out of bed in the morning, would indulge in a prolonged scratching of his genitalia. He would grasp his penis in one hand, pull it up, then begin scratching along its length all the way down to the scrotal sac before working round and round his balls in the methodical manner of a dog ridding itself of fleas. The first few times, I must confess, it was rather mesmerizing, but thereafter the noise of it worked on me like nails on a black-board.

Women love to accuse men of being lousy communicators, but it occurs to me that we're not much better. The sloppy kisser and the scratcher, for instance—did I make either of them aware of how I was feeling? Of course not. I just calmly made my way to the nearest emergency exit. In fact, I have never told *any* lover what it is I want from them. That's because my prize-winning, number-one sexual turn-off is being asked that very question: What turns you on?

It's no secret that when it comes to sex, men are as straightforward as women are complex. Still, now I'm wondering. Am I hypocritical? Relentlessly fickle? Is this the reason I've motored through lovers and been married twice? "Am I a monster?" I ask my husband as he wanders by, with a bunch of freshly picked wildflowers in his hand.

"Why, yes!" he says.

Clearly, the issue merits further investigation.

For the record, I'm happy to be asked "What turns you on in bed?" over dinner, at theater intermission, or even during the play itself if it's dull enough. I'm happy to be asked at any time except in the throes of passion.

In general, I love talk. I'm a woman, for Christ's sake, and communication is my oxygen. Plus I'm a writer, so words fascinate me. I'm turned on by lectures and debates; I can even work up a thrill over slander, slur, and insult. Give me dialogue any which way you want, only don't give it to me in bed.

I tend to get lost inside of sex. If I'm into it, then I'm out of it, if you know what I mean. Sex is a drug better than any other, and it takes me to a wonderfully primordial place of touch, sight, smell, and taste, a metaphysical Utopia of the senses, where, even at the best of times, we are granted only temporary residence. Thus, it is a place from which I do not wish to be unnecessarily extradited in order to face humdrum interrogation. In this ephemeral country, the only sense that does not hold an elevated position, for me at least, is sound. The minute I cross that border, my audio is all but switched off. I don't hear phones, I don't hear police sirens. I'm sorry to report that if some poor old lady was being mugged on the street, I'm afraid that someone who isn't having sex would have to come to her aid.

Making love to another person is an elemental and powerful thing. Words—dropped, disconnected, uttered involuntarily: great. But talking and questioning are entirely extraneous to the proceedings. If I can't manipulate a lover into giving me pleasure any other way than by ordering him about and if he can't make a vaguely instinctual guess at how he might do it, chances are he and I won't be having sex very often. Besides, it's not as if I'm the silent type in bed. I may not whinny like a horse or swivel my head around in an *Exorcist*-like fashion, but I don't believe I have ever left anyone in doubt as to whether I'm having a good time.

But there's another reason being questioned about my sexual predilections makes me nervous. Once you identify a liking for something in particular, it takes all spontaneity out of the erotic act and may even set a dangerous precedent. I know this because it happened to me.

Owen and I met at a party I threw and he crashed. He was adorable. By the early hours of the morning, we found ourselves hunched in a corner, our bodies pressed together, so deep in conversation we were oblivious to the fact that everyone else had left. Owen was a journalist. He was funny in a self-deprecating way, attractive in a charming, crooked way, and he would have been extremely good in bed but for his relentless pursuit of an answer to the dreaded question.

It started right at the beginning. We were having sex, I was totally into it—and, God knows, making enough noise about it—yet there it was, the thread of a whisper in my ear: "So, is this good?" He'd been licking my armpit or some place very close to it and I really didn't want him to stop.

"Mmmm..." A question requiring some version of a grunt, I can just about handle.

"And this?" He traced a finger along the inside of my thigh. "Is this good?"

"Mmmm..." Quickly, I found his mouth and kissed him in hope of promoting silence, but he was having none of it. He pushed himself onto his elbows and regarded me soulfully. "So, what do you want me to do to you?"

I stared at him stupidly. Had this been an actual question requiring an actual answer? It had. Smell, touch, taste, all began to fade as I was forced to turn up the volume on my audio.

"What?" I said.

Up until that moment, the movement of our bodies had been as fluid as currents in a river. Now it was as though two rusting pieces of machinery were being crunched against each other. Owen duly repeated the question.

"Huh? Oh, hey. No, listen, everything you're doing is, you know. Just great."

"Good, I'm glad." He kissed me. "But I mean, I still want to know what you like...as in exactly."

At first I tried fudging it, a few murmurs here, the odd confidence-inspiring generalism there, but he wasn't satisfied. And the more specific an answer he required, the more evasive I became. What to do? It felt too schoolmarmish and crushing to sit him down and discuss it, so we floundered on until one night the axe fell. Exactly what he was doing or how he was doing it, I can't recall, but whatever it was, I must have made some extra-happy noise because suddenly his head shot up.

"Ah-*hah*!" he said triumphantly. "So you like *that*, do you?"

And now I was in trouble. What exactly did "that" refer to? His hand was on my breast. Had he been fondling it in a particularly imaginative way?

"Yeah," I said. "It was great; I mean, it was all...great. Everything you do is perfect, you do know that, don't you?" But it was too late. From that moment on, it was as if whatever action he had performed and whatever fatefully ecstatic bleat it had elicited from me were indelibly associated in his mind. Every time we had sex, he would enthusiastically perform this same movement with the panache of a concert pianist who'd finally mastered Rachmaninoff's Third. It seemed that with one extra-enthusiastic moan, I had turned Owen the journalist into Owen the sportsman on a winning streak, who, out of superstition, refused to change his socks until the end of the series.

Before long my breasts were being serially aggravated, yet I was powerless to protect them. I tried gently maneuvering Owen onto the fresher erogenous pastures of my neck, ear, knee, but it was like separating a dog from a bone. No matter where I buried them, my breasts would be dug up and the nipple worried between his teeth until the pain became such that I ended up barring them with my hands. Here's how the ensuing conversation went:

"What's wrong?" he asked.

"Nothing. I just, uh...nothing."

He tried to pull my hands away.

"I... er, no, *no*, don't, I mean, oh dear."

"What?" Then, suddenly, he got this alarming, knowing look in his eyes. "*Oh*, I get it. Oh, my God... you're about to come! Wow, I can't believe I can make you come just by touching your nipples!!"

Ah, the irony. "Um... ha-ha, no, look, it's not that so much, it's just—"

"Wow. I had no idea they were so sensitive!" he said admiringly.

"Yes, they are very sensitive," I agreed miserably.

But Owen was on a roll. "Well, baby," he growled, "you ain't seen nothin' yet."

And right then and there, I felt the chill wind of sexual doom blow through my heart. If I had to pluck a single word from the dictionary of dirty talk, if I had to name and shame a word I never want to hear in bed, particularly when uttered in über-sexy tones, that word would be *baby*.

Let's be clear. I have no problem with actual babies. As it happens, I have several of the little critters myself. Equally, I don't object to being called "baby" outside the bedroom by friends whether male or female. I actively love being called "babe," "my babe," or "poor baby" (particularly in a sympathetic manner when I have the flu). I'm even partial to "whoa, baby!" as in the very memorable "Whoa, baby! Yo pussy as shiny as yo face?" question put to me by a gentleman pushing a wheelbarrow of lamb chops through Manhattan's meatpacking district as I staggered out of a spa after a particularly abrasive facial.

No, it's the peculiarly breathy, velvety, all-knowing Barry White version of "baby" that I find a cold turn-off and cannot take, from anyone, not even from Barry White himself should he ever find himself in my bed. I understand that as phobias go, my "baby" fear is silly and illogical, but like all silly and illogical phobias, it originated from a bad experience I had when I was younger.

I was nineteen, embarking on a career in the fashion business, when I found myself being photographed for a magazine story on my company. The photographer had a lazy eye and almost the first thing he said to me as he fixed his camera to a tripod was "Okay, baby, look at me. Look me straight in the eye."

But, oh dear, which eye? One of his pupils pointed north; the other was roving around the room like a planet cut loose from its universe. His entreaties soon graduated from "Look at me, baby" to "Come on to me, baby" and from there to the gruesome "Make love to me, baby," all murmured in generic porn undertones. Under any other circumstances, I might have risen to the occasion. As it was, I had spent much of the previous evening at a nightclub in the company of no small quantity of drugs. I was raw from lack of sleep, my hair looked as though it had been deep-fried, and for some reason I was being photographed in a pair of shapeless men's pajamas. Making love to anything was not at the top of my agenda at that moment. But it was his ghastly, deep-throat addendum of "Baby, baby" to every command that ultimately undid me. I began to get an appalling case of giggles.

"You're not trying, baby," the photographer said plaintively. I was trying, but every time he repeated the word, I fell about laughing until my mascara and makeup were swilling around on the floor in a pool of oily tears. After that, if anyone ever called me "baby," even in a half-sexy way, it quite finished me off. And so, finally, Owen began to sense that something was amiss.

"What is it?" he demanded. "You've gone all...I don't know...stiff."

"I'm sorry, it's just that . . . well, I'd rather you didn't do that."

"I thought you liked it."

"I do like it. I mean, I did...It's just that..."

"It's just that what?" Owen's ego was deflating like a balloon, I could see it in his eyes. It was equally noticeable in his erection.

"Look," I said. "I love it sometimes. Just...not *all* the time."

"But you made that noise," he said forlornly, as though I'd not only thrown his Christmas present back in his face but had somehow managed to convince a stray cat to pee all over it first.

"Well, I like it in the way I like pineapple on pizza, sort of once in a while, a surprise ingredient, just not on every slice."

"You like pineapple on pizza?" he said weakly, because by this time he'd gotten it; all the other breast-fondling sessions were passing before his eyes. Now he was really embarrassed and so was I, and when we English are embarrassed we take refuge in our humor so that we never, ever, ever have to discuss the source of our embarrassment.

Afterward, I tried to rationalize it. Why had Owen felt the need to ask, and why did I have such a problem answering? Was it simply that he wondered if he was up to scratch? Did he have bases to cover and boxes to tick? I don't know. All I know is at that time I spent much of my workday giving out reassurances to colleagues. (I need hardly tell you that the fashion business is populated by extremely fragile egos.) Sex was one thing I really needed to have taken on faith.

I've since come to believe that for women, "What do you want?" is a key question, one that opens the door to all our conflicted desires and uncertainties. If men only knew how badly a woman longs to be sat down and asked what she wants, not in bed but in the bigger context of life, they might do it once in a while, simply in the name of charity. I suspect, however, that men are too frightened to ask because what a woman really wants is a door more safely left closed.

Owen and I never quite recovered from the harassed-breast incident and parted ways.

Ironically, my next significant lover managed to turn my aversion to dirty talk on its head. This time, though, it was dirty talk on paper—quite a different matter. In the days before the mobile phone and texting, I fell madly in love with Michael, an architect who happened to be a master of the smutty written word.

Unlike seductions whispered in the here and now, then lost in the heat of the moment, committing desire to paper makes it forever. It started in Japan. I was in the middle of a trip spent almost entirely in the back of an air-conditioned company car contemplating the neck of my driver, a man who spoke no known language. I was cross-eyed with jet lag and loneliness and had another week to go when one night, as I was lying on my beige bed in the beige surrounds of my beige hotel room, an envelope appeared under the door. Inside, there was a handwritten fax of such indescribable filth, I find myself turning pink at the thought of reproducing it on this page. Over the course of the week, the envelopes kept coming: on a waiter's tray, in the hand of a bowing concierge. In fact, they appeared with such regularity that when my revered fashion licensor invited me to admire the giant carp in his ornamental pond, I half expected the revolting beast to open its mouth and spit out an envelope.

Once I was back in London, Michael, who was in the middle of a divorce and therefore keeping our affair secret, took delight in getting messages to me whenever I was in any kind of half-grown-up meeting. It got to the point where only about 40 percent of my brain was focused on work; the remaining 60 percent was concentrated on the knock on the door I knew was coming, the entrance of an apologetic secretary bearing a note with my name on it.

I am an easy blusher. It's a trait my mother assured me would disappear along with teenage acne, but, regrettably, it never did. I'd unfold these notes and read something along the lines of "I am imagining my fingers inside you" or "I can still taste you in my mouth." Feeling the knowing eyes of the secretary upon me; the heat would begin rising until my cheeks burned hot.

"Good Lord!" my colleagues would exclaim. "Are you all right? Not bad news, I hope?"

"No, nothing like that," I'd say, blushing even harder, and hastily downing the proffered glass of water. Exactly how Michael charmed every assistant, every air steward, every concierge to take down his dirty dictation or deliver his faxes he never revealed, just as I never discovered how he managed to acquire such a good working knowledge of my itinerary. He turned up for surprise trysts with impressive regularity— at hotels where I was staying or restaurants where I was having dinner. Receptionists, maids, and assistants the world over seemed to be in his pay, including a couple of my own. He should have been a CIA agent. Maybe he was. Either way, it didn't matter, or last. For nearly a year, we had a lot of fun.

Then, one day, it wasn't fun any longer. Things didn't end badly. There was simply nowhere to go. Michael was the stuff of fantasy—spontaneous, mysterious, wicked, the very epitome of a turn-on. But he was also an incorrigible flirt, a bolter who could manage a relationship only in bite-sized chunks of excitement. The sex was always great but the emotional emptiness that followed began to erode my soul. I was no longer looking for uncertainty and mystery. Indeed—guess what?—they had become a turn-off.

*   *   *

A woman's desire is a fragile thing, blown this way and that by the winds of change. Our likes and dislikes flip-flop depending on where, exactly, we are on our personal evolutionary curve, what phase of life we are in. Women have far more roles to play than men, and each comes with its own emotional and physical wish list. We want to be held! We want to be screwed! We want security! Danger! Comfort! Passion! I don't know a woman who isn't constantly torn between the mutually exclusive needs for the intimacy of a long-term relationship and the thrill of a one-night stand. Frankly, we should consider ourselves lucky if we get enough of both.

Men regard the question of what turns them on and off as solely a sexual one, and thank God they do—if this question was as complicated and loaded for them as it is for us, then the human race might find itself in a state of impending extinction. Personally, I find it humbling that men are prepared to ride the roller coaster of women's ever-changing emotional needs. I am beyond grateful that my husband always wants to make love to me while my own libido rises and falls like the Dow, dependent on the vagaries of my work, children, and whatever body dysmorphia I might be suffering, foodie religion I'm propagating, or even book I'm reading.

I'm forty-six now. Does this mean that when I'm sixty-four, I will long for a Barry White look-alike in my bed calling me "baby, baby" and begging to know what turns me on?

Okay, let's not push this theory too far.

But right this moment, watching my husband busy at the sink with the purple thistles and sprigs of cow parsley he has brought in from outdoors, I remember a girlfriend of mine text-messaging me something my husband had said to her at a recent dinner party: "I don't flirt, I like to fuck, and I arrange flowers. P.S.: Wow, I can see why you married him!"

So let's consider. No flirting and flower arranging... would these attributes have set my pulse racing at eighteen? At twenty-five? At thirty-five, even? Definitely not. Do they today?

Hell, yes.

Overcome

LAUREN SLATER

I could chalk it up to getting older, the fact that sex interests me these days about as much as playing checkers.

Granted, at the unripe age of forty-four, my estrogen is probably plunging and my periods, although still regular, are brief and bright, more like a wink than a flow. But the fact is, I've never much liked sex, even though it has on occasion captivated me. Says my proverbial therapist: *Sex threatens you, Lauren. You feel overcome.*

Another distinctly less sexy possibility than feeling over / come, or at least over coming, is that I have never much liked sex because, when all is said and done, there's not much to like. I mean, really: What is the big deal? Especially when it's with the same person, over and over again; from an evolutionary standpoint, that simply couldn't be right. I, for one, have always gotten bored of sex within the first six months of meeting a man, the act paling for me just as the sun pales at the approach of winter, and as predictably, too.

I met and fell in love with my husband for his beautifully colored hair, his gentle ways, his humor. We were together many years, and so sex faded. Then we decided to get married. Predictably, almost as soon as the engagement ring slid onto my finger, I fell in love with someone else. I fell madly, insanely, obsessively in love with a conservative Christian man who believed that I, as a Jew, was going to hell. We fought long and hard about that, and then had sex. This is so stupid it pains me to write about it. This man...he played *golf*. He wore shirts with those nasty little alligators on them, and I fucking *fell in love with him*. A terrible thing, I know. And yet this affair, I sensed, was absolutely necessary for me to move forward with my marriage. The affair was a test. I believed, but could not be sure, that just as sex had cooled for me and my soon-to-be husband, it would cool with this man, with any man, no matter what or whom, in which case my fiancé was the person I wanted to marry. Except suppose I was wrong? Suppose there was someone out there with whom I could have passionate, slick sex my whole life like one endless Christmas morning, which, since I'd never actually celebrated Christmas, held all the more magic and mystery for me?

So I continued on with my conservative Christian, very smart, very handsome, and we had fantastic, obsessive sex while, the whole time, I had one eye on the clock. I was waiting to see when, or *if*, this affair would run out of fuel. I prayed to Jesus and anyone else who might be up there that it would, so I could marry the man I loved. And yet night after night I left the man I loved to have sex with the man I was *in* love with. I could not stop. I was like one of those bonobos with the scarlet butts. Yuck.

Actually, I never had intercourse with him, though we did everything else a man and woman can do. He did not believe in sex before marriage. Therefore, when my fiancé asked me if I was having sex with someone else (why was I coming home at 3:00 A.M.?), I could answer no. On the Christian man's end, when his God asked him if he was having sex with someone else, he, too, could answer no, and so we both lived highly honest, righteous lives filled with perpetual sex.

But because I am not a bonobo, the inevitable started to happen. The alligator-wearing man lost his appeal. Sex turned tepid, then revolting. While the revolting part was particular to this crazy relationship, the tepid part was wholly within my experience and proved, for me, that there is no God of monogamous passion. Thus freed from the tethers of this affair, I returned to the gentle arms of my pagan husband. We are going on our tenth anniversary. He wants hot sex. I turned tepid long ago.

*   *   *

A University of Chicago study found that 40 percent of women suffer from some form of sexual dysfunction, usually low libido. There are treatments for this sort of thing— Viagra or a prescription for testosterone. I had breast cancer, which nixes the latter option for me. As for Viagra, I've read that since it increases blood flow, it is as likely to make your nose as your genitals active, the end result being more mucus production. Can you imagine sex while honking into a wadded tissue?

The real issue, for me, is that I'm not sure I have a dysfunction. On the one hand, I am miserable about our lack of a sex life. I am miserable that sex interests me only about as much as checkers. I am miserable about it because it makes my husband miserable and withdrawn and it is so unhappy, living this way. "Have sex with someone else," I tell him, and then look down at my open hands, my pinkish palms cracked from wear and weather.

"The problem with that," my husband says, "is falling in love. If you have sex with someone else, you just might fall in love with them."

"I'd fucking kill you," I say.

Of course I wouldn't. But I just might kill myself.

*   *   *

I have no answers for how one exists without a sex drive, or with a sex drive that is equal to interest in checkers. A gulf of loneliness enters the marriage; the rift it creates is terribly painful. I could get treatment, but I've had so *much* treatment—for cancer, for depression—that in this one small area of my life, can I claim, if not health, then at least the absence of pathology? Especially because when I say I don't have an interest in sex, that might be a misstatement. Maybe I do have an interest in sex. It's simply that, comparatively speaking, I have so many other competing and stronger interests, crammed into a life that is already overloaded, but which I nevertheless love.

There are so many things I love, once I manage to throw my feet over the edge of the bed in the morning. I am captivated by the idea of thousands of solar systems, by smooth stones and colored glass, which I cut and solder, silver liquid lines bringing the scraps together in purposeful patterns. I love my wheeled mosaic nippers, how they take tiny bites out of solid opalescence and how these pieces assemble into quilts of glass, into tabletops, into garden balls of deep cobalt blue. I love my garden; I love finding wild coneflower, black-eyed

Susan, even loosestrife. When I see them in fields or growing between bricks, I pull them up as gently as I can and bring them back to where I live, then nurse them along, hoping through the cold winters that they will pull their perennial magic and reappear again. And half the time they do! I love seed catalogs, especially in the winter, when the pictures of the glowing globes of red-hot tomatoes remind you to have faith that warmer weather will come. I love horses and riding them. I love my dogs, of course, and my children I love so much it hurts; they pull on me painfully, and I love them. I love words and writing, although that love is complex and fraught, a tense, toothy love that has made its marks on me forever. I love my router, my planer, my circular saw. I love wood, especially salvaged wood I can pull off old barns, then restore until it's gleaming. I love clay. I like to sew and cook.

I have recently acquired a love of stones and am making a new floor for our bathroom entirely out of polished pebbles I found in the streambed by our house. Right this minute, as I sit here typing, I am literally weighed down by dozens of stones crammed into the capacious pockets of my tattered sweats, stones I found this morning. For the past three weeks, I have spent most of my mornings with a shovel, occasionally on my hands and knees, scraping madly to expose the pearly surface of a solid piece of the past. Stones. Where did they come from? Is it possible they landed here by way of an asteroid that broke free from its planet billions of years ago, and so I am finding not only stone but space? Is it possible we will one day run out of stones as we are now running out of oil or water or trees? Could we survive without stones? Would we miss them, and, in missing them, retrospectively discover their value?

*   *   *

My first orgasm happened more than two decades ago when I
was nineteen. I was in a roominghouse with a moody, broody
bad boy who had a muscular chest and a head roiling with glossy
curls. He did downers and uppers and acid, none of which I did.
But we both loved the Grateful Dead. Every time I slept over, we
woke in the mornings and listened to their song "Ripple," the
clearness of the music, the pure simplicity of it, affirming for me
again and again that I was part of a people, a species, capable of
creating and of great beauty. *Ripple in still wa-ha-ter.*

We'd gone out all summer before the start of our respective freshman years; not once did he ask me for intercourse,
even on our last night together. The very absence of his question underscored its implicit presence. *When?* I confided to my
roommate that we had not yet done the deed. Hers was a
pause of shock. "You haven't gone past third?" she said. (This
is how teenagers talked back in the Reagan days, when you
said no to drugs and yes to sex, back before AIDS, when—and
probably still now—girls tossed their cherries out car windows or dropped them in the dirt like they were nothing, those
fruits, that single stretch of skin. *Snap.*) I didn't want to snap.
Bright blood on a white sheet. I didn't want to bleed. Sheer
fear of that plunging pain is what held me back; I couldn't use
a tampon, never mind a member, its pale smooth head with
that single, squinting eye, asking, accusing. Instead of telling
my would-be lover the truth, I made up an elaborate lie. *I
was raped. Too traumatized to have sex. I need more time.*
Remembering this now, for the first time in a long time, I do
not judge myself. I consider it a great deal to ask of a relatively
newly minted woman that she offer her intact body up for this
frankly difficult deed. I also find it interesting that shame, an

emotion that's supposedly deeply rooted in the human limbic system, untouched by time or class, is in fact very much subject to time, class, and culture, too. In the nineteenth century, to be raped was to be shamed forever. In the twentieth century, to be a virgin was to be shamed, and so I lied, to save my skin.

Except one time, on a May night, through the open window, warm liquid breezes poured over our naked bodies. Then he touched me just so and I tipped into the orgasm and was grasped. This was different from whatever I'd achieved on my own. This was softer, gentler, full of a wide-open love, a deep falling-down love. When it was over, I hated him. I hated that man (that boy, really; we could not have been more than nineteen). The intimacy was too much, too wrenching and shameful.

*   *   *

There is nothing as intimate as the sounds of sex, which are a shared secret between lovers, part of the glue that binds them together. They are the most private utterances in any relationship, trumping language so completely that words themselves are squashed beneath their primitive weight. We have our regular speaking voices, and then we have our sexual voices. While these voices may be odd, disturbing, even disorienting, especially if overheard, they serve a special purpose: to bring us close. My husband's sounds draw me near to him, when he allows himself to have them, when I do. In the right situation, with the right sanctions, these nighttime sounds—what we say and what we do not—would be preserved, bottled, so they did not wash away with the laundry, the toothpaste foaming down the drain, the home-from-work-at-9:00-P.M. nights, you angry, me angry.

*   *   *

In our culture, sex has lost its sacred quality. If I were mayor or president, I think I would institute some rules for the good of the American marriage, a prohibition or two—no touching allowed until Tuesday—because longing springs from distance. It is ironic, but also absolutely understandable, that proximity can kill sex faster than fainting. Devout Muslims are not even allowed to touch each other until marriage. Ooh la la. Imagine the long courtship, in which every gesture is observed to be sure the lovers land not even the slightest flick of a finger on one another's skin. Imagine the buildup of tension as time passes, as the wedding day nears, as the woman is sheathed and wrapped for the pure and only purpose of being later unwrapped, after months of imagination.

That ritual makes sense to me. I've always found it odd that on a Tuesday night you might go about the bizarre bodily act of having sex and then, the next morning, amidst a chattering group of children, eat Cheerios. It seems to me that if sex was separated out from the daily wheel of life, it might survive monogamy more intact.

I am a woman in love, but I am not in love with sex. I am in love with glass and stones and skin. I am in love with my children, my animals. I am in love with *making,* as opposed to making love. Someday I hope to build a house. And inside this house I want to live with my family—my children and my animals and my husband, whom I love so imperfectly, with so many gaps and hesitations. I hope he does not leave me for a woman who likes to make love.

* * *

The Grim Reaper, who for me is not death but mental illness, visits me from time to time, drawing me down with his sword. Each time this happens I never know if I will return to love. Each time I do I am more grateful than the time before. And so I see my life, my large, unwieldy, disorganized life, as a banquet, so much! So rich!

I am a person captivated by things, by solid, actual, concrete things that can be assembled, made, be they books or babies. In our living room there hangs a huge canvas sign I made. It spells out my simple mandate, all in buttons: MAKE THINGS, the edict by which I live my life, hung up where my children can see, the buttons vintage and collected over many years. My sign does not say MAKE LOVE. I wish it did, as love is so much nicer to make; at least it sounds that way. But for me, sex does not even come close to the thrill of scoring gorgeous glass for a window I will use, of hearing the grit as the grains separate and the cut comes clean and perfect.

Sex cannot compete with the massive yet slender body of granite I excavated out of the ground last week, six feet long this stone, packed with time and stories if it could only speak. I'm going to spend months carving it with a silver chisel. I am going to figure out a way to make this stone into an enormous mantel under which, in the home I share with my husband and the babies we made, our fire will flicker. The stone will give off waves of warmth in the winter, and it will keep the night coolness captive all through the summer days. I imagine my mantel, my windows, my glass, my gardens. I cannot believe how lucky I am. I have so very much to do, such wide and persistent passions, so little time in which to explore their many nooks and curves. Here. Now. Don't bother me. I'm busy.

Ouch, You're Lying on My Hair!

VALERIE FRANKEL

Woody Allen once said sex and humor don't mix. Apologies to Mr. Allen (I can't say "woody" without snickering), but sex and comedy most definitely *do* go together. It's damn near impossible to wrench them apart. For starters, just look at the penis. The shiny bald head, the squat shaft, the tilt, the way it jerks around like a puppet on a string. How did the first sentient chimp/woman hybrid keep from snickering at the sight of it? When my eight-year-old daughter saw a penis for the first time (Graham Chapman's in Monty Python's *Life of Brian*), she turned to my husband and me and asked, "Is that what it really looks like?" We told her it was. And then she burst into laughter.

Think of the funniest sound in the world. A fart? Burp? Slurp? Squish? Suck? Plop? If you don't make at least three of those noises during sex, you're not doing it right. How about the silliest positions you could get yourself into? Ankles around your ears? One leg sticking straight up like a cat? On your palms and feet like a camel? Ass high in the air? If an alien landed on Earth, looked through a bedroom window, and saw a couple humping this way and that, he'd laugh himself to death. Granted, we might find it equally amusing to watch him mate via frantic thumb wrestling. But that only reinforces my point. Sex is universally the stuff of comedy.

Don't get me wrong. Like everyone else, I started out with fairy-tale notions of what sex should be: two people with clean, trim, hairless bodies (in soft focus, of course), moving with the fluidity and flexibility of Olympic gymnasts. I clung to this vision for years, inevitably feeling a crushing disappointment when sex turned out to be badly lit, sweaty, stubbly, and fumbling, complete with feet caught in the sheets, wet spots, flying boobs, goose bumps, stomach flab, and the humble homeliness that is pubic hair.

Take the afternoon I lost my virginity. My deflowerer took me to his uncle's house in a neighboring town; his uncle was away and we'd have privacy, he assured me. We went out back to the pool, our plan to do it on the lawn so as not to leave evidence on the patio. We'd only just begun when the uncle, his wife, and their two kids arrived home unexpectedly to find us in flagrante delicto (like you didn't see that coming). The uncle hurled accusations at us as I scurried around, clumps of grass in my hair, hunting for my shorts in a juniper bush. "I'm not a slut," I said in my own defense. "I'm an honors student!"

Things didn't get much better once I was out of school and living in the adult world. As long as I clung to my romantic vision of sex, I wasn't doing much laughing. Where was the soft focus? I wondered. Where were the simultaneous orgasms? For that matter, where were my solo orgasms?

Once, in my early twenties, I went to see a friend's band at a New York City club that no longer exists. I met a guy there who bought me many drinks, which I accepted greedily. The band was two hours late. By the time they hit the stage, I was hammered, dancing frenetically and starting to feel green around the gills. I told the guy I needed air, which he thought was code for "screw in the back stairwell." We started making out there, until I warned him that I felt a teeny-tiny bit sick. He told me to relax and unbuttoned my jeans. When his hands pressed against my exposed belly, I returned every drink he had bought me in a florid, explosive arc, onto his shirt, pants, and combat boots. I still remember the stuff trickling gently down the stairwell wall like drops of rain.

Even my first honeymoon lacked all conventional sense of romance. My then-husband, Glenn, and I were on an Alaskan cruise, and we'd brought along some massage oil as a special treat. It was apple-scented and thick. I rubbed a ton of it on him and began what I intended to be the erotic massage to end all erotic massages. About three minutes in, he asked, "Is it supposed to tingle?" I said, "I don't know," and continued. A minute later, he asked, "Is it supposed to burn?" and I noticed that his skin felt hot under my hands. He jumped in the tiny cabin shower, barely tall enough for him, and washed off what he could. He started to break out in hives "everywhere" and we had to rush to the infirmary and wake up the ship's doctor to get Benadryl. Glenn recovered in a day, but he was scented-oil-phobic forever after. Turned out, for him, it *had* been the erotic massage to end all erotic massages. As for me, it is entirely possible that I was born to be sexually accident-prone. I'm just lucky, I guess.

Eventually, thanks to a rutting dog-man of a lover, I realized that picture-perfect sex did not mesh with the grunting honesty of colliding genitals. This guy wasn't satisfied until we were both covered in fluids, our hair tangled, the covers on the floor. He made snuffling sounds and offered an endless stream of coarse commentary. I couldn't help laughing at how unashamed he was of his swinging balls—and appreciating it. Once I accepted the squalid, seamy, earthy reality of sex, it suddenly got a lot more fun—and funny. The revelation was like being hit over the head with a rubber chicken. Satisfying sex should never look like a Hollywood movie, unless it's one starring Will Ferrell.

Most men I know figured this out long before I did. Take farting in bed, which, I concede, is embarrassing. You have a choice there: Either cry about it or laugh. Guys will laugh just as hard at the hundredth fart as they will at the first. They have no hang-ups about being the ridiculous human animals that we are. Perhaps their acceptance of bodies as gassy, lumpy, leaky amusement parks is why men have orgasms as easily as they say, "Pull my finger." Men know they're imperfect. They embrace their imperfections. Any guy would be pig-in-shit happy to do the goofiest, stupidest thing in bed, as long as it felt good.

I've come to feel the same way, which is why my now-husband, Steve, and I are a sexual match made in Catskills heaven. We tend to conduct ourselves with a certain abandon that makes us forget where the edge of the bed is or that a shower curtain isn't weight-bearing. I've pulled leg muscles, sprained my neck, nearly dislocated my jaw. My husband has bloodied his eyebrow, twisted his knee, and bent his glasses. We've broken lamps, a lawn chair, the towel holder in the bathroom. I've had splinters in my elbows. He's endured bruises and bug bites. We've both had rashes, chafed skin, cramps, and carpet burns.

Neither of us intends to harm the other, or ourselves. We're not into bondage or S&M. The most outré we get is light spanking, and even that we do with ambivalence and witty mockery. Apologies to sadists and masochists everywhere, but I don't see how pain wormed its way into pleasure. I suppose, if you really are a very bad boy and need to be punished, fine, then bend over and take the paddling you deserve. But my husband is a well-mannered grown man. He deserves kisses and clenches. If, during a position change, my elbow happens to fly into his nose, the *pow!* is an accident of passion. And I feel worse about it than he does. You wouldn't know it from the tittering, but really I do.

Just this week, we started kissing in the hallway, hot, steamy, with blazing intensity. In an energetic fit of passion, Steve picked me up, threw me down on the bed, lay on top of me, and pinned me beneath him. If I were writing a sex scene, I'd describe how I then exposed my vulnerable throat for his delectation, swooning and writhing beneath him, already eager, urgent for the dizzying, shattering release of long-built-up tension. What actually happened is that when Steve lifted me in his arms, his back gave out. Throwing me down on the bed? It was more a drop than a toss. His release of long-built-up tension? It arrived a day later, under the ministrations of a chiropractor.

Even worse, at a friend's party one night, where we both drank too much to compensate for the fact that we didn't know anyone, I friskily pushed my game husband into the powder room and knelt in front of him. The crunch of my kneecap on the tile floor should have been a warning. But I was feeling no pain (yet). I reached for his belt and started to unzip. I tried a supersexy move of pressing my cheek to his bulge, only to ensnare a portion of my hair in the zipper of his jeans. The disentanglement took forever—longer than the blow job would have, had we ever gotten to it. I eventually had to yank out a clump of my snarled curls to free myself. By the time we left the bathroom, a line had formed. Each smirking person assumed we'd begrudged his or her inalienable right to bladder relief for our own selfish pleasure. The next day, I hobbled to the hair salon with a dislocated kneecap. I had to get bangs that took months to grow out.

One of my fondest romantic memories is of an evening we spent in the Bahamas a few winters ago, when my intrepid husband and I took off from our hotel one evening after dinner in search of a deserted strip of beach. The moonlight bathed us softly. The waves lapped. We started going at it. Before long, a rock was digging into my back and my husband's knees were shredded on the sand. Beach fleas savagely attacked. We completed the act on principle and we both came. Then we tried to clean off in the ocean, wading into the water in the darkness, stepping on broken shells that cut our feet. Sexually speaking, it was okay. The recollection, however, of the two of us limping back into the resort lobby—our feet oozing, limbs covered in sand, clothes wet and torn, flea bite welts surfacing, busboys and guests staring as if we'd just been resurrected from a shipwreck—always makes me laugh. It's a shared treasure from our past, a sexy, funny home movie of the kind that, whenever we replay it, bonds us more deeply than if we'd had some majestic, music-swelling *From Here to Eternity* moment. Because when it comes right down to it, nothing is quite as life-affirming as a rousing climax while accidentally head-butting the man you love. When our bodies collide, I don't care that I'm not trim, hairless, or gymnast flexible. I don't care if I fart in bed—and, God knows, neither does Steve. The ultimate secret of our unique chemistry: Much as we love sex, we love to laugh even more. We are real (clumsy) people, having real (sloppy) sex, and very real *(pow! biff! boff!)* orgasms together.

Quite possibly, we'll die in some bizarre sexual mishap. Given the options, it's not such a bad way to go.

Turning the Other Cheek

DEANNA KIZIS

Of all the twenty-nine-year-olds throwing a New Year's Eve party simply for the chance to flirt with their ex-boyfriend, I was the most confounded by the state of my romantic affairs. I was enduring a five-year losing streak in love, and although I'd taken my previous four breakups on the chin, with my thirtieth birthday approaching, I was starting to feel victimized. What seemed most unfair was that, unlike friends who had gone to bed with a guy after the first date and ended up happily settled, I didn't do casual sex. I'd abstain for weeks, even months, giving nothing beyond a blow job until a guy demonstrated genuine affection and promised fidelity, conditions that were supposed to save me from heartbreak.

They didn't, and so I found myself chatting up said ex at my party; I'd invited him despite his recent proclamation that he preferred being single (postcommitment and -coitus, naturally). Then P. walked into my Beverly Hills apartment. (Not that Beverly Hills; the one south of Olympic Boulevard and miles away from a stable income.)

P.'s entrance was a sock to the chest. For one thing, he was exactly my type, over six feet tall, boyish, very indie rock, with the soft, broken-in T-shirt to prove it. He had a mop of sandy hair, laugh lines around his eyes, a mouth that at rest curled into a little smile as though it had ideas of its own. One look at him and I got that nervous feeling you get when you think a guy is going to be great yet you're holding your breath, desperate not to have your fantasy shattered when he actually opens his mouth.

P. had been invited to my party by a concerned friend who was hoping he'd distract me. He seemed willing. When I snuck into my bedroom for a cigarette, he followed. He produced a lighter, then took his own pack out of the threadbare pocket of his vintage Levi's. I asked why we'd never met before, and he told me he was in L.A. for two months finishing a screenplay. He thought he might even move here. When we finished our cigarettes, he asked if I wanted to go out for dinner and I accepted.

A few days later, after Mexican food and margaritas, P. opened a bottle of wine at his place. He had a guitar and knew how to play Radiohead songs. He strummed decently and I sang badly and we both drank heavily until we fell into his bed laughing. P. was a gentleman in the sack; I rewarded him with a hand job.

Our relationship progressed from there. Since he was also a writer, P. had time to procrastinate with me, to linger over long lunches and sneak off to matinees, which quickly graduated to regular dinners and rock shows together. He wanted to get to know the city, and I was his enthusiastic tour guide. P. was available, smart, and curious. He wanted to meet my friends, asked about my upbringing (lapsed Catholic, though nun-like axioms—"If you have sex out of wedlock, you're going to hell"—still knotted up my logic the way gum sticks in hair). P. held my hand when we walked down the street. He talked about how maybe we should take a trip up to Big Sur so he could see the coastline. Soon, I became obsessed with the way he smelled: coffee, cigarettes, and something unidentifiably sweet. I started sleeping in an old T-shirt of his that he said I could keep. (Like a teenager, I didn't wash it.) After about three weeks of heavy petting and romance, I broke my rule about sex and commitment and went for it, first because I was dying to sleep with him, but also because we got along so well, I was sure we'd end up together. Besides, P. was only in town for a short time; I figured I had to be flexible if I wanted things to work out.

P. was an adventurous lover. Soon he was making suggestions, each more titillating than the last. There were finger fucks in the car as we sped home from a day at the beach, then sex in the bathroom at a party, which gave way to you-watch-me-masturbate/I'll-watch-you-masturbate. He wanted to see my vibrator, wanted to use it on me; he wanted phone sex; he wanted surprise sex, a new genre for me, which involved him letting himself into my house in the dead of night and taking me by surprise in a rape-by-permission scenario that made the feminist in me cringe and the burgeoning sexual adventuress scream in ecstasy.

One night we were at Coach and Horses, the dive bar of *Swingers* fame, when P. coyly mentioned, apropos of nothing, that if I got a strap-on, he might let me use it on him.

"Are you serious?" I asked, almost aspirating beer out my nose.

"Maybe."

"Have you done that before?"

"No, ma'am."

I laughed. He said he was just kidding. But I could tell he was kidding about the kidding.

The next day, his suggestion was still on my mind; I didn't know what to make of it. P. was straight, and as far as my experience went, a request for anal action from a hetero-sexual male—apart from the stinky pinkie—was completely off the map. Not that I was going to explore the proposal. I'd never wanted to use a strap-on in my life. I had never fanta-sized about it, and I can confidently say that if I hadn't met P., I would have gone through the rest of my days without ever thinking about it. I'd seen dildos in sex shops when buying bachelorette party gifts, sure, but they always struck me as bizarre, icky, brutish. Not for me.

*   *   *

On a warm February evening—exactly the kind of night a guy from New York would marvel at, since normally he'd have been home freezing his ass off—P. and I were sitting on the patio of an Irish pub in Hollywood, sharing a plate of bangers and mash, when he said that he was pretty sure that at some point he'd mentioned his ex-girlfriend, M. "Yes," I said, remembering that he'd mentioned her in passing about five weeks before, sometime shortly after our first date. Something about a bad breakup, a fight over who should get the dog. At the time, it had set off warning bells, but he had never mentioned her again. I'd thought the situation had been resolved in my favor for some time. ·

"Deanna." P. said my name like it was a statement all on its own. "M. and I are talking about giving it another try when I get back to New York in a few weeks."

I was stunned. I said as much. He told me he didn't think he needed my permission to readdress a relationship that had begun years before we'd met. I asked if he was breaking up with me, then backpedaled: Well, not breaking up with me, since we weren't going out, but ending it. Not at all, he said. In fact, he would really like to keep seeing me. He really cared about me. Besides, he said, you never knew which way a situation like this could go. The whole thing with his ex... it could be a speed bump, nothing more. Maybe he was just afraid of starting something new, he said. Afraid of a long-distance relationship. He was so confused.

"In the meantime," he said, "we're having fun, right?"

I wanted to tell him to go fuck himself. I wanted to tell him I felt misled. I wanted to tell him I didn't have casual sex—especially kinky, wanton, anything-goes casual sex. For weeks P. had been pounding himself into me like I belonged to him. I thought we were falling in love. I wasn't sure if I was going to scream, cry, or both.

But my nethers and my brain were no longer acquainted. A friend calls this syndrome "smart girl, dumb vagina." I calmly told P. I wanted to see how things progressed, that even if this was just a casual thing, I was happy with it. We were having fun, and I was fine—no, really, fine. My vagina asked him if he wanted to sleep over.

We continued this way, me maintaining the charade that I was happy when I was miserable, him comfortable with the stated casualness of our arrangement. If anything, the underlying tension upped the ante on our sexual risk taking. Every now and then, he would mention that if I got a strap-on, he just might let me use it.

Perhaps I wanted to embarrass him when I mentioned this to a good friend over lunch. I figured she would either dismiss him as a closet homosexual—in which case he didn't love his ex or me—or a pervert, in which case we could have a good laugh at his expense.

"Oh my God, you have to do it!" she said, practically jumping out of her chair. "How many guys are gonna give you this opportunity? It's the chance of a lifetime!" She hastily motioned for the waiter to bring us the check, saying that she was pretty sure she'd have what I needed in her trunk.

I should explain that at the time my friend was a struggling artist, supporting herself by writing porn reviews for a sex industry trade magazine. She really was quite normal, and like many other journalists, she got her fair share of swag in the mail, most of it X-rated. Her gifts were a huge hit at birthday parties: gigantic baskets of videos, vibrators, and cock rings that everyone would pass around and pretend to be shocked by.

We went to her car and it turned out that she did indeed have everything I needed, including an adjustable rainbow-striped harness that I assumed was marketed to lesbians who liked their strap-ons to make a political statement. She also had an array of dildos in a variety of sizes, colors, and shapes, all still in their original packaging. She insisted I take two—a four-inch and a six-inch—so P. would have a choice of size. Pressing a sample of K-Y into my hand, she gave me a significant look. "You'll need this," she said.

I stuffed the strap-on and accoutrements into my bag, brought them home, and shoved them in a bathroom cabinet, convinced I wouldn't ever use them. But then P. started talking about his ex all the time. I was great, and he really cared about me, but he had a whole history with her. Our sex was better, but they'd put in so much time it seemed a waste not to give it another chance. I listened and said nothing. I wanted to be his girlfriend, damn it. I was convinced I was in love with him, but it wasn't merely about love anymore; my dignity—my whole worldview—was at stake.

One night we returned to the Coach and Horses, and amidst the amber haze of beer, cigarette smoke, and several mentions of his ex, P. brought up the strap-on again. If I wanted to do it, he might let me, he said. If I was mad at him about his ex, this could be the way to "punish him."

We went back to my house. As I opened the door, I realized how angry I was. I couldn't believe how many times he'd mentioned his ex-girlfriend, both that night and in the past few weeks. My humiliation was vast and deep: I'd been hanging on, hoping he would choose me, sinking deeper every time I slept with him. The deeper I sank, the more I clung. The strap-on beckoned. Even if it's what he wants, even if he's goading me, I thought, if I use it on him, I can't lose. If he liked it, I'd be the woman who made his sexual dreams come true, ex be damned. If he dumped me, I'd still be the girl who fucked him up the ass, which had its own appealing ring. While he continued to moan and groan about his ex, I went to the kitchen and opened a bottle of Champagne that had been sitting in my refrigerator since New Year's.

"What's the occasion?" he asked.

"I got you a present," I said.

"What is it?" P. looked wary. On to me and my sad commitment fantasies, he probably thought it would be some thoughtfully guilt-inducing gift.

I told him I had gotten a strap-on.

He asked if I was joking. I said I was not. He said he wanted to see it.

I didn't want him to see the actual harness—the rainbows, the Velcro, so silly. Instead I went into the bathroom and took out the dildos. "You get to choose," I said, placing them on my dining room table.

The four-inch one was friendly: a glossy, smooth abstraction of a phallus in ironic hot pink rubber. The six-inch one was mean: jet black with molded veins, a thick shaft, proudly stiff, and shaped like, well...like a cock.

I was sure he would pick the pink.

He tapped the black. "If you're going to do it," he said, "may as well go full tilt."

We laughed nervously. We drank some more. We went into the bedroom and started messing around. He went down on me. I gave him some head. Then I said, "Stay here."

He lay back to wait for me and I went into the bathroom. I still wasn't sure I could do it. The more I thought about it, the more the act seemed potentially messy if not disgusting. What mortifying stains would a strap-on leave on my 300-thread-count sheets? What if the strap-on changed me from a peppy writer girl from California into a sick, twisted sex addict destined to end up stripping somewhere off the 5 freeway?

My hands were shaking. I'd never really examined the harness, a bewildering mass of straps and Velcro and plastic buckles. After a few tries, I figured out I had to step into it and adjust the buckles to fit snugly around my legs and my butt. I put it on and suddenly felt very odd. I was wearing Mork and Mindy rainbow suspenders with a big hole in front of my pussy. It was not a sexy look. I reached for the black dildo. A voice inside me said, *You're way out of your depth.* It was true. How, really, does one fuck another? I'd been on top, of course, and bounced up and down until I lost my breath. But that was really a pantomime of fucking. I had never penetrated, merely enveloped with gusto. Actually penetrating a guy—fucking the shit out of him—was something else. What if I didn't have the nerve to go through with it? What if I had lousy technique? What if I hurt him? Heavy is the head that wears the crown.

"Are you okay?" P. called from the bedroom.

I called back that I would be another minute and struggled to get the black dildo out of its packaging. Those hard plastic packages are impossible to open even when you're dressed and completely sober. I finally managed, then I had to loosen the harness, slip the dildo through the hole, and tighten it back up. I did it all without really looking down at myself. I was so embarrassed already, I didn't know if I could take any more self-degradation. But of course I had to see. I slid my eyes down my naked torso, past my little breasts, down between my legs, and . . .

I had a dick.

If I moved left, it moved left. If I moved right, it moved right. It was snug to my body—it didn't flap around or wiggle. I had complete control over it. When I jumped, it jumped. If I thrust my hips forward, it thrust forward. It moved, it looked, exactly like a penis. It was heavy but erect in the way that a penis is heavy but erect. It was attached to me. I turned to go, bumped my new appendage into the sink by mistake, and almost apologized to it. I couldn't believe it. I was delighted. I felt strong and masculine and crafty and feminine all at once. I had a dick! I had a dick! I had a dick!

I walked into the bedroom. "I want to see," he said.

"Don't move," I commanded, his words ringing in my ears: *If you're going to do it, may as well go full tilt.*

I straddled him, my knees pinning his shoulders to the bed.

"Kiss it," I said. He did, and I watched, agog.

"Lick it," I said. He did. I was getting wet just watching him do my bidding, taking orders, a slave to what I had, to what he wanted. Our roles had been reversed. He was suddenly me. If he wanted my dick, he had to be compliant. He was excited, and tried to sneak a finger up inside me.

"No," I commanded, wanting to stay in charge. "Turn over."

He rolled onto his stomach. I crept up his naked body. My breasts tickled his back, but my strap-on poked him, bluntly stating its purpose. I was a girl-man, a man-girl. I started to toy with him, to kiss his ears, the back of his neck. He groaned. I was terrified but emboldened. I took out the K-Y. Like a guy, I slathered the jelly onto my cock. I pulled him up by the waist, so his ass was in the air, and I spread his legs open cruelly with my knees. I held my breath. There was no turning back. With no ceremony and no apologies, I pushed the tip into him. He tensed for a moment. I felt his body resist. I felt his fear. Something inside me told me to be merciless and I pushed in deeper, then deeper still, then all the way. He started groaning. He started panting. He was clutching the pillow. He was terrified. He was in ecstasy. Eager for more, I started to fuck him. I was so in the moment, so connected to my strap-on and the feeling of his body giving way to my presence, that I quickly got more excited. I was dripping wet, yet I held back. I would not give him the satisfaction of coming first. I wanted to fuck him and fuck him and fuck him hard, harder, hardest. Now he was screaming,

screaming! He was making crying sounds and mewing sounds and gasping and carrying on like—like a *girl!*—and I was fucking him and holding back and holding back and trying not to come and commanding, "Tell me you love it."

"I love it!" he yelled.

"Tell me you love it!"

"I love it!" he screamed. "Fuck me! Fuck me! Fuck me! *Fuck me!*"

We both came at once and I collapsed on top of him, exhausted, spent, delirious.

*   *   *

The following morning, I bundled up the strap-on, the sheets, all the evidence of what we'd done, and threw it in the wash. Over bagels and coffee, P. and I exchanged some "wows." We determined that he liked it and I liked it. He made jokes about how he was sore and I made jokes about how now he knew how the other half lived. We discussed whether we would ever do it again, and we were both unsure—it had been such a momentous evening, we couldn't even consider trying to replicate it. Not now, anyway. Maybe not ever.

P. went back to New York a week later. We had a farewell date, and it was fun but anticlimactic. I wasn't sure where we stood, but I wasn't sure I wanted to know. After he left, I moved the strap-on and the dildo from my bathroom to a paper bag in my hall closet until I changed apartments a year later and finally threw them away. One time turned out to be enough. The strap-on had granted me a kind of supervision, a gift. I had seen—experienced—how a man could have sex with a woman and love it but not love her, and it was okay. It was natural, and I was no whore. I'd glimpsed a power in myself I'd never known I had, and I wasn't ashamed. Suddenly, everything clicked into place. I might have sex without love again, but I was sure I would know the difference. It would be a decision I could make, or not.

One night P. called to tell me that he was, in fact, getting back together with M. I was stung, yes, but not as much as I thought I would be. I was even a bit amused, because P. was not simply P. anymore. He wasn't another guy who'd fucked me and left. He was also the guy *I'd* fucked.

He and M. eventually broke up, of course. He visits Los Angeles occasionally, and when I run into him, I can't help thinking about how he looked, how he sounded, how he felt when I pounded myself into him that night, after so many weeks of him pounding himself into me. I think of his terrified eyes and his cries of pure ecstasy and I smile. P. and I are now as we will always remain: even.

Pregnant Pause

PARI CHANG

One of the reasons I married my husband, Geoffrey, was that we had great sex. Before him, I gauged compatibility by quality of conversation: the Jewish jabbermouth school of thought. But Geoffrey is Chinese, and the Chinese are generally not a schmoozing tribe. Geoffrey is not a ruminator, a neurotic, or a bullshit artist. He doesn't say "What if I kissed you?" or worry about kissing you or tell you a story before kissing you. Geoffrey kisses you when he feels like kissing you. I might be pulling my hair back into a ponytail, getting ready for the gym, when he'd curl into my neck, jolting me out of that ordinary moment. His breath smelled like Coca-Cola, a sweetness welling up from inside. Plus, he had the athletic, exotic good looks of those Calvin Klein underwear models on billboards in Times Square. When he'd kiss me while my hands were tied up in twisting the elastic band, it thrilled me that a quiet man could be so bold.

We met at a bar, coincidentally sharing a booth with mutual acquaintances. He put down his scotch glass too close to my martini and his pinky brushed against mine. *Don't look at him*, I thought. *Keep your eyes on the olive.* But the energy of our two pinkies touching made me unable to sit still, so I shimmied out of the booth and zigzagged through the squeezed crowd to lose myself in a forest of tall people. Geoffrey followed and suddenly pressed his palm against the small of my back. Not just a pinky this time, but the whole hand, and on purpose. With the music blaring, I couldn't rely on repartee to control his flirtation. Instead, I acquiesced and let Geoffrey lead me to the dance floor, where he never took his eyes off mine.

For our first date, Geoffrey suggested Central Park. I'd never before been asked out for the afternoon. I took it as a challenge by Geoffrey: Get to know me without buffering the awkwardness with a few drinks. In the taxi, I asked him where he was from. "I don't know really," he said. "I was born in California. Then we lived in Boulder, Colorado. After that it was back to Cali, then Boulder again, and then New York. My father was a scientist, so we moved around a lot. What's your story?"

"I'm from New Jersey," I said. It actually sounded enviable. We took out a rowboat. Alone on the still water, I dug deeper. "So, after all of that moving around, what feels like home?"

"That's the million-dollar question," Geoffrey replied. Then he pulled the rowboat onto a muddy bank, dragged a log from the brush, and fashioned a bridge to a waterside boulder like an urban Tom Sawyer. He sidestepped across and I followed—touché. Our postures on the boulder were the same, shoulders rounded, hands atop bent knees. For many minutes, he made me brave silence. "Granola bar?" was all he said, then fished one from the pocket of his board shorts.

We spent the rest of the afternoon lounging together in the Sheep Meadow. I finally asked him what he was thinking. "I'm not thinking," he said. "I'm just lying with you on a blanket in the grass."

I always assumed I'd know, really know, the man I married, but Geoffrey was more like a scent I followed. I thought I'd end up with a Jewish guy who had my wiring: a running internal dialogue, a need to be organized, prompt, and approved of. Or else I figured I'd fall for my perfect opposite, that we'd yin and yang like pieces of a puzzle. But Geoffrey and I weren't mirror images or halves of the same whole.

The first time we fooled around, he climbed up my stomach and exhaled, whispering, "Feels like poetry." The second time, he said, "Does it frighten you that I think I love you?" We'd only been dating for a few weeks.

"A little," I admitted, "like being outside when it's about to storm."

He tucked the top sheet behind the headboard so that it arced above us. "A tent for two, then," he said. "It's going to be a good rain."

Soon we were making love, all the time, *love*. He'd undress me, peeling off one item at a time. I'd close my eyes, raise my arms above my head, and listen to his chest heaving. Holding my face in his hands, he'd kiss me hard, without opening his mouth. Then he'd gently take off my pearl earrings. In our tangle of lovemaking, I'd stop thinking, for once. Looking at Geoffrey, I'd see his black hair stiff as a paintbrush; his diamond-shaped face, a leopard; his smooth muscled legs, a sculpture. And after sex, the whir of bliss kept coming. It was a primordial kind of pleasure. Letting him inside me put me deep inside myself.

While looking for a like mind, I found belonging in a lover. A life mate isn't always calculable on paper, by check marks next to a list of traits. Sometimes rightness is ascertainable by instinct, like other gambles. I pinned my star on the psychedelic rush I felt just relaxing beside Geoffrey on that blanket in Central Park, watching the trees sway against the sky.

We were married for four years, both thirty-two, when I got pregnant somewhat unexpectedly. Though I'd stopped taking the pill, we weren't officially trying. Geoffrey liked to say that we pulled the goalie but still played defense. I'd purchased a pregnancy test mostly as an indulgence at Rite Aid, along with hot-oil treatments and tortoiseshell barrettes. I peed on the stick, propped it against the soap dish, and settled into a bubble bath. Squinty-eyed and rinsing my hair, I saw the blue plus sign develop like a Polaroid picture. When Geoffrey heard the urgency in my voice, he shut off the barbecue mid-grill. He greeted me with a sausage wheel on a paper plate, the most foreboding of meats. I pointed to the evidence by the soap dish.

"Plus sign means addition, but to me this looks like an *x*," he said. "What does *x* mean?" As if semantics could get us out of this one.

"X means we're multiplying."

My husband sat on the cover of the toilet seat. "I was just about to watch the Yankees game," he said. Our dog, Iverson, lapped at the sausage wheel. "That's my dinner," Geoffrey snapped, then picked up the dog and tossed him into the tub.

"You're mean to pets!" I shouted as he stormed off to

the television. I thought of how I never would have agreed to name our Boston terrier after a basketball bad-ass with corn-rows, but Geoffrey knew that I knew nothing about sports, so he posited that Iverson had a literary air, like Emerson. "Mommy's pregnant," I told the poor dog now, scooping him into my arms. I was hoping for a lick, some sign of en-thusiasm that I hadn't gotten from my husband. But Iverson shook the water from his coat, spraying the entire mirror with bubbles.

As I plodded past Geoffrey, I started to cry. "Because of you, I have to Windex!" I wanted to get into what I was really crying about: Geoffrey's reaction to my news. The downside of being married to a passionate man is his temper. It made him behave like a real jerk sometimes even though he wasn't one. I resented the way our communication occasion-ally broke down, but I knew from experience that the only way to connect with Geoffrey at times like this was to wait in silence until he composed himself.

"I'm sorry I threw the dog in the bath," Geoffrey sighed later, when he finally came to bed. He rolled Iverson onto his back, scratched his tummy, and said "Forgive me, little buddy?" with such tenderness that it softened me. He nuz-zled Iverson a little, and I cuddled in, too. "Look, a guy is used to trying not to get his girl pregnant, so when you told me, my first reaction was ... you know." But I didn't know. "Dread," he said. He kissed my shoulder, then my neck. "But I can't tell you how excited I am now."

"Yeah? How excited?" I pushed his shoulders back against the mattress, kissing him, on top of him. I slid my hand into his boxers, but he giggled.

"You're tickling me," he said, but I kept kissing him.

"Can we take a rain check?" he asked. "I just feel really ticklish tonight."

He rejected another overture a few nights later. My ob-gyn had just confirmed how far along I was, so Geoffrey and I were Googling "pregnant + 5 weeks," clicking on the first link that came up: *Your baby is the size of a sesame seed,* it began. Geoffrey asked me to scoot over to make room on my desk chair for both of our butts. We read along together. "This feels nice, sitting thigh to thigh," I whispered.

"Don't get any funny ideas," he said. He sounded like a teenager at a drive-in movie whose date has just tried to cop a feel.

The same thing happened the next week, and the week after that: We tracked fetal development online every evening, then went uneventfully to bed. *Your baby is the size of a lentil...a raspberry.*

I spooned Geoffrey to mimic the shape of a kidney bean on the night we read that our baby had grown to that size. When he told me to stop, I apologized. I tried to convince myself that it wasn't a big deal that we weren't having sex. After all, Geoffrey was being a loving partner in other ways—attending ob-gyn appointments, even boycotting sushi as an act of solidarity when the doctor said I couldn't eat it. Still, after he fell asleep, I snuck over to the computer and logged on to our favorite pregnancy Web site. I scrolled past kidney bean, my heart thumping like a wily spy, and read ahead, even though we'd agreed not to do that. Next week would be grape, I found out, and after that, kumquat. *If he doesn't fuck me by kumquat, we've got a problem,* I told myself. *Kumquat.* The word itself sounded evocative of orgasm.

When kumquat came, I wore a lace demi-cup bra with

matching panties to bed and draped a bare thigh over Geoffrey's hip. He pulled the duvet up to his neck. "It's too weird," he demurred, and kissed me chastely on the forehead.

"Weird?" I snapped. "Weird is for things in formaldehyde!"

"Lots of guys get freaked about having sex during pregnancy," he said.

"I'm not even showing! My tits are fabulous! What's your problem?"

Geoffrey lowered his head and gripped his hair in his fists. "I never imagined having sex with a pregnant woman," he blurted. The truth always comes out in the dark.

I never imagined falling for a Chinese guy, I almost shot back. "Love is full of surprises," I said, instead.

"Maybe it's evolution. The male's desire drops once the female is pregnant." He was grasping at straws, talking propagation of the species.

Frustrated, I slipped into something more comfortable— an oversized T-shirt and drawstring pajamas. Then I sat on the bed, took a deep breath, and interrupted him. "Hello? Your problem isn't biological. It's psychological." Geoffrey had never seen a shrink or even been a pot smoker. He had the just-do-it mentality of an athlete or a warrior. "Imagine this scenario," I began. "You see me pruning the African violets on the windowsill, but I don't know you're there. You feel mischievous. You take the watering can and sprinkle my back, then trace my spine through my wet, clinging blouse. Then you push me onto the easy chair. I'm pregnant and we are about to make love. What goes through your head?"

"Poking the baby. The sonogram, this little tadpole swimming around, and then *bam*! A giant spear butts up against his bubble, stabbing and stabbing like a punch to the gut."

A punch to the gut—that was exactly what his explanation felt like to me. *If sex with his pregnant wife is weird,* I told myself, *then shouldn't he wade through the weirdness? Isn't that intimacy?* I wondered if our problem had a cultural component. On the Internet I learned that Chinese women don't have sex during pregnancy. But I wasn't Chinese, and besides, when I ran the cultural precept by American-born Geoffrey, he told me that he was unaware of it. Still, maybe the tradition had seeped into him, the way ham grosses me out even though I don't keep kosher. Kumquat. I never should have picked a Chinese fruit for our week of sexual reckoning.

"You have to meet me halfway here," I told Geoffrey. "My hormones are raging. I've been having orgasms in my sleep."

"Doesn't sound so terrible." He laughed.

"I dreamed the super of the building next door followed me up a ladder, wearing his tool belt and whispering to me in his Irish brogue. Okay?"

"That old man with the belly?"

"Please touch me," I said. "I need you." I reminded him of those times that he'd asked me to pleasure him as a courtesy of monogamy, when he woke me in the middle of the night because he'd had a stressful day at the office and wanted release. I had always obliged, just as a neighbor lends a cup of sugar. So now he did.

During my second trimester, at my urging, we visited a New York sex shop called Come Again. Geoffrey chose an erotic book and a porno. I picked out a vibrator. The woman behind the counter had a crew cut and bound breasts. She looked at my pear-shaped belly but didn't smile collegially or ask when I was due. "Can I ask you a question, miss?

Ma'am?" I stammered. "It says 'two-in-one' on this box. What exactly does that mean?"

She shrugged. "You get penetration. You get stimulation."

"American Express?" I said.

At home, we began with the tamest item in our bag of booty: the dirty book. Then Geoffrey clicked off the bedside lamp and reached for the vibrator. "How does this feel?" he whispered. *Like a buzzing gelatinous carrot,* I thought. Here I was, pregnant. I wanted our connection to feel organic, not manufactured.

"Maybe if we lit some candles," I said.

"Is that better?" he asked. It wasn't.

"Honey, no dice," I finally said.

Physical closeness became even more awkward when I had to resort to sleeping on my side with a special pregnancy pillow between my legs, its big U cushioning my back and front.

"That stuffed snake takes up too much room," Geoffrey would say.

"It's called a Snoogle, and I need it."

I'd get up to pee in the middle of the night and he'd toss, turn, and mumble, "This damned Snoogle."

One Saturday evening, I woke up and found him sleeping on the couch. I missed him so much in that moment that I gently straddled him, hoping he'd be too groggy to protest. But when he felt himself inside of me, he freaked: "The baby! Get off!"

I guess he felt guilty the next morning, because as he folded the spare blanket he'd slept with, he offered, "How about we go shopping today?" I took that to mean *Forgive me for last night.*

I put down the *Times*. Sitting Indian-style on the living room rug, I had just heard the knock of opportunity. So I slunk toward my husband on my hands and knees and kissed my way up his thigh.

"No way," he said. "You just threw up." True, but now I felt better than ever, and I'd brushed my teeth twice. "I don't do well with sick women." I wondered aloud if it triggered bad memories for him, since he had lost his mother to cancer. "Must you get Freudian?" he asked. The moment had passed.

I'm a proud woman, not at all masochistic, so I had to ask myself why my desperation intensified with every rebuff. I thought about the word *pregnant*, how it meant "having a child developing inside" but also "full of meaning, significant." That was just it: Pregnancy had a way of magnifying issues, so our sexual impasse seemed suddenly portentous, as if we had some major marital problem that I had somehow overlooked. I wondered whether we communicated well enough to weather parenthood.

Midway through my second trimester, we took a trip to the Greek islands to reconnect. At the beach, Geoffrey dug a hole in the sand, then spread a towel over the indentation so I could lie on my stomach and read my book. In our villa on the cliffs of Santorini, I modeled my white silk lingerie for Geoffrey by the light of the moon. "How do I look?" I asked him. When I wore it on our honeymoon, he'd said, *Good enough to eat,* and bit me on the hip.

"Radiant," he said now, and stepped back for a wide-angle view, as if I were a museum piece to behold behind glass. He regarded my body with respectful awe, as if I were a goddess. But I didn't want to be rendered too sacred to fuck.

"What don't you feel that you need to feel in order to make love to me?" I asked.

"Aroused?" he ventured, which I found shallow, unenlightened, and a little bit mean.

As the window sheers puffed like a sail in the Mediterranean breeze, I wondered if I belonged with a loafer-wearing Jewish guy in the suburbs, driving an SUV with GPS. Geoffrey and I didn't own a car that told us which way to turn. We didn't even own a car. We borrowed one from Geoffrey's dad, rented our Manhattan apartment, and partied on weeknights. My life with Geoffrey had no blueprint, and I had always relished the possibilities. But with pregnancy, we bid an abrupt adios to Champagne Tuesdays. Now that we had a peppy little dog and a bun in the oven, the vista seemed to be narrowing.

The following afternoon, we meandered through the island streets buying a Greek baby bonnet, a European rattle, and a watercolor painting for the nursery. At outdoor cafés along the way, we dipped pita in a shared plate of hummus and ate ice cream in giant waffle cones. On our last day in Santorini, we spent sunset at the beach. At the water's edge, I faced the sea, stretched my legs into a wide V, and hung my head, the tide lapping the ends of my hair. From this upside-down view, I admired the figure of Geoffrey sitting in the sand, bent-legged, palms cupped around his knees. *He's not thinking,* I knew, without having to ask. *He's simply watching his pregnant wife do yoga along the orange horizon.*

A few days later, in Mykonos, Geoffrey ran his hand down the curve of my side while we napped one afternoon. I pulled him close against my back, all sunscreen and salt, his breath a conch sound in my ear. He reached under my cover-up and tugged down my bathing suit bottom. My belly was too big for us to lie face-to-face, too big for me to reach my arms over his head and let him slip off my top, too big for him to toss me onto an easy chair with abandon. We made quick, silent love, then we fell asleep. When we rose at dusk, the sheets glowed white and the pillows were as cool as clouds.

Neither of us mentioned it afterward, and when we returned home, we settled back into our abstinent routine. I didn't expect otherwise; our Internet research no longer alluded to small fruits or salad beans and instead referred to an actual baby. Geoffrey and I connected physically in a different way now. He rubbed shea butter on my stomach at night or rested his head on my belly to feel a little foot kick.

In my eighth month, he left on a business trip. I made popcorn and rented *Mona Lisa Smile*, free to watch a Julia Roberts movie in peace. I opened the DVD drive and recoiled from what I found inside—the Come Again porno. So on those nights when Geoffrey had stayed up late in the living room and I called from our bed, "What are you watching?" it wasn't the Patriots game after all.

Now it was my turn. I fast-forwarded past the raunchy plumber laying the pipe to the housewife on the kitchen counter. In fact, I skipped all the scenes with men in them. The lesbians did it for me. The lesbians! A female lover would not hesitate to make love to a pregnant woman, I thought. She'd watch the Julia Roberts movie with me, then make my Mona Lisa smile all night long.

Geoffrey called me from his hotel room before going to sleep. I told him I'd found the porno in the DVD player and asked why he hadn't copped to watching it.

"You would have asked me to watch it with you," he said, the telephone allowing him to be more frank than if we had been speaking in person. "I'm sorry I lied about the Patriots," he said before we hung up. And with that, I forgave him.

In bed, I cozied up with my Snoogle, but all I could think about was the baby. So I got up, gathered my jars of sample paint, and let loose in the nursery, brushing swatches of periwinkle on the walls. Geoffrey maintained 99 percent certainty that the baby would be a boy, but as a favor to a friend, I let a Hollywood psychic read my belly for an *Access Hollywood* segment and, as broadcast on national television, the psychic predicted a girl—and an easy labor, to boot.

A few months after our baby was born—a boy by emergency C-section (so much for the psychic)—Geoffrey and I celebrated our fifth wedding anniversary. While my mom babysat, we spent the day at the Brooklyn Botanic Garden, the site of our wedding. We walked through the Shakespeare garden, passed the Japanese pagoda, and ambled up Celebrity Path, a trail of stones, each carved with a name of a celebrity from Brooklyn. Somewhere between Marisa Tomei and Judge Judy, Geoffrey squeezed my tush. We arrived at the amphitheater where we'd said our vows and he slid his hand up my skirt. Call it adolescent exhibitionism; actually, it was love. Beyond the cherry esplanade and rose garden, past the signs for compost and native flora, we ravished each other, trusting the moment.

Suddenly, Geoffrey noticed a man up ahead whom he took for a park ranger. Frantic, he buckled his belt and tucked his BlackBerry and our bottle of Poland Spring water into his pants pockets. "That's a uniform he's wearing," he whispered.

"A polo shirt and khakis?" I whispered back.

"I think I saw a wire in his ear." The only other tourists

we'd run into were two bearded Deadheads, hard-core environmentalists, and now Geoffrey was convinced they'd reported us to the botany police.

"Sir, madam, you're under arrest and charged with one count of fucking by the ferns, two counts of coming in the compost," I teased, but Geoffrey couldn't be calmed.

He grabbed my hand and we ran like Hansel and Gretel through the forest, looping to the parking lot and sliding into his father's car. In the shelter of the capsule, sun-warmed leather kissing the backs of our thighs, Geoffrey loosed a loud "Wooooey!" and gunned the gas, my husband and I like the Dukes of Hazzard making our getaway in the General Lee.

On the Brooklyn Bridge, I opened my window all the way and let the wind pull at my cheeks. Then I craned out to see the water, a vantage both terrifying and irresistible. When traffic slowed to a near halt, I sat properly in my seat. Geoffrey's wedding ring flickered with light on the steering wheel. I knew what he'd reply if I asked him now: *What does home feel like?* He'd say, *Home feels like this.* At the crest of the bridge, Manhattan sprawling, Geoffrey said, "Happy anniversary." It came out like a promise reiterated, as if he was declaring *I do. I still do.*

Under the Influence

ANNA MARRIAN

I was about to have sex for the first time—sober. I was just past thirty. Michael and I had both been off booze and drugs for a year and had met recently in a sober summer share on Long Island. In the old days, I'd have screwed him first then introduced myself. But so far, in the three weeks we'd been dating, our physical contact had been limited to a sheepish mutual application of sunscreen at the beach.

I lay beneath the blankets, arms clamped to my sides like a mummy. The bathroom light clicked off and Michael padded toward me in his white T-shirt and knit boxers. Without a word, he slipped under the covers and lay alongside me. We stayed that way—like two stiffs sharing a sarcophagus—not talking, just waiting, the room filling with the noise of our breath and the sirens outside.

Interrupting our paralyzed silence, Michael reached over

and placed his arm, motionless, on my belly. I wanted to make the next move but instead remained still, too nervous to show that I wanted him. Suddenly, he rolled on top of me, our mouths mashing awkwardly, hands fumbling with buttocks and boobs. We raced forward to intercourse—to be done with it—our bodies jammed together like mismatched pieces of a jigsaw puzzle. Was this what I'd gotten sober for? I wondered. Had I traded in the lush life for a future of anxious humps? In all my years of getting high, I couldn't remember a night as unsexy as this.

*   *   *

My first drink and kiss came together on my fourteenth birthday. The boy was tall with soft brown eyes and he worked at my riding stable. He made me laugh. And the more I laughed, the more my crush grew. By midsummer, I was going to the barn to clean my saddle daily, simply to be near him. When my birthday came around, I invited him to my pool party and after everyone left he stayed behind.

My family lived in a sprawling three-story colonial house in the New York countryside that was easy to creep around in unnoticed, especially since my mother and stepfather were hosting a noisy dinner party in the dining room down the hall. We swiped a bottle of Jack Daniel's from the well-stocked bar, then made for the far end of the back lawn, near the edge of the woods, under the summer shadows. It was a hot July and we were still in our bathing suits from the party, passing the bottle back and forth until everything turned misty. I took gulps of the sickly brown stuff until I could no longer feel the bottoms of my feet against the damp grass.

I blacked out and came to in his arms as he carried me up the three long flights of stairs to my room. I held his neck tight. He delivered me to my wrought-iron bed and placed his lips, soft and gentle, on mine. He kissed like we had all the time in the world. It felt sweet and good and I could have gone on like that forever. Then his hand slid down the top of my suit and rested on my lower belly, and a fear in my gut started circling like a school of sharks.

I'd never been kissed, but I had been touched once before, a year earlier, by a man fifteen years older. He was a distant but favorite cousin on my father's side, one I didn't see often since he lived overseas. I'd met him while visiting my father; my parents had divorced when I was three and my dad moved abroad. I craved this cousin's attention, as I did my father's. So when he said he wanted to spend a month on my stepfather's farm to get a taste of American life, I hoped we would grow close. Instead, he doted on my younger half sister, who'd captured his attention with her crooked bangs and missing front teeth. With my bush of frizzy hair, metal teeth, and oily T-zone, I couldn't compete, so I sulked instead.

Finally, he noticed.

That's when he suggested we grab some drinks—a martini shaker and two glasses—and take a drive up to the back fields to watch the sunset, just the two of us. As we lay in the cut hay, warm from the August heat, his hand suddenly pressed on my small, braless breast. He was smiling down at me and I flinched but tried not to show it, my eyes searching for something to focus on in the sky overhead. The smell of hot skin and cut grass passed over me, and I froze as his hand slid under my shirt to feel my newly budding breasts, my heart hammering beneath his touch. I wanted to tell him to stop but by then his hand had made its way down into my pants and had taken my voice away. A prickly sensation scorched my skin. My body—still so new and foreign to me—suddenly felt appropriated. Stiff with fear, I slipped out of it, leaving it like roadkill.

I looked up at his raised eyebrows and lopsided smile. "This is what cousins do together," he said. I tried to hold his gaze but my eyes wouldn't stop darting. He asked me how I felt: "Happy, scared, confused?"

I was terrified but answered that I was confused. I'd masturbated a few times but had never been touched like this by any boy, let alone a man twice my age. When his fingers rubbed me, it was like sandpaper on rough board. Perhaps another girl could have found pleasure, let herself go beneath his touch, but I was not that girl. When he was done, he stood up tall above me, my stepfather's pewter martini shaker in his hand. A chill blew out of the navy blue sky and again he asked what I was thinking. I shrugged and shook my head, so he did the talking. He told me this was something just between us and that I mustn't tell anyone, especially Mom, in whom I still confided my secrets. He made me promise. I tried to convince myself this was all normal because betraying him would mean betraying my father's family and my tentative place within it. This I wouldn't do. I carried his touch locked inside, my body wrapped tightly around it.

And so, on the night of my fourteenth birthday, I stiffened reflexively when the boy with the soft brown eyes ran his fingers along my thigh and tried to push in underneath my bathing suit. The room was spinning and my throat was tight and dry and I grabbed his wrist and held it firmly. He didn't fight me and we kept on kissing. My body relaxed again and I pushed my lips into his as softly as I could, feeling for the sweetness that had slipped away.

A week after, I found my first crush laughing with another girl, one who was easy, everyone said. He wouldn't look at me. My heart sank. I wanted to tell him why I'd been scared but I couldn't. Instead, I drank some beers and right in front of him kissed the guy who worked in the barn, the one who was handsome but kind of dumb and not funny at all.

My cousin taught me how to separate from my body; my father showed me how to stay that way. When I was sixteen, I went to visit him on my own for the first time. Before, I'd barely gotten to see him alone. This time, he promised, he'd tour me around, just the two of us.

Days after my arrival, I was lying on his bed, a king-sized canopy floating overhead, as he got ready for dinner in his adjacent dressing room. The ceiling fan wafted a warm breeze while we chatted through the open door. He wanted to know all about my life back in New York, so I told him everything: about my mother's disintegrating marriage, how she and I had grown apart. I told him I was relieved to be living at boarding school, where I got wasted on booze and pot with my friends. I told him I'd snuck into my boyfriend's dorm room and had sex for the first time. I felt comfortable telling him the things I'd stopped telling my mom. According to my mother, my dad was easy, permissive, bohemian. Mom told me he'd smoked pot with my half siblings when they were teenagers and I knew she didn't approve.

As he sauntered into his bedroom in navy slacks and a freshly pressed shirt open at the neck where he was tying a scarf, he casually asked me if I'd tried anything other than pot, such as cocaine. I wanted to be grown-up for him, so I lied and said I had. "Oh yeah, once. It was pretty cool."

"You want to try it again?" he asked, arching his brows.

"Uh, yeah, I guess," I said in disbelief, thinking this would never have happened back home. My mother once told me she'd had a bad trip on hash brownies and hadn't wavered from her vodka-on-the-rocks regimen since.

"This will be our little secret while you're here," he said as he clapped and rubbed his hands together, his habit when he got excited. The bright lights and white walls of his room seemed stark against the black night leaking through the big open windows, the breeze carrying unfamiliar screeches and hissings. "You can only have a very little bit. It's top-of-the-line pharmaceutical. Very pure stuff," he said, retrieving and opening a small brown leather case that held a thimble-sized glass vial, small mirror, razor blade, and matching brass spoon and straw. "Go get us two glasses of whiskey on the rocks," he said without a glance. I hated whiskey, though I'd never tell him. I wanted what he wanted.

As I hurried down the long open-air hallway from his bedroom to the bar, the terra-cotta tiles cooled my nervous feet. Geckos clung to the walls, their red necks ballooning for their mates. When I returned, he was snorting a line, and then he let me do one. We passed the straw back and forth and he smeared his finger across the residue on the mirror and rubbed his gums. I copied him and my mouth felt thick and frozen.

I held my breath and gulped at the whiskey, washing away the bitter coke drippings clinging to the back of my throat. As I watched him clean up the paraphernalia, I caught a scent of jasmine. I breathed it in deeply, a velvety bloom slipping under my skin, and breathed out a shinier version of myself, more perfect, more certain, more lovable. I felt close to my father in a way I never had, bound by our special secret.

After doing coke most nights with my father, I returned to New York with a new sense of rebellion in my step. I wanted to go to parties in Manhattan in short skirts, tight

shirts, and stilettos. In the disapproving words of my stepfather, I was "hot to trot." When I went back to boarding
school, I moved into the party dorm and spent long weekends
with my boyfriend, smoking pot and having sex. I'd get so
high that my limbs felt cut off from my body when he rocked
on top of me, his naked shape hulking and foreign through
my haze. After he graduated, I started fooling around with
my best friend's boyfriend, drunkenly rubbing up against him
in the dim light of the English classroom, the heat between
my legs stoked by the thrill of our clandestine encounters.

By senior year, my grades were erratic and I was placed
on probation for drinking. On the eve of Christmas vacation,
I got drunk and fell down a slippery flight of wooden stairs,
only to be revived by the paramedics and expelled the following afternoon. Mom was not pleased. We fought most days
as I finished up my senior year at the hippie progressive
school near home.

It seemed perfectly natural then, quite adult in my mind,
that on my eighteenth birthday, on the cusp of my so-called
independence, I would discover sex on cocaine. I was living
in London with my mother for the summer and had quickly
hooked up with the son of one of her acquaintances. He was
older, as would become my pattern. At my birthday party, he
put his hand on my ass and whispered that he had a surprise
for me. He led me out the back door and I slid into the slick
bucket seat of his Porsche, where he gave me a few bumps of
powder off his car key. We'd indulged once before but he
hadn't been this generous. It was 1985, the postpunk era, and
as the drug kicked in, I looked at myself in the reflection of
the windscreen: a teased-out platinum bramble around my
head, black Cleopatra eyes, scarlet lips, black bustier, pink
poof skirt, and pointy lime-green stilettos. I could feel his

eyes greedy on me. The drugs, the outfit, his desire, made me feel like someone else—someone who could command power, make men ache for me.

After we did lines of cocaine on his glass coffee table in his basement apartment, he pushed me up against the wall and stripped me naked, laying me out on his bed. I enjoyed being taken this way, being the object of his hunger. I stretched my body out for him to see and he draped his olive-skinned body over mine. His appetite excited me more than the sex; in truth, I felt nothing physically as he pumped from above. When we returned to the party, I ran in and out of the bathroom taking more bumps off his fat car key. Each time, his hands slid along the back of my thighs and into my black lacy underwear, and each time, I left him wanting more.

At the end of the summer my mother returned to her place in the States and I stayed in London, quickly finding other older men along with the drugs. The combination gave me a sense of home. But by winter, I'd lost my job, run low on money, and moved into an abandoned office building with some North London squatters. Like everyone else there, I survived on the dole and the occasional temp job, rotating drugs and men like goods on an auction block. Some boyfriends lasted a few months, others were one-night stands, but the drugs were a constant. I wasn't picky as long as I could get high, though the anarchic crowd I ran with preferred hallucinogens, which they considered to be more refined than the powders.

Ecstasy was my favorite; it made me bold yet vulnerable, filling me with a happy, achy love that drove me to paw the arms of strangers indiscriminately in the clubs I frequented. The wide-open feeling in my heart was what I imagined sex should be like, and was the reason I loved it. I always expected the drug to lead me to transcendental orgasms, but that never happened.

One morning, I stumbled home in my short skirt, my dyed pink hair covered by a velvet leopard-print cap, my pot dealer's arm linked in mine. Normally he was aloof and introverted and I was shy and awkward during our transactions, yet three hours into the previous night's Ecstasy high we were pledging our undying love. We clambered into his bed below a window lit by the glow of the rising sun. His coarse hair felt like silken threads, his skin like velvet against mine. As we rolled and wrestled, he slipped inside of me, and I knew he was my most trusted friend. After a few hours, the warm, fuzzy feeling changed into a heavy lust that demanded satisfaction. We adjusted and repositioned, working it, grinding, seeking relief, but it was always just out of reach. After five hours of sexual acrobatics, our hunger and the drug's effects waned. The air was heavy and stale. My once again aloof pot dealer told me he wanted to sleep, alone, and I receded like an intimidated mouse, skulking out into the afternoon sun.

Sex on acid was more unpredictable. One afternoon, I found myself sitting on my bed sandwiched between my boyfriend the petty thief and an Australian traveler who had a certain lumberjack appeal. We each had a tab melting on our tongues. I was younger than both by a decade and thrilled to be the center of attention, figuring on another lost afternoon of giggles, hallucinations, and deep conversations.

I knew the stuff was working when I felt the familiar sensation of wetness all over my skin and noticed the burning halo pulsing around the bald lightbulb hanging overhead. The Aussie man placed his hands on my shoulders from behind, then started rubbing my breasts through my sweatshirt, giggling softly. My body felt rubbery under his spongy touch. My boyfriend watched, then said he was cold, so we scrambled under the covers, all three of us. I wedged myself between their bodies and my boyfriend started stripping naked, so we all did.

I touched the skin on my boyfriend's chest and it, too, seemed soaking wet. Aussie man was still giggling, his body cupping mine from behind. Our legs were all tangled together. I felt as if I was enmeshed inside hundreds of limbs, as if we were three trees growing together, me at the center. My heart was speeding, racing up my throat, and I was shaking lightly all over. I wasn't sure if my nerves or the drugs were to blame for the trembling (I'd never had a threesome). But when my boyfriend started stroking me, I began to relax. The room shone brightly, golden trails following my hand as I gently clung to my boyfriend's neck. The nerve endings along my skin stood up and smiled.

Then there was a shift and I noticed I was no longer the center of the tangled limbs. The guys were reaching over me to touch each other and my heart began beating fast again, like a manic cartoon character's. My body tensed and I felt as if I were falling through a forest canopy. I sat up to scan their faces; they looked like two grinning schoolboys.

"Mmmm," said the Aussie man as he moved toward my boyfriend, meeting his lips. I tried to insert myself between them but they ignored me. A sickening dread pulled deep inside me like a fast-receding tide, and I collected my clothes and hurried out of the room. Not long after, I left this boyfriend after discovering him in bed with his best friend, a bottle of Thunderbird in one hand, his pal's prick in the other.

*   *   *

I met the writer, the one with the demon drug habit that would eventually bring me down, in a pub over a half ounce of Moroccan black hashish. I was immediately drawn to him: the way he sat quietly in the corner bobbing his brown Chelsea boot, a glass of brandy on the table before him, the *Guardian* open on his lap. The tails of a long pink silk scarf spilled into the open neck of his Liberty print paisley shirt, like Dad used to wear. He was twenty years older, owned his own place, and received a small weekly stipend from his wealthy father. I'd grown weary of the squatting life; such stability seemed enticing.

Six months later, I moved in. He was the only man to tell me, "No one will love you as much as I do," and I thought this was something to hold on to, clinging to the idea that he'd take care of me as my father never had. I liked our life, the long evenings at home smoking hash and drinking snake bites, a potent cider and beer concoction. There was a certain domesticity to it. Each night, I'd return from my new job as a secretary and he'd tell me about his latest idea for his book. Brian Eno played in the background, the TV flickering on mute. He rolled a joint, I mixed the booze.

The first hit of hash filled my chest with a warm buzzing sensation that drifted up to my brain and down between my legs. Everything became funny and easy, the day's stress sliding away. At first, I'd feel uninhibited and vaguely sexy. We'd crawl on top of each other, enjoying the slow, sweet hum of the first hit, rubbing through our clothes on the shag rug while time stood still. A more secure woman might have stopped after the first few hits. I never did. I wanted to keep up, to be his best girl. Another joint came around and I sucked it down. Once we were good and high the clothes came off and I let him take charge. He was thin and pale, slighter than me, but he liked to grab my wrists and hold me down as if he were conquering me. I played along like a good little submissive, convinced this was the way to keep his love alive.

By then, I'd be so high nothing mattered anyway, my head floating off my body, which was anchored to the ground, heavy as lead. As my boyfriend moved on top of me, I felt as if I was hanging from the ceiling looking down, watching some other girl. Over time, our evening ritual diversified into benzodiazepines along with the booze. Sex on the pills, when we bothered to have it, was sleepy and languid, our skinny bodies going slack, barely making contact, like we were cocooned in a pair of mittens.

Then he introduced me to his longtime love, heroin. And still I tried to keep up. Sex on smack wasn't so much sexual as surreal, like falling into a giant powder puff. We moved slowly, without a destination. I felt safe, the drug licking and coddling my body as his engulfed me. Sometimes his eyes closed and he disappeared, a little smile on his face telling me he was somewhere sweet. Sometimes I sank into a warm, underwater sleep, eventually bobbing up above the surface to find our limbs intertwined but our bodies barely moving. Time drifted; we'd be in bed in the afternoon and wake up in the middle of the night as the first shivers of sickness rolled in.

As my habit took hold, sex ebbed away, paling next to the satisfaction of dope. The drug gave me everything I needed in a partner, like having an orgasm with God. Three years passed and my world became small and simple: Score, use, work, get sick, repeat. As I visibly deteriorated, my only friend at the office encouraged me to get clean. I tried to wean myself off with methadone and downers but my boyfriend was still using, so I inevitably fell back.

One afternoon, I returned home to find him sitting in a chair in the low light, nodding out, spittle dangling from his lip, his fingers holding a dead cigarette with a long curling ash. The curtains were drawn against the bright spring outside. His eyes fought for light as he saw me come in, only to flicker closed again.

I kept my coat on, sat on the bed, and smoked a cigarette. I'd seen him like this before, but on this day, tired and tentatively sober, I saw him for what he was, for what I was fast becoming. The thought of laying my body against his sad, bony form sickened me.

I went to the closet for my luggage and found an old photo of us, taken when we had first met. My legs are swung over his and we're sitting in a garden alcove. I remembered how we'd made our way from the pub, weaving a bit but animated by pints of Guinness, hands sliding into the back of each other's pants. We'd found a quiet garden and necked like lovers at a fifties drive-in, fingers navigating snaps and flies and buttons, hungry to get at each other.

When I looked at his sleeping face again, it was haggard, drawn, and creased, a thousand years old. Not quite forty, he'd been a junkie half his life. I was at the beginning of that road looking through the long lens of my future. I got up and opened the curtains; streams of light flooded the room, trapping swirls of dust. I took my bags and left.

*   *   *

Eventually, I made it back to New York and, with my mother's help, went to college at twenty-five. I struggled to stay clean, swearing off the hard stuff, but I made up for it with booze, pot, and pills. Nights, I trawled the downtown clubs, driven by a palpable desperation, believing that every man I brought home would wake up and be my boyfriend, my savior, not understanding why they never called. At thirty, I finally got sober for good after my mother discovered I was partying again. Our confrontation was angry and tearful, and for the first time, though I couldn't quite grasp how much I was hurting myself, I could see what I was doing to her. So I got clean and took a vow of celibacy for a year, until I met Michael.

Our sex gradually got better, though I inevitably grew agitated when he went down on me for too long. When we made love, I could not meet his gaze, preferring to stalk the sweetness in my body by myself, my eyes closed, rushing after my orgasms as if they were rare butterflies to be netted and contained, body clamped down, grinding Michael into me to squeak out an itchy little orgasm. At least I was feeling something, I reminded myself, more than in the old days.

One evening, he cradled me naked in his lap and asked me how he should touch me. I held onto his neck and guided his hand tentatively, frustrated and embarrassed that I was a grown woman with no sense of what she liked. Though I was typically playful and provocative with him, teasing with my ass, eager to please, I was guarded when it came to my own pleasure. He moved slowly, waiting for my cues, for my permission. I could feel him tracking my darting eyes but I couldn't stand to be watched, so I sealed my lids, trying to give myself over to the possibility of surrender, my body's tightness defying his touch. Finally, I opened my eyes and fought the impulse to look away. One of Michael's first observations of me had been that I looked at the world as if I were a deer in headlights, eyes wide, unfocused. But now I met his eyes directly, without looking away, and let his gaze hold me, soft, sober, and steady.

The Sweetest Sex I Never Had

HOPE EDELMAN

He lumbered into tenth-grade home ec class about a month into fall semester, a big bear of a boy with a short, neat haircut and a freshly washed T-shirt and jeans. He was recently out of juvey, according to the high school rumor mill, something about a robbery and a gun and, depending on who was relaying the story, someone might have gotten shot. It wasn't impossible to believe. In ninth grade, he'd punched his right hand straight through a closed window in third-period English class. No one knew why.

Mrs. Rabinowitz, the home ec teacher, added him to the cooking pod on the far left, which until that moment had consisted of me and my friend Nadine in our own little L-shaped, blond-wood kitchen.

He plunked himself down on a chair at our matching little blond-wood table. He didn't look all that dangerous to me.

"Hey," he said, nodding slightly. David was his name.

"Hey," we said back.

Then he smiled.

This was the fall of 1979. Jimmy Carter was, more or less, running the country. In India, Mother Teresa had just been awarded the Nobel peace prize, and a few dozen miles from where we sat the shah of Iran was receiving cancer treatments at New York Hospital, which meant relations between the United States and Iran were about to get much, much worse. But in suburban Spring Valley, our most pressing concerns were when the Who would return to Madison Square Garden and whether Mrs. Rabinowitz would notice that David had just dropped a chunk of hash into our bowl of brownie mix. She didn't.

As he poured the chocolate lava into the square silver pan, I saw the ragged scar winding up the side of his right thumb where the skin had been stitched back together. He asked me to put the pan in the oven for him because he'd lost enough feeling in his hand that he couldn't tell if he was getting burned until it was too late. He said this matter-of-factly, not in the kind of overdetermined, attention-getting manner I'd come to expect from other fifteen-year-old boys. When I took the pan from him, my knuckles bumped into his, and an electric current ran up the front of my body like a zipper from my thighs to my breasts.

I had no sexual experience to speak of, other than a few sloppy tongue kisses in the ninth grade with a tall, pale boy I'd found about as sexually exciting as a dial tone. I'd agreed to "go out" with him for a few weeks simply because he was the first boy who'd ever shown interest in me. In the spring of that year, I'd traded my silver aviator-rimmed glasses for contact lenses and let my unruly neck-length hair grow into long, bouncy curls. The suddenness of the transformation startled everyone, not least of all me. Overnight, I'd gone from being an object of ridicule, tall and awkward, to an object of interest to men. My mother had predicted this would eventually happen, and despite my stubborn insistence that she understood nothing, *nothing*, about me, she was right. Boys on the cusp of manhood were everywhere now, miming air guitar riffs at public bus stops, hanging out of car windows brandishing half-empty bottles of beer, taking cigarette breaks at loading docks in lower Manhattan on days when I accompanied my father to work, all signaling their appreciation of the female form with catcalls and low whistles and invitations to accompany them into dark movie theaters, into their cars, into their bedrooms when their parents weren't home.

Plenty has been written about the objectification of women in our patriarchal culture, but if anything, it felt as if the girls I knew were objectifying the boys, using them to affirm their own sexual currency. To me, boys existed exclusively for my own purposes, to be ogled, teased, and cried over, their behavior providing raw material for endless hypothesis and analysis. Showing interest in one meant positioning yourself somewhere in the vicinity of his orbit, then manipulating your behavior to get him to notice you. What to actually do with his attention once it was obtained was a far less thought-out plan. Like a preschooler who believes that teachers sleep at the school at night, it was hard for me to imagine that boys had regular lives when they stepped outside my range of vision. The idea that they brushed their teeth in the morning, fed cats, or bought black concert T-shirts at the mall was so foreign to me as to be incomprehensible. Still, I badly wanted one of my own.

In our sophomore class of more than six hundred, stu-

dents paired off, broke apart, and paired off in different com-
binations weekly, with the rapidity—and, sometimes, the
randomness—of a reshuffled deck of cards. In the loud, echo-
ing hallways of our enormous high school, couples walked
cemented at the hips, pausing for long, meaningful kisses outside the doorway of the girl's class until the buzzer finished
ringing. Then the boy would hightail it to geometry or social
studies, skidding through the doorway thirty seconds late in a
public announcement of devotion to his girl.

Probably some of those couples were sleeping together.
For sure, some of the seniors were, although all my fifteen-
year-old girlfriends were still virgins. The one couple in our
tight group who might have gone the distance had broken up
in the spring when he wanted to and she didn't, the kind of
cat-and-mouse game I imagine makes us look like relics to
high-school sophomores today. Well, so be it. In middle-class
Spring Valley in 1979, fifteen was still awfully young to be
having sex. Which is not to say that we didn't think about it,
constantly, or didn't want it. Sometimes I would make excuses
to put myself next to David in the home ec kitchen simply so
I could catch a whiff of his shampoo. I imagined what it would
feel like to have his hands on me. Or what his scar would feel
like against my skin. At night, I could hardly keep my hands
off myself. When the class ended in December, I signed up for
speedwriting, not because I had any idea what speedwriting
was, but because he told me he was taking it, too.

Winter arrived, and stayed, and stayed. Riding the ski
lift at Mount St. Peter, the rinky-dink slope where the ski club
brought us by bus every Friday night, David and I passed a
clandestine bottle of blackberry brandy back and forth and
debated, among other things, how eleven people could have
been crushed to death at the Who concert in Cincinnati. Had

people *really* mistaken a sound check for the concert starting? Could that many people have been *that* stoned?

We'd become sort of friends by then, David and I, the kind who sat together in speedwriting class and sometimes had brief, utilitarian conversations on the phone. "We're just friends," I explained to anyone who looked at us slightly askance. He was an established member of my group of friends by then, though he usually stood on the perimeter in his olive-green army jacket, refusing cigarettes with a benign smile. He seemed to me to regard the action around him with a sort of detached bemusement, as if to say *I'm a friendly visitor just here to observe.* He was trying hard to stay out of trouble, I knew. "I don't want to go back to that place," he once said about his past, and I got the message that he didn't care to elaborate.

When he and I both wound up taking a junior lifesaving class that winter at the local pool, it was all I could do to sit still when I saw him in a Speedo. He had actual chest muscles, and dark hair on his legs. When the teacher asked him to demonstrate a survival hold on me, his grip was both firm and protective, not as hard as it should have been but not timid, either. The feel of his skin against mine felt so good it made me want to sob. Because, damn it, we were just friends.

Then one bright cold morning, he met me in front of my locker before first period and propped the door open with his hand.

"Hey," he said.

"Hey back," I said.

"You want to get out of here?" he asked. His parents were both at work, he explained, and we could hang out at his house for the day. I'd never cut school before, never even considered it, but I knew, even at fifteen, that small miracles like this one didn't come along every day.

It was April by then. Two weeks before, my mother had walked through our front door with news of a malignant tumor in her left breast. I was home babysitting my younger sister and brother, annoyed that my friends were all at Nadine's house, unaware that my parents were in a Manhattan surgeon's office that Tuesday afternoon, trying to grab on to inflexible terms like "three-centimeter tumor" and "unilateral mastectomy." When they returned home and told me, I shouted "No!" and ran to my room, pulling the door shut behind me.

This could not be happening, I remember thinking. Not to a forty-one-year-old mother. Not to my mother. Not to me.

My mother was fast on my tail. "Hope, we can talk about this," she said through the closed door, but I was already on the phone with Nadine. "My mom has cancer. Can I come over?" I blurted out, then pushed past my mother and fled from the house, running a mile and a half through a church cemetery, two neighborhoods, and the high school ball field, where my friends were already waiting for me, huddled together for warmth and grinding cigarettes into the third-base line under their Adidas sneakers. The circle broke open to receive me as I ran up and closed behind me without a word. Later, we all went back to Nadine's bedroom and sprawled across her matching twin beds, nodding in time to Pink Floyd's *The Wall* on her portable eight-track tape player while her parents prepared dinner downstairs. *Hello? (Hello, hello) Is there anybody out there?* David was in the group, sitting on the carpet with his back against a bed. He didn't say much, but I could feel his eyes on me, and whenever I glanced in his direction he didn't look away. It didn't feel threatening; exactly the opposite. It felt as if he were trying to hold me safe in his gaze, and the thrill of this pulled my attention fully and palpably into that room, diverting it from whatever might be going on back home, from whoever might be crying or not crying in their bedrooms, from the surgery already on the calendar.

And then, two weeks later, David was inviting me to walk out of school with him, to turn my back on everything that was confusing and hard and wrong. So I tossed my books back into my locker and followed him out the double glass doors.

At eight-thirty in the morning, the inside of David's house was utterly still, freakishly still, as if we were stepping into an illustration where we provided all motion and sound. He gestured me upstairs to his bedroom. He was much bigger than me, and a hell of a lot stronger, but I walked up the carpeted stairs without the slightest bit of reluctance or fear. I trusted him completely. The possibility that he might hurt me, or force me to do anything I didn't want to do, never crossed my mind.

His room was long and narrow like a ship's galley, with a dresser, desk, and stereo along the right wall and a twin bed pushed against the left. The space was tidier than I'd expected, not that I'd really known what to expect. Dirty socks piled up on the floor? Album covers strewn across the bed? Empty, crushed beer cans underfoot? This was the first time I'd been inside a teenage boy's bedroom, and I realized, like a light switch being flipped, that these boys who high-fived it in the school hallways and shouted to each other by last name, who slouched around in dark parking lots in hooded sweatshirts and army surplus coats, actually had mothers who looked after them and kept their bedrooms clean.

David with parents? It was impossible to imagine. An older sister was off at college somewhere, too, but I didn't even try to wrap my mind around that one.

He picked up an acoustic guitar that stood angled in a corner by the window. "You play guitar?" I asked. I hadn't known that either.

"I'm learning," he said.

"Do you sing?"

He laughed, a low, throaty waver. "Really badly," he said.

He strummed a few chords: the opening to Emerson, Lake, and Palmer's "In the Beginning." All the boys who played guitar knew it, the first few bars as familiar to all of us as any lullaby, the way the opening notes did a quick backflip into a deep pool and swam a few steady strokes across before turning a backflip again. He knew more than just the opening chords; he played the song all the way through. I closed my eyes and hummed along with the chorus. *You see, it's all clear, you were meant to be here...* I couldn't help thinking it was prophetic, if not preplanned.

When he finished, he rested the guitar back against the wall. I might have said something about what we were missing at school. He probably asked how my mother was doing, and I would have said fine, just fine. We may have smoked a joint, though, hash brownies aside, he was still trying to avoid anything that might land him in front of a judge again. So maybe not. Somehow, enough time passed to bring us to late morning, where we were leaning back on the top of his bed, shoes off, talking. Then we wiggled down a little further, still talking, and a little further, still talking, until we were nose to nose, whispering like twins, two heads of dark hair, two pairs of dark eyes.

It was a game now. Who was going to make a move first? I closed my eyes and inhaled deeply. His skin smelled bright and fresh, like springtime. Then he tilted his head slightly to the left—finally—and kissed me, a soft, slow kiss, gently parting my lips with his.

It was a sweet kiss, tender and careful, not urgent and sloppy like the others I'd had. When we finished I pulled back and stared at him, my face a quiet question mark. *What do you want?* He smiled enigmatically. I rested my head against his chest, which felt warm and solid. I could feel his heart beating as fast as mine.

"I love you," he whispered, barely loud enough for me to hear.

Until that moment, I wouldn't have believed it possible that an entire body could shake from excitement. A boy! *This* boy! Loved *me*! This was no small miracle. This was colossal. Monumental. Epic. Bigger than what my chest could hold.

I'd never said "I love you" out loud, not to my parents nor my siblings, not even to the dog, never even written "love ya" at the bottom of a notebook-paper letter to a friend. My parents weren't verbal or demonstrative, offering each other no more than a perfunctory peck hello when my father returned from work every evening at five. Occasionally they'd say they were proud of me, but that they loved me? It would have been so out of character that I might have had to ask "What do you mean?" We all simply took it for granted, I suppose, that the cohesion we felt as a family was, well, *that* thing. Still, when I whispered back to David, "I love you, too," these felt like the most solid and true words I'd ever spoken. I liked the way they made me feel. I. Love. You. Three steady drumbeats. Decisive and resolute. There was no room for misinterpretation there.

We kissed more that morning, listened to some albums, tried to expand time to push three o'clock as far away as possible. Somewhere around lunchtime, we went down to the kitchen, where David pulled a loaf of bread and some cold cuts from the refrigerator. He took two plates down from the cabinet next to the sink.

He knew how to make a sandwich? Truly, there was no end to what this boy could do.

I sat at the table and stared at him, noticed the ease with which his broad shoulders moved under his denim shirt, the casual way he took a bite from his sandwich or reached for his glass of Coke. It was like witnessing a perfect choreography. Unlike me, whose every move took place in a fog of self-conscious deliberation, David either didn't realize someone was watching him so closely or didn't care. I reached out and lightly traced the scar on his hand with my index finger.

"Yeah," he said around a mouthful of sliced turkey breast and white bread. He paused a moment to swallow. "That was really fucked up."

I admired him in that moment for having had the courage to act on his anger instead of keeping it bottled up, and for being able to bear the mark of his own rage. I imagined it must have felt good to act on impulse, without letting fear of the possible consequences hold him back. I wanted to tell him all this, but I didn't know how. Instead I just asked, "Does it hurt?"

This time it was he who studied me carefully. "Not so much anymore," he said.

When he walked me back to school, we slid both our hands inside his glove and held hands the whole way. I didn't know enough to wonder if he'd see me in school tomorrow and pretend nothing had happened. He called my house that night to say he missed me. When he asked if he could see me again and I heard his little exhale of relief as he realized I hadn't changed my mind, I handed him my heart. *Here, beautiful, vulnerable boy who loves me. Here it is. All for you.*

*   *   *

My mother was loading the dishwasher when I walked in, her bright yellow rubber gloves reaching all the way up her elbows. She looked the same as she always looked: short frosted hair, dangling gold earrings, a buttoned-down print rayon shirt. A little wooden plaque that she loved hung above the sink: BLESS THIS MESS in wide blue calligraphy. I could almost convince myself that nothing in our house had changed.

"Is it okay if David comes over after school tomorrow?" I tried to sound nonchalant. It wasn't unusual for me to ask permission for a friend to come by, though it was a first for me to ask about a boy.

"David? Do I know him?" She tilted her head, trying to place a David.

"I don't think so."

"What's he like?" She was trying so hard to be a normal mother having a normal conversation with her teenage daughter. I wanted to help her out, yet at the same time I needed to know, with tremendous urgency, if I could see David the next day. I shifted from one foot to another impatiently.

"He's just this guy from school. So? Is it okay?"

Maybe, in that moment, she decided not to take more from me than was absolutely necessary. She smiled a tiny smile and went back to rinsing dishes. "I don't see why not," she said.

So that's how the divide began. She had cancer. I had a

boyfriend. She had a mastectomy the following week. I had David in my bedroom that afternoon, when I returned from seeing my mother in the hospital. And the next afternoon, and the next, and the next. My parents didn't encourage his presence, but neither did they object. They weren't particularly hip or progressive parents, not like Nadine's, whose stash of pot Nadine snuck from her mother's lingerie drawer, or like Lynne's, who spent weekends at an ashram in upstate New York. So it wasn't about that. Perhaps they were relieved to have one less child whose needs they had to meet for a while. Or maybe they were just too preoccupied with the pathologist's report to divert energy toward anything that wasn't liable to cause them immediate heartache.

David and I were tentative with each other at first, then inquisitive, then bold. Within a few weeks, we were spending long afternoons on my green shag carpet with our hands underneath each other's clothes while my father sat sentry in a black vinyl swivel chair in the family room on the other side of the wall, doing *New York Times* crossword puzzles, listening to Frank Sinatra, and smoking Tareytons as my mother recovered from her weekly chemotherapy treatments upstairs and, quietly and imperceptibly to all of us, slowly began to die.

My parents were no longer sleeping in the same room by then, my father exiled to the family room couch because, as the excuse went, his snoring kept my mother up all night. It wasn't clear to me how she'd endured twenty years of snoring only to pull the plug on it now—I suspected it had more to do with her finally being fed up with him than with getting a good night's rest—but it was indisputable that she needed her sleep, so I didn't question the arrangement.

This new sleeping arrangement meant a lot of things to me. First, I was now the one listening to my father snore all night on the other side of the wall, which meant I wasn't going to get much sleep that year. It also meant that my parents were no longer having sex, a fact that was not lost on me. I was guessing they hadn't been for a while, not if my father's unpredictable temper and my mother's frustration with his drinking and his tendency to clam up when things got tough were indications. Knowing they had no sex life made me feel both terribly relieved and uncomfortably squeamish at the same time. But most of all, having my father on the couch outside my room meant I had to be exceedingly, exceptionally quiet when I climbed out of my basement bedroom window at night.

David would be waiting for me in the cemetery behind my neighborhood, a solitary figure backlit by moonlight, weaving among the headstones of Revolutionary War soldiers and babies who hadn't made it more than a few days. As I ran to him, his features slowly took shape in the darkness—the same way he was starting to come into focus as a real person, a person who loved art and guitar and me. Then it was him, David, right there in front of me, pressing his face into my neck. We'd only been apart for a few hours, but no reunion had ever felt so necessary or sweet.

We had the whole cemetery to ourselves after dark, to lie on the cool grass and press up against each other, me flush on top of him, rubbing and touching and inhaling until we both thought we might explode. When he gently stroked my breasts with fingertips callused from steel guitar strings, I lost all power of reason. This was far beyond anything I could make myself feel in the shower or in bed alone at night. The first time he took my hand and slowly guided it behind the waistband of his jeans, my eagerness to do this for him was rivaled only by my curiosity. Everything I knew about penises came from Judy Blume's novel *Forever,* which my friends and I had passed around in the ninth grade. The male character called his penis Ralph, a detail we all found hilarious. The boys we knew called theirs *dicks* and *cocks* and occasionally *peters* or *schlongs.* Somehow, I'd gotten the impression they were hairy and bumpy and rough, and that erections made them inflexibly hard all over, like broomsticks. David's was surprisingly soft on the outside—circumcised, though I had no way of knowing that then—with a layer of smooth, velvety skin encasing what felt like the arm of a rubber doll, firm yet so unexpectedly pliable that it made me wonder if I was touching the wrong thing.

It didn't take much to get him off: just a few timid strokes up and down and then a warm, viscous liquid filled my hand. When I pulled my palm out of his pants, a woodsy, organic smell emerged with it. I looked at the cloudy white syrup slowly dripping between my fingers. It seemed like something more likely to have come out of a tree than from the body of this boy shuddering and sighing in my arms.

"Ah," he said, sounding embarrassed. "I'm sorry."

"It's okay." I wiped my hand on the tail of his denim shirt, but I was careful not to remove it all. I wanted some to come home with me, to hold on to it as a piece of him that would remain with me all night, cradled under my pillow, even after he was gone.

Long after midnight he'd walk me to the edge of my neighborhood and we'd solder together for a final kiss, then I'd walk the last block home alone with a wetness and warm ache between my legs. Once home, I'd lie in bed and silently recite my nightly prayer to keep my mother healthy and safe, adding a new and special plea to protect David because, God, I loved him, I loved him *so much*. Sometimes I gripped my pillow hard and cried over how much I loved him, my body pulsing with desire, while my father—my *father!*—snored out his banishment on the other side of the door.

*   *   *

We were now one of those couples kissing passionately in the school hallways, and I finally understood what made it so hard for those pairs to peel apart. In the few minutes we had between the time David met me at the doorway of one class and delivered me to my next one, I wanted—no, *had* to have—as much physical contact with him as possible. It was literally painful to be apart for long. Every pore in my skin hurt for him. The phys ed teacher gave me an especially hard time, frowning whenever she saw us sucking at each other's faces in front of the gym. "All right, Hope. Enough," she would say, holding the door open to usher me in. I imagine— in the way it's convenient for teachers to reduce students to stereotypes—that she saw me as the honor student tossing my smarts in the trash for the chance to screw a former out- law. But she didn't know him, not really, not as the sweet, gentle boy I knew him to be, the one who touched me so care- fully, so perfectly, that I needed his hands on me all the time.

If you define sex as an act of penetration, we weren't having it, but that feels beside the point. What we were doing had plenty of sex attached to it, the best kind of sex, pristine and uncomplicated and sweet. It was sex without an agenda, no my orgasm or your orgasm, no expectation or disappoint- ment, and without any of the preposterous, tired sentences that would later come to characterize full-on fucking, like "Do you have protection?" and "Are you done yet?" and "Did you come?" This was sex simply for the gorgeous sen- sation of it, two people touching each other in all the right places because there were no wrong places then, doing it for no reason other than that it felt good and to keep doing it felt even better. It didn't matter if an orgasm was the final result, though it usually was for him; rarely for me. That wasn't the goal. This was something primal, instinctual, and more tender and reciprocal, I've come to realize, than most fifteen-year-olds ever know. On nights we couldn't see each other, we tied up our respective family phones for hours, doing our individual homework in comfortable silence, content simply to hear the other breathe. "If we were older, I'd ask you to marry me," he said one night with an aura of wonder in his voice, as if he'd just discovered feelings could have such density.

My heart stopped, then started again. "A hundred years ago, we could have gotten married at sixteen," I told him. I had no idea if this was true, but I liked the way it sounded. It didn't seem all that far-fetched. We could get an apartment somewhere, and use my bat mitzvah money to eventually buy a car. I could cook, I don't know, spaghetti or scrambled eggs. We'd do our homework on the couch together at night. For jobs, we'd . . . well, we'd figure that part out. We'd be together all the time, that was the thing.

My mother, who'd met my father at nineteen, was on to me. Or thought she was, at least.

"I've been thinking," she said, "that maybe you need to see Dr. Rosen about getting some birth control."

We were floating in the backyard swimming pool on a late Saturday morning, just passing time. I remember I had on a purple string bikini decorated with iridescent butterflies. She was wearing the navy blue postmastectomy bathing suit we'd picked out together the afternoon we went shopping for her wig. I'd turned the event into a comedy routine, parading through the store in blond Farrah Fawcett curls, just to mask the sobriety of what we were doing, and it had felt good to make her laugh.

"Birth control?" I asked. *What?*

"You know," she said. "You and David."

"Me and David?" I couldn't seem to do more than echo whatever she said. Me and David? My mother didn't like David, not even a little. She'd made that clear the day she told me she'd seen him hitchhiking back from our house in the rain. I could tell from the way she said it that she'd driven right by. (My father, on the other hand, reluctantly but occasionally would make a U-turn to give him a ride.) At best, my mother would give David a little smile and a nod when he walked through our front door. He was growing out his hair, which she hated. "Scruffy," she called him. "Handsome," I said. So was she actually *giving me permission* now to have sex with him? Or did she think we were already doing it? On my bedroom *floor*?

Either way, she wasn't trying to talk me out of it. That much I could see.

I shook my head. "I don't need it yet," I said.

"You might soon."

"Mom! I'm only fifteen!"

"Not for much longer."

"We're not *doing* it." We weren't even talking about doing it, which for the first time struck me as possibly a little odd.

"Uh-huh," she said, sounding unconvinced.

"Fine. You make an appointment so he can examine me and tell you I haven't done it. Is that what you want?"

She bit her bottom lip and looked the other way, like she did whenever she was trying not to cry. I couldn't believe how bad this made me feel.

"Forget it," she said, treading water in the opposite direction. "Forget I even said anything."

Later that night, I called Nadine to tell her about my crazy mother, my so-far-out-of-it mother, because that's what you did when your parents acted too weird for words and you didn't know how to react: You immediately told your friends.

"You and David haven't done it?" she asked.

Jesus. Was I the *only* one around here who thought I was too young?

"Come on! I would have *told* you," I said.

"I just thought, because..." And then there was a long patch of silence.

Oh. He'd done it before. Damn it. I should have known.

"With *you*?" I said.

"No! With someone older. He told me a long time ago, before he started going out with you."

Well. If I could put the image of someone else's hands on his skin out of my mind, I could handle this. What he'd done before he met me didn't matter, I decided, which marked the first and last time I ever believed this about a boy.

"I figure we'll do it eventually," I told Nadine, which felt like what I was supposed to say. "We've got plenty of time." The truth was, I would have done it without hesitation or regret if he'd wanted me to. But he didn't push for it, so neither did I.

*   *   *

We were fifteen, and because we were fifteen, when it ended it ended badly. I went off to summer camp in July for a waitressing job arranged months in advance. For two months, we wrote tortured letters filled with professions of our love, his growing increasingly more lonely and depressed as the weeks stretched on. Nadine wrote to tell me he carried a photo of me in his wallet and stared at it all the time. "It's painful to watch," she said. At night, I snuck down to the pay phone in the counselors' lounge to call him, but what was there to say, really? *I love you. I miss you. I'll be back soon.* I asked questions; he answered in monosyllables, distracted, or sad, or bored, I couldn't tell. The night I came home he walked to my house, where he sat on my bed, hands hanging between his knees, and confessed that he'd screwed around with Rhoda Kaminsky while I was gone. She was a year younger than us and known to do anything with anyone just to have a boy by her side. He was so, so sorry, he said. He'd never meant to hurt me. He didn't know why he did it. And more of that.

I started shivering uncontrollably, even though it was the end of August.

"Rhoda *Kaminsky*?" I said. Then I told him to leave.

Later that night, a Saturday, I gathered with my friends, who immediately closed ranks around me, shouting obscenities at him across the parking lot. "Cocksucker! Motherfucker! Dickhead!" The scene had all the drama fifteen-year-olds were capable of producing. At one point, David took a hit of acid and sat in the middle of the street, daring a car to hit him. His friends tried to drag him back to the curb. Mine shouted, "Let him die!"

"He's making the biggest mistake of his life," Nadine assured me.

"He's just screwed up, man," his friend Brian told me.

"You were too good for him," my mother said, as if that settled that.

She was lying in bed after a chemo treatment, swollen from prednisone, baby-fine tufts of new hair pushing through the top of her head. Five straight months of chemo, and now the doctors had decided to pound her with a stronger set of drugs. You'd think we would have known.

Something inside me snapped when she said that, and I spun on her in a fury. "I loved him!" I wailed.

Her head jerked up as if I'd yanked it with a string. I'll never forget the expression of shocked sadness on her face. Not because I said I'd loved him—that much she must have known—but more likely because, in spite of her attempts to hold on to me over the past few months, she'd just realized I'd been gone for a long time.

I walked around in a daze after that, unable to bear the idea of another girl stroking David's bare stomach, or sucking on his bottom lip, or inhaling the scent of his freshly washed hair. I couldn't stop picturing them rolling around together in the grass. The only way I could tolerate the image was to turn it into something vulgar and cheap, to picture him sweating and grunting piggishly on top of her and her lying bored and unresponsive beneath him. So convincing was this picture that when, two weeks later, David came back, claiming he'd made a big mistake, he was so, so sorry, and could I possibly ever consider taking him back, I was so repulsed by the image of my own creation that I couldn't stand to have him touch me. I told him no, and then I kissed him, on the cheek. Which, suddenly, made me feel terribly old. And so my first great love ended right there outside of Mr. Polochek's AP American history class, while Lisa Colavito and Manny Goldstein got it on against the lockers alongside us.

*   *   *

The ardent feminist in me keeps trying to reframe this story as a cautionary tale of how a fifteen-year-old girl with very little sexual experience was taken advantage of by a boy with much more, who then dumped her for someone who'd sleep with him. After all, it could be a useful parable: "Mothers, don't let your daughters grow up to mess around with delinquents." But nothing about that version feels true. In fact, what I began to learn at fifteen was the critical distinction between sex and love. Because if you'd been the girl in this story, you would never have felt taken advantage of. You would have known all along that everything you did in that cemetery, and on your bedroom floor, and in his bedroom one Saturday afternoon when no one was home and you both stripped down to nothing but your underpants and rolled around on his bed for hours, until your father started honking the car horn outside, was consensual. You handed it all to him willingly. And if you were the forty-three-year-old woman, now a wife and mother of two girls, looking back on this story twenty-eight years and more than two thousand miles from your girlhood home, you still wouldn't be able to find a way to make him the bastard and you the victim. Eventually, you'd have to acknowledge how rare and precious and exceptional your first sexual experience was, compared to the kind of stories your friends tell. You might even wish something similar for your own daughters when their time comes. Well, minus the delinquent part. But still.

It took me a long time to figure out what my own mother had been trying to tell me in the swimming pool that day. It wasn't that she thought I was having sex with David, or that she thought I'd need birth control soon. It's that she realized, even if she couldn't say it, that she might not be around to help me when the time to really need it came.

As for David, he didn't take my innocence at fifteen. It went the following July 12, at 2:43 A.M., as I was sleeping on a couch in a hospital waiting room. In his own way, David helped keep it intact until then. Consciously or not, he and I made a choice together, an unspoken agreement between the boy with too much experience and the girl so eager for more, an implicit understanding to preserve her childhood just a little longer, in light of what they both understood was lying in wait around the next corner, and all that she was about to face, against her will, too soon, too soon.

Sexercise

ABBY SHER

The first thing I did when my boyfriend Jay and I moved into an apartment together was put five boxes of high-fiber, low-fat cereal on our new shelves.

I'd been obsessive about my weight in the past, studying food labels and exercising until I almost fainted. For a period in high school, I refused to eat more than hot dog rolls with mustard. After college, I added raisins to the menu. Then I fell in love with a pale-eyed male bulimic who taught me how to exist on coffee each day until sundown. Instead of having sex, we gorged ourselves on deli meats at one in the morning and I rubbed his back while he gagged. When he dumped me I swore I would never love again. I also said to my therapist, "He's the sick one, right?"

Two years later, I met Jay at a holiday party. We both worked for the Second City theater group in Chicago but had never officially met. We began talking. At one point, he placed his hand on the small of my back and every cell in my body yearned for him. His eyes were the color of untouched water. His freckled lips had a way of curling up shyly as he said, "See ya later, darlin'."

After our second date, he brought me purple hyacinths and told me he couldn't stop thinking about me. I was so excited I got the hiccups for two hours straight. He took me to French restaurants where we feasted on buttery crêpes, tapas bars with mountains of glistening mushrooms, bistros with roasted chicken that made me moan. I had never been treated like this before. I told myself I was not going to mess this up. I went back to starving myself all day so I could get tipsy on the first glass of wine with Jay and forget all my food restrictions (low fat, low carbs, low sugar, low everything). I took up a more demanding exercise regimen. I wanted to be tiny for Jay—sculpted, cut, perfected. I was also onstage every night of the week now, and was determined to be *that girl*. As in that girl with raw, crazy, hilarious depth and unstoppable energy and she is *so skinny*!

I added more rules to my existing ones: No eating before the show. No eating in public. No less than an hour and a half at the gym a day. I started drinking diuretic teas and devouring magazine articles about how to feel full from your daily intake of water. Then I announced I was quitting my job so I could "do my own thing." Jay was thrilled until he realized it meant I was devoting all my energy to longer workouts and cardio classes. By the time we pulled up in our moving van with my cereal boxes, I had dropped about twenty-five pounds. At a hunched five foot eight, I hovered just above 100.

One day, Jay caught me in our kitchen on the way out to

the gym. He started kissing me below my ear, his mouth traveling up into my hairline. "Not now," I said. "I have to go."

I felt his breath on my neck, soft and warm. "Where you goin', hot stuff?" he whispered.

"You know where."

He pulled away, his eyes steely.

"Why do you have to go there? Why can't you spend this time with me?"

I wanted to tell Jay it wasn't up to me. I had an immutable obligation, and no time to waste explaining it to him. Nearly an hour ago, I had eaten a Toasted Nuts and Cranberries Luna Bar—170 calories, 3 grams of unsaturated fat, 24 grams of carbohydrates. I knew only one way to get rid of it, and that was by pushing, pumping, climbing, the lights of the gym pulsating around me, until I was breathless and the world was spinning almost as fast as it was inside my head.

Since we had moved in together, our sex had gone from heated to sullen. Like everything else in my world, it felt flattened out, the only peaks and valleys the electronic kind on the stair machine. I didn't understand life outside of interval training and I found it annoying and inconsiderate of Jay to interrupt my routine. He had no idea of the urgency of my mission, that as we sat in the kitchen discussing his selfish proposition, I was digesting and depositing fat on my hips.

We fought. He said I cared more for my disease than I'd ever care for him, his face traveling from bewilderment to righteous fury. I told him it wasn't a *disease*, it was a strong habit. He stocked our pristine freezer with frozen meats and pizzas. I told him it looked crowded and messy. He begged me to eat with him, offered to make whatever I wanted, but I told him I wasn't hungry. Which I almost believed, though I couldn't stop staring into restaurant windows and grinding my teeth on the way to the gym.

He clenched his fists and shook the cereal boxes.

"This? This is what you're hungry for? This cardboard... *shit*?"

I gave him my most menacing silence in return, then made a point of filling my evenings with "writing meetings" or trips to the local café for coffee. When I did get caught at home around supper, I sat on the floor watching TV while Jay ate next to me, chewing his food slowly, thoughtfully, until there was nothing left on his plate but shadows of hamburger grease and stray bread crumbs.

I always made sure Jay was asleep before I slipped into the kitchen for my own dinner of cereal and chicken broth. Crouched over my giant mug, I chomped ravenously, bitterly. Then I went back for seconds and thirds, praying he wouldn't wake up and see me.

Clearly, this couldn't continue. I rationalized by telling myself the situation was temporary: I'd come to L.A. for only a few months to house-sit for friends and for some work, and since Jay was between jobs, he came, too. But he'd only do it, he warned, if I promised to go into an outpatient program for eating disorders as soon as we got back. He'd already made sure my insurance covered it. I told him okay, but in truth, I secretly hoped we'd both fall in love with California and end up living there for good.

We fell into a routine quickly. Wake up and have coffee together, marveling at the lemon tree in the garden. Then I'd take a Ziploc baggie of dry cereal and walk to the local Bally's, where I'd gotten a temporary membership. I raced from the bicycle to the elliptical trainer, then did weights and a few sets of sit-ups, triumphantly counting each leaden step back to the locker room. Afterward, I went to a café and had mint tea and pack after pack of Extra sugarless gum while I tried to write. In the afternoons, I walked to a Bikram yoga studio and slipped from one pose to another as the temperature rose to 112 degrees. Jay picked me up just as the sky was turning lavender. He had spent most of his day on Craigslist looking for odd jobs and watching ESPN. One night he showed me a listing for a carpenter job starting as soon as possible.

"That sounds great, sweetie!" I enthused.

"Yeah, except they probably want something permanent. And we're going *home*."

"Well, we might both find work, and then..."

"We made a deal, Ab," he said resolutely. Jay was a man of his word and he expected the same from me. My two months in L.A. were almost up and then I'd be starting an outpatient eating disorders program back in New York, 9:00 A.M. to 6:00 P.M., five days a week.

"I have an idea. Let's go to the Pig 'n' Whistle tonight!" I squeaked eagerly.

"And do what?"

"I dunno. See who's there?"

"La Brea tar pits," Jay muttered, because this was a common topic of discussion among our L.A. friends, though none of them had actually been there.

That night, before we went out, I took a shower in the master bedroom while Jay ate spaghetti for dinner. I threw my wet gym clothes in a ball and stepped lightly onto the pink tile. I lathered and rinsed, then reached for my rusting nail clippers and carefully snipped off a line of skin along the right side of my waist. I had been cutting myself like this for a few months now; I'd read about it in a book for teenage girls and was curious how it felt. I loved the way it focused my senses on the sharp line of pain, silencing the voices in my head telling me to run, jump, climb, sweat.

The water stung as it hit the new layer of skin underneath and I had to step out of the spray to let the beads of blood gather, marking my territory, my handiwork. I made three fresh incisions on my stomach before putting in conditioner and getting out of the shower. I liked the number three.

"You almost ready?" Jay called.

"Almost!" I sang back. I pulled on my control-top panty hose and my jeans and counted out the notches on my belt. I was hoping to get to the fourth hole in the next week. Over my jeans, I pulled on a black, shapeless dress.

Jay met me at the bathroom door.

"How's my girl?"

"Okay."

"You look sensational."

"Please don't."

There was nothing sensational about me. My skin was gray and my hair was falling out. I had slices up and down my arms and torso. My best friend had stopped talking to me because she said she couldn't watch me do this, and my mom called every day to beg me to please come home already. I told her that I had everything under control. Still, Jay was the only one who knew how bad things had gotten. Whenever I dared to look at his face, his eyes were angry and scared, his arms helpless at his sides.

That night, the Pig 'n' Whistle was hopping. Cell phones and designer sunglasses on every table and talk about the biz. I greedily gulped three glasses of pinot grigio and started shimmying my hips, crying "Yes! Yes! Yes!" when my friend Martin suggested karaoke.

We went to the back of a small Japanese restaurant in a strip mall. There was nobody there except for us and a few regulars at the bar who looked to have been hanging around as long as the limp Christmas tinsel on the walls. It was such a relief to forget myself in Paula Abdul's ferocious beat, to dance giddily at Martin's impersonation of Boy George. Jay got up to sing "Easy Like Sunday Mornin'," his eyes closed and his head tipped up. There was such peace in his face, I had to press my back against the wall for support. I hadn't seen him that happy in forever.

When we got back to the house, we were still humming, *"The tide is high, but I'm holding on..."* This was usually the time of night when I broke down and ate: high-fiber cereal covered with chicken broth and melted fat-free cheddar cheese on top, sometimes hummus and carrots, washed down with watery cocoa. Whenever I didn't think I could make it another mile on the stationary bike or felt light-headed on the treadmill, I imagined this banquet awaiting me and tried to pedal faster, harder, stronger.

But Jay had another idea for that night.

"I'm sorry, but you do look hot in that scarf," he said as I began to unwind it from my neck.

"Please don't." It was what I always said now.

"Just let me tell you even if you don't agree." He pulled me to him and traced kisses down to my collarbone.

"Keep the lights off," I whispered, and reached for his belt. He knew this rule by now, but I still reminded him. The thought of him seeing my distended belly and fleshy thighs drew a shiver up my spine. I squeezed my eyes shut so there was no chance of my seeing anything either.

He lifted my dress over my head and threw it across the room.

"I hate that dress," he said. I tried to laugh but it came out more like a whimper. "I hate it because I can't see your body, and I love this body."

"No talking," I admonished sharply. I pulled down his pants and then my own, following a sequence of events that had been plotted out long before me, events that had nothing to do with desire. I felt no desire. I was able to feel hot and cold, maybe even itchy, but besides that my sensations had been numbed to a slow haze. I had stopped menstruating months ago.

He took off my panty hose, his fingers grazing my new markings. "When did you do this?" he whispered.

"Tonight."

"Why?" he asked.

"Shhhhh," I commanded.

It was the saddest sex I'd ever had. Quiet, tense, contrived. We knew each other's bodies, the smell of each other's hair, the curve of each hip. I did what I thought he wanted, grabbing his back and licking his ear. He kissed the raw skin along my waist, then up between my breasts, gently gyrating, holding my hips with a soft but steady grip.

"Yes, yes," he murmured.

"Oh, yes," I whispered in return, trying to echo his soft cries, to fill up the space between us. I wanted to mean it, urging my chest forward, pressing my ribs into his warm skin. But I heard my voice as if it were a stranger's, as if I were lurking somewhere in the shadows watching these two bodies collide, his trim and determined, hers flailing, bony, all pointed angles.

All the while, I envisioned my midnight meal, the bran flakes tumbling into the white porcelain bowl as Jay moved inside me. Then I remembered my friend Megan telling me

how she used to count sex as one of her calorie-burning activities along with jogging and strength training. I clenched
my buttocks and imagined a referee with a starter pistol, vi-
sualizing the network of muscles and tendons pulling my butt
cheeks together. Jay had to slow me down.

"Easy, girl, easy."

Anorexia is an isolating and egocentric disease. As Jay
and I were rising and falling, I was thinking only of myself,
about how I could use sex to make everything in me leaner
and stronger. I was disgusted with this body—its lumps and
scars, its breasts hanging in small sorry sacs, its pubic hair a
dark and wiry nest. I wanted no part of it. I wanted it to perform for me, then disappear.

Jay came and I was so relieved.

"Did you like it? Was it good?" I asked anxiously.

"What do you think? Did you have fun?"

"Yeah." I put on long johns and a T-shirt and scuttled
under the covers while Jay lay naked on top of the bed, looking up at the shadows of palm trees on the ceiling. I wondered how long I had to politely wait before I could go
downstairs for my late-night snack, before I could lift that
first soggy spoonful to my mouth, lick the soft sludge of fake
cheese. If Jay truly loved me, wouldn't he feel my body's true
longing and let me go? Wouldn't he know that my whole being was writhing with a hunger I had no name for, a hunger
bigger than both of us, bigger than our bed, bigger than this
beautiful house on a hill, tree branches tapping on the glass
windows?

I couldn't wait any longer.

"Be right back," I whispered, and hurried down the
stairs to the pantry. I added an extra slab of cheese as a re-

ward for being so patient. It was better than any orgasm I could remember.

It must have been only an hour or two later, but it felt as if it were a different day entirely. I opened my eyes. The streetlights were still on and the sky was a quiet, clouded green. My empty dinner tray was on the dresser. The television was still chattering: *Call now! What are you waiting for?*

I felt cold and wet, a weight pressing down on me. I pulled the comforter aside.

I was thirty years old and I had just wet the bed.

"Jay!" I whispered. "Jay, please wake up!"

"What, sweetheart?"

"Jay, I think I wet the bed."

He stood there with me, staring at the sodden mattress. There was the outline of a ghost on my side, dark and forboding. I didn't know what to say or how to make this better. I just knew that if I started to talk, I would break into a thousand pieces. So we just watched the bed, waiting for something to change as the Earth moved in its slow, meditative rotation. It had taken me thirty years to get here and it might take thirty more to get somewhere else. I wondered where else I could go. I wondered if Jay wanted to spend those years with this body, my long johns clinging to my shrunken legs, my belly sticking out like a sulking toddler's. But this was all I had left.

Jay told me to change into dry pajamas while he stripped the sheets and laid down a fresh pink towel. The mattress looked too big for the room now. The towel looked too bright for this light of day. There was a certain danger in the air, in the back of my throat, just underneath my fingernails, that demanded to be recognized. It was not going away. It held me.

"Do you want to come back to bed?" Jay asked.

"Nah. You can, though," I said, wishing he wouldn't.

"I'm sticking with you," he said, and pulled me in tighter, so all I could see and feel was the broad wall of his chest. And he held me, stilling me with his even pulse, nourishing me, our two bodies finally one.

Look Both Ways Before Crossing

MEREDITH MARAN

I'm lying in a twin bed in a cabin at a gay resort, quaking so hard the bedsprings are rattling. An arm's length away from me is another twin bed, with another woman in it. A woman who's wearing only a white T-shirt and white Jockey bikini panties. A woman who has breasts, for Christ's sake. Nine months after we met at a conference and began an exchange of increasingly incendiary calls and letters, mere days after my husband of ten years moved out of our house, this woman, R., has flown those breasts—and other body parts too breathtaking to consider—from the East Coast to the West to spend time with me.

Maybe she just wants to be friends, I tell myself now, hoping she can't hear my teeth chattering. *Maybe I'm just making this whole lust thing up.* After all, when R. wrote a month ago to tell me she was coming to California, she suggested that she stay at my house, meet my husband, hang out with my kids. Whether inadvertently or by design, her letter brought to a rapid boil the simmering cauldron of my marriage, in which I'd been drowning alive.

Running my fingers over the unmistakably feminine handwriting on the page, rendered weak-kneed by this bit of proximity to the woman who had become the star of my sexual fantasies, I asked myself: *Do I want to invite R. to stay in the guest room of my suburban tract house, meet my husband, hang out with my family?*

No, I do not.

Well, then. Do I want to tell her that I'm not quite ready to trade in my hetero hope chest for the lesbian equivalent— silk lingerie for flannel, designer shoes for work boots, my fantasies for reality—and ask her to reschedule her trip for a later, braver time?

No, I do not.

Do I want to forgo a hot tryst with a woman I'm falling in love with to save a marriage to a man I no longer love, a man whose anger has been steadily escalating in direct correlation to my diminishing enthusiasm for him, for our vows, for the torturous counseling sessions we've subjected ourselves to?

No, I do not.

So I screwed up my courage, phoned R., and made a counteroffer. "Let's go away together," I said. "I'll book us a room someplace nice."

From three thousand miles away, I heard a sharp intake of breath, followed by thick silence. I knew that R. was waiting for me to clarify the terms of my invitation. "Okay," she said finally, adding, "Can you make sure it's a gay-friendly place?"

This girl's got balls, I thought, but "Goes without saying" is what I said. And then I canceled my next marriage counseling session and called the one lesbian I knew. I asked her what someone would do if someone needed to find a gay-friendly hotel. Hooting, she sent me to A Different Light, the bookstore in San Francisco's Castro district, for *Gay Travel A to Z.* I went home, flipped through the pages with sweating hands, then called to make a reservation at Bridges, a resort on the Russian River.

Not all that friendly, I thought when my request for twin beds sent the clerk into fits of laughter. "Wow. That's a first," he sputtered. "Pulleys, whips, butt plugs—I've been asked for a lot of weird things. But twin beds? That's kinky."

Lying in the dark now on stiff, scratchy sheets, I wonder if this is all a bad dream. Am I really about to wreck what's left of my heterosexuality, my marriage, my family?

R. sighs and sits up. Across the dim reach I see her eyes glowing at me. My heart bangs in my chest. Will she...? What if she...? No. She won't start this. Until we touch I'm a straight woman, a mother, a wife. If anyone's going to wrench me out of my suburban ranch house and into Lesbian Nation, it's going to have to be me.

"What do you want, Meredith?" R.'s voice wafts hoarsely through the dark. *I want you to jump on top of me,* I do not say. *I want you to pin my arms over my head, quiet my ecstatic cries with your mouth, do all the things I've been waiting for a woman to do to me since I had my first crush on Judy Zimmer at age six, when her father caught me kissing her and threw me out of the house; that taught me there were advantages to kissing only boys. Or since I fell madly in love with Debbie Taylor at twenty-two; when I confessed my feelings to my Catholic boyfriend, he told me it turned his stomach to think of making love to a dyke. Or since I started lusting after you last year at thirty-two.*

I will myself to say something. Do something. I throw the blankets off my shaking legs and stand up, swaying on my feet. R. holds her own covers up: *Come here.* I slip into her bed, lie flat on my back, arms at my sides. Our hips are touching. I think the heat of that junction will set fire to the sheets.

"We don't have to do anything you don't want to do," she says.

I'm standing on the edge of a cliff. I suck in a breath. I jump. "I want to do everything," I say. *It's been so long,* I do not add. As we fought more and more, my husband and I had sex less and less. After years of neglect, my whole body now feels like one big throbbing clitoris. My skin, my insides, my soul are starving for touch.

I turn and put my arms around R. Touching her back shocks me: It's as smooth and hairless as my three-year-old son's. Our nipples collide. *Just like in the porn movies,* I think. My insides bubble like lava. R. runs her hand down the length of my body. Her hands are so delicate, so soft. Juices gather and drip between my legs. Her breathing is ragged, rasping in my ear. Or is that me who's panting? After all these years of wondering, I'm stunned to realize how different and yet the same it feels to want this woman. I've felt exactly this way many times before, every time I was in bed for the first time with a man. Lust is lust. Making love is making love. But how will I know what to do?

R. presses herself to me, works her leg between my legs. "I can't," I moan. "I've never...I won't..."

I can, as it turns out. We do.

*   *   *

Thirteen years after my husband and I agree to the terms of our divorce, twelve years after R. and I become lovers, R. leaves me. She denies my accusation that she's having an affair. She says it's because I don't understand her. We don't speak for a couple of months, and then she calls. "I thought we should talk," she says. My heart lurches. She has come to her senses. She wants me back. "About how to keep from running into each other at Gay Pride."

"Oh," I croak. Every June for a decade R. and I marched in the Gay Pride parade together. This year she'll be marching with her new lover, the thirty-three-year-old who was the object of my "paranoia," the hot younger thing she left me for.

"That is," R. says into my silence, "if you're going to the march. I mean, if you're still gay."

If I'm still gay? I've spent the past month crying, meeting with my lawyer, crying, refinancing the house, crying, seeing my therapist, crying, and trying to explain to my kids where their other mother went. Sex—let alone a reevaluation of my sexual orientation—has been even lower on my to-do list than eating, sleeping, and feeling any emotion other than grief.

"Of course I'm still gay," I manage. "But I'm not going to the parade." I hang up the phone, go to the bathroom, and stare at myself in the mirror. Am I still gay? I don't look gay. (What does gay look like?) I don't feel gay. (If I could be interested in anyone at the moment, it would be a man, now that I've been screwed, literally and figuratively, by a woman.) Why should I be gay? I've learned the hard way that, contrary to popular opinion, women aren't any nicer than men. I left my husband, splintered my family, crossed the line from hetero to homo floating on a cloud of dreamy delusions: Surely a woman would understand me, mirror me, nurture me as no man ever had, as no man ever could. But my life with R.—a long-running, high-pitched, poorly scripted dyke drama—had proven me wrong. Sure, R. understood the take-no-prisoners power of PMS and the social implications of shaving or not shaving one's armpits and legs. We could finish each other's sentences, rattle off each other's psychological résumés, wear each other's clothes. But when R. and I weren't paying one lesbian-affirmative therapist after another to mediate between our childhood ghosts, we were fighting about lingering ex-lovers (hers), whose turn it was to cook dinner (mine, always mine), or which of us was secretly attracted to this mutual friend or that (both of us). My inflated expectations of R., of being in a relationship with a woman, served up extra helpings of pain when she left. No man had ever, could ever, hurt me as much as she did.

Besides, as much as I liked touching her breasts, her lips, feeling what she was feeling inside me, knowing that she was feeling what I was feeling inside her, I'd missed having a penis inside me, too, a broad chest enveloping me, the guttural grunts of a man's thrusting orgasm, the suffocating, satisfying weight of a man's postcoital collapse.

Staring at myself in the mirror, I have a revelation. I've crossed the line once. I can cross it again.

*   *   *

D. and I have been friends since we met in an activist group ten years ago. Our shared politics brought us together, but our shared sexual curiosities are what have kept our bond strong. I've always loved hearing about the vicissitudes of his open marriage. He couldn't get enough details of my girl-on-girl sex with R. Telling each other erotic stories from our relationships gave me a little crush on his wife and gave him a little crush on R. When the four of us had dinner together the meals were spiced by attraction, sparks sizzling in every possible direction.

So much for that. Now D. and I are both slogging through divorces. We've been spending more time together, smoking pot, taking walks, sharing tips on what to tell the kids. One foggy July night we meet for dinner at our favorite Thai restaurant, the one that's halfway between our former marital domiciles.

"What are you doing about sex these days?" D. asks me over pumpkin curry.

I stab a chunk of zucchini with my fork, trying to convince myself to eat it. I've lost fifteen pounds to heartache. On the list of things I've vowed to never do again—along with depend on anyone, stay in a relationship that requires a team of therapists to prop it up, and believe someone who says they're not cheating—is drive myself crazy wishing I could lose five pounds.

"Nothing," I say, shaking my head. "I'm pretty sure I'll never have sex again."

D. stretches his hand across the table, laces his fingers through mine. I look up at him, surprised. We're as huggy as any other good citizens of Berkeley: We kiss hello and goodbye, sit on each other's lap when the car that's driving to the demonstration or the party is too full. But this feels different.

"I've always wanted to make love to you," D. says. "And now there's nothing in the way." He smiles, a handsome, friendly smile. "Want to go to your house and fuck?"

The word shocks me more than the question does. Sex was "fucking" to me until I met R.; she called what we did "making love." It took me a few years, but eventually I started saying it back to her. Why go to all the trouble of becoming a lesbian—reading my sons books about kids who have two mommies, hiring only gay-affirmative doctors, therapists, and housecleaners—if sex with R. wasn't going to be more meaningful, more spiritual, more emotional than it had been with men?

I look at D., then at the chunk of zucchini on my fork, then back at D., deciding which one I'd rather put in my mouth. I've never really liked zucchini.

"Okay," I say.

He jumps up, hands me my jacket, throws a few bills on the table, puts his arm around me, and speed-walks me toward the door. "Keep the change," he calls to the waitress.

"Your kids are with their dad tonight, right?" D. doesn't wait for my answer; we know each other's joint custody schedules as well as we know our own. "I'll follow you to your place." He kisses me hurriedly, rushes to his car. He seems to think my offer will expire if he doesn't redeem it in the next five minutes. He could be right.

What's the point of having my heart broken if I can't fuck who I want? I ask myself as I drive through downtown Berkeley, D.'s face in my rearview mirror lit by eagerness. A familiar buzz is building in my lower chakra. I press my thighs together. My body wants this.

I unlock my front door. D. leads me upstairs to my bedroom, starts taking off his clothes. "I know you don't want a relationship," he says, his voice muffled by the white T-shirt he's pulling over his head. "Neither do I. We can be fuck buddies for as long as we want to be." Muscles! "Then we can go back to being friends."

I stare at his barrel chest, furred with whorls of wiry black hair. No breasts! His face reappears. A beard!

My head is spinning. Twelve years with R., and now in

one night I'm throwing away my passport to Lesbian Nation. *Oh, well,* I think. *Been there, been done in by that. Why would I ever want to go through all that again?*

D. bends to unzip his jeans. White Jockey underwear! What do my sons call those ugly things? Oh, yeah. "Tighty-whities." But D.'s wife must have taken the bleach with her when she moved out; his underwear is more gray than white, splotched with faint yellow stains. I struggle with a moment of pure revulsion. Is it too late to cancel my defection and beat a hasty return to my adopted homeland?

If you're still gay. I hear R.'s voice in my head. I want her out of my head. Out of my body. Fucking D.—crossing that line—will help.

D. tosses his jeans onto the chaise, lies naked on his back across my king-sized bed. I busy myself undressing. And then I'm naked, too, and there's nowhere else for my gaze to go. A penis. That goose-bumpy sack, its baggy skin like a plucked chicken's. I try not to stare. Thick, sinewy legs. He even has hair on his feet. Can I really do this?

"You're beautiful," D. says huskily. He and I have seen each other's body before, in hot tubs, on beaches. But not like this. Not for this. *You're beautiful, too,* I start to say, because he is, even if I can't quite appreciate it. But wait: Am I supposed to call a man beautiful? Straight sex, I realize, has become foreign to me. I don't speak the language anymore. I don't know the culture, the protocols, the rules. What's sexy? What's insulting?

"Come here," D. says, reaching for me. Eight weeks ago, she reached for me in this bed. I take his hand, let him pull me down on top of him. He's longer and wider than I am, than R. was. His erection presses urgently against my thigh.

He caresses my breasts, my belly. His hand snakes

between my legs. I push it away, raise myself above him, lower myself down. *Ahhh.* How could I have done without this for so long? He tries to caress me again. I push his hand away impatiently. I don't want this to be anything like it was with her. I don't want to feel anything—surrender, orgasm, heartbreak—I felt with her. I just want to remember what it's like to fuck a man.

D. and I go on this way for months: buddies by day, fuck buddies by night. Over time the tenderness we shared as friends evaporates in the heat of the rough, recreational sex we favor: exactly the kind of sex I longed for when I was trapped in predictable, passionless married sex with my husband, the only kind of sex I can tolerate in the wake of my crashed-and-burned affair. But the acrobatic high jinks I engage in with D. seem to simulate, not stimulate, genuine passion. Has fucking D. ruined a friendship I counted on? Has loving and losing R. ruined me for sex as well as love?

Then in December a friend says she wants to introduce me to K., a Frenchwoman she swears is perfect for me.

"I don't do girls anymore," I say. "And I don't do love."

My friend pulls out a photograph and hands it to me, smirking expectantly. Sure enough, K.'s beauty—glossy shoulder-length hair, chiseled nose, voluptuous lips, curvaceous body—hits me like a brick. But it's her eyes... her eyes are on fire. Staring at this sexy, sparky woman, I feel my resolve and cynicism melting. Maybe this could work.

"You should meet her, at least," my friend says. "Tell you what. I'll have a very special sale at my store tomorrow night. I'll invite only her and a few other people."

"Now you're bringing in the big guns," I say. Even if I could resist the Frenchwoman with the glowing eyes, I'd never miss a sale.

K. and I fall in love the moment we meet, in the dressing room of our friend's Berkeley boutique. She drapes me in velvet, smooths satin over my shoulders, speaks to me throatily, poetically, her voice adorned by an accent that heightens her allure. Maybe I'm not quite finished with women after all.

"Closing time," our friend announces, beaming at us proprietarily. Is our mutual magnetism already that apparent?

"Come to lunch tomorrow," K. urges me. I start to agree, then stop myself. Am I really doing this again?

"I'm on deadline," I stall. A shadow falls across K.'s face. "But I'm turning my book in on Friday," I say. "I'll have lunch with you then."

K. greets me at the door of the mansion in the hills where she's staying, a confident smile on her pouty lips, the scent of expensive French perfume in the air. She's dressed for seduction in a fluffy angora sweater, flowing velvet skirt, buttery leather shoes. It won't take much to get me there. But first, she says, touching my face lightly, first, we will have lunch.

She cooks for me in the cavernous gourmet kitchen, sits me down at a table dressed in flowered linens, feeds me mouthfuls of curry- and saffron-scented rice. I'm surprised by how much pleasure I take in her company—not just anticipating what is to come but sinking into what's happening between us right now: the laughter, the storytelling, the connection across languages and cultures. Like me, she has a history with men and women. Unlike me, she was raised in a culture that doesn't padlock people into sexual cages, so she's light about it. Flirtatious. Delicious. *Uh-oh,* I think. *This one I really like.*

"Want to see the house?" K. asks when our bowls are empty, a ruse I fall for willingly. She leads me upstairs. We never get past the bedroom. She builds a fire in the floor-to-ceiling fireplace, spreads a sheepskin rug inches from the hearth. We lie down together in the center of the heat. Our ankles are touching, our elbows, our hips. *Don't let this happen,* I warn myself, but it's beyond reason, beyond memories, beyond control: that burning in my belly, that clenching in my groin.

K. and I talk, the way women talk to each other. We tell each other important things. She cries softly, telling me about her mother, who died ten years ago. I choke out the deepest, truest version of my breakup with R. As K. talks, I pull the elastic from her ponytail, run my fingers through her corn-silk hair. She kisses me and I know for sure that this is dangerous, more than I bargained for. But certainly we won't be falling in love. We live a continent and an ocean apart. Certainly K. won't be leaving her big life in Paris. Certainly I won't be leaving mine in Oakland, where I have a teenage son about to move away from home and another in the throes of a rough adolescence. Plus, I'm still having sex with D.

I kiss K. back, our tongues intertwining like swans on a glassy lake. *Stop this now,* I tell myself. But it's too late. My heart is blooming, blooming, blooming in my chest.

"*Déshabille-moi,*" K. murmurs, and I undress her. Silk chemise! Her shoulders are broad; her waist is narrow. Breasts! I gasp at the sight of them. Her nipples are pert and rosy, beckoning to me. The faint scent of cardamom, turmeric. Her skin is velvet; no beard scratches my face when we kiss. No fur blurs the perfect contours of her alabaster ass.

By the time K. goes back to France three weeks later I've made reservations to visit her in six weeks' time. No ambivalence or equivocating for us: Already we are a couple. Over dinner in our favorite Thai restaurant, I tell D. about K.

"You just got over R.," he argues. "Aren't you afraid of getting hurt again?"

I shrug. "I'd rather get hurt again than miss a chance like this."

"You're getting caught up in romance," D. says.

"Guilty," I say. I've always liked D.'s honesty, but now, compared to K.'s gentle sensitivity, his candor feels like aggressiveness. And when did he start chewing with his mouth open? It grates on me. He grates on me.

I tell him it's time for us to go back to being friends. We give it a try, but the time between our dinners and racquetball games grows longer and longer.

Six months later, K. leaves her own country, a continent and an ocean away, and moves in with my younger son and me.

*   *   *

"Did you have sex with anyone else?" K. still asks me twelve years later, whenever I come home from a business trip or a writing retreat. "Remember the rules," I warn her whenever she leaves home—the home where I once lived with R., then had recreational sex with D., and now live with K. She knows the drill. As she's packing for a hiking trip or a visit to France, she recites our terms of engagement: "Use condoms or dental dams. Don't come home with a phone number or an e-mail address. Make sure he or she is someone who lives far away, no one we'll run into at the grocery store."

"Get rid of the boyfriend," she calls to warn me when she leaves work early. "Must be your other girlfriend," I say when I pick up the phone and someone hangs up. We laugh, because we trust each other: to want something or someone else, and to tell ourselves and each other the truth about it.

We entertain and titillate ourselves, plotting ways to bring home a man to share, talking about what we're missing. But the truth is, when K. is composing a bouquet from flowers she's grown in our garden, or hand-washing my underwear as tenderly as she bathes our infant grandniece, or panting in my arms, it's hard to remember what, exactly, I'm missing.

Our arrangement was as easy for us to come to as it was for us to come to each other. Neither one of us wants to feel that someone else is making our decisions for us. Both of us want to leave our options open to other adventures and our hearts wide open to each other.

In twelve years, neither K. nor I has exercised the elasticity of our agreement. But we keep it in place, along with our wedding vows. We both like sex with men and sex with women, and we both like sex with each other—even more, apparently, than we like the excitement, the exoticism, the eroticism of that other thing: whatever it is we don't have.

Lost in Space

JULIE POWELL

You like that, don't you, bitch?

When I first learned about the story of Ptolemy's spheres in junior high, I thought it was one of the saddest things I'd ever heard, in science class anyway.

What a little slut you are.

Claudius Ptolemaeus was an astronomer, mathematician, and all-around talented guy in Hellenistic Egypt. In his book *Al Magestt,* he put forward a gorgeously baroque planetary system that explained and could predict, with admirable success, the movements of the heavenly bodies. He envisioned an intricate system of orbits and counterorbits, each with a mysterious name like *epicycle, equant,* or *eccentric deferent,* planets spinning in a complex but achingly precise dance around the earth, the center of the universe. It is a beautiful theory, brilliantly conceived.

It is also, of course, dead wrong.

How desperate he must have been, I thought. An old man, peering up at the stars for something he has missed, adding circle after senseless circle to his cluttered pages. Another orbit, another layer, anything to make the numbers come out right, to prove the centrality of the earth and mankind, the only possibility he could conceive.

This is what you want, isn't it?

I see it differently now. Ptolemy's certainty was a gift, not a curse. There were things he simply knew. He believed, for instance, in what Plato called the "Spindle of Necessity"—literally, the spindle purported to run through the center of the earth. It is said to have been created by Ananke, goddess of necessity; also of compulsion and inevitability. Ptolemy knew the Spindle of Necessity existed and that the earth spun around it. In his mind, all he had to do was discover its workings. To him, the rotation of the planets was basically the world's greatest Sudoku puzzle. If he kept drawing those circles, eventually he'd figure out why a phenomenon he already knew to be true was true. And the thing is, he managed to do it. What comfort, what pride, he must have taken in that.

Say it.

It doesn't matter if you're right or wrong. It only matters how blissfully certain you are. It's when the certainty falls apart that the dread sets in.

Yes. Please. Do it again.

*   *   *

The first time D. slapped me, I flinched. He didn't apologize. Instead, he gave me a conspiratorial smile and slapped me again, hard across the face. I gasped, but in truth, it didn't hurt much. Not, I realized with a small prick of surprise, quite enough. I giggled nervously when he slapped me again. And again. What I noticed was this: As my cheek burned hotter and hotter, I began to feel more and more deliriously... free. *So this is it,* I remember thinking. *This is much better.*

The next day, my jaw ached. It wasn't the only ache I had, but it was the one I found most enthralling. Alone in the bathroom, I cradled my cheek in my palm and made exaggerated chewing motions, smiling dreamily as I felt the grinding click at the hinge of my jawbone. No one had ever treated me like this before, yet it felt astonishingly natural, as if I were finally home.

I had succumbed to D.'s charms something less than a year earlier, after a lunch of Indian food and beer. He made me laugh for the first time since the 2004 presidential election, two days earlier. I say now, only half joking, that I must have been mad with grief.

Unlike my handsome husband, D. wasn't much to look at: small, with heavy-lidded eyes, crooked teeth, an oddly shaped thatch of wiry hair on his chest, and an angry red wart on his thigh that suggested some kind of contagion. Though naturally thin, he'd begun to develop a shade of a paunch, the result of a principled stance against all forms of exercise that didn't take place in a bedroom. I found his looks, like his languorous, almost feminine movements and purring low voice, both enticing and off-putting. People tended to grimace uncertainly at the mention of his name. "Oh, he's funny, and kind of sexy, I guess, in an annoying way, but..." No one could really put a finger on him. He was unfingerable. Yet despite the highly suspect nature of his allure and my very-much-married status, there was a touch of inevitability about my ending up in D.'s mussed California-king bed.

A little background is in order.

I was already in deep with my future husband, Eric, by my senior year in college. High school sweethearts, we'd made it with enviable, almost unbelievable ease through nearly four years of a long-distance relationship, years marked by weekend bus rides and late-night phone calls. For me, they were also marked by a certainty that came on strong and got stronger. Perhaps as only two people who fall in love very young can do, we filled each other out, providing filters through which we saw ourselves and the world. We had kissed for the first time on a sun-dappled river after hours of silent, side-by-side inner-tubing. We both should have been elsewhere that summer afternoon, but caught up in the dream of floating together, we kept on until we were both hot and pink with the sun and delicious inevitability. In my mind, our story was a pitch-perfect fairy tale. If I ever experienced any doubts or temptations, this fairy tale chased them off. I knew I was young but I was also sure I knew what I wanted—in fact, knew what I would have, in the fullness of time: a wedding, a marriage, a dog, and some kids, all with Eric. Boys could, and did, attempt interference, but I was a rock of fidelity, a paragon of hip faithfulness.

I suppose because I had my unshakable faithfulness to stand on, I was able to pull off the neat trick of being a thoroughly untouchable sex fiend. I might not have walked the walk, but I talked the talk with both relish and expertise. I heartily approved of every deviant practice I read about, in any dirty book I managed to get my hands on. After a visit to the woman-friendly sex shop Good Vibrations, I became a vociferous advocate of sex toys. One of the first proud moments of my college career was the day my floormates voted me the girl with the "wildest fantasy life" during a drinking game. It seemed to me I'd found a wonderful way of having my cake and eating it, too, of being perceived as a sexy adventuress without taking any risks. My universe was in perfect order.

So it was with surprise, confusion, and a good dose of shame that I found myself with a strange boy in my dorm room one night, fucking to the strains of Al Green. This didn't make sense. I couldn't understand how it had happened. There had been a party, an introduction to D., a friend of a friend visiting from a nearby college. Then, suddenly, kissing, an invitation to come upstairs, an R&B disc slipped from his pocket in the CD player, clothes coming off.

At the time, the distance in my long-distance relationship was even longer than usual. Eric had been gone for months, off on his year abroad, in Siberia no less. *That must be the reason I cheated,* I thought, tense and sleepless in D.'s narrow college-issue bed. A momentarily weakened gravitational pull, an abnormally vast orbit had led to an aberration in my usually stately motion. A wobble had led me to fall, briefly, under the influence of another nearby body.

I was lonely and horny and drunk, I reasoned. *It won't happen again.* That's what I told myself each night D. knocked on my door. I'd consider not answering, then think of the multiple orgasms. *This is the last time. I am not attracted to this man,* I'd remind myself, even as I hungrily licked and kissed my way down his chest to his nearly concave belly. *I don't even like him,* I'd tell myself as I cuddled against his shoulder, explicating the details of my photo albums, which he pored over with touching attention. At night we fucked, and we talked and giggled, too. But during the day I was distant, even rude. After graduation, as my parents and I bustled out of the dorm with boxes of my belongings,

D. loitered nearby. I barely acknowledged him; soon enough, I was in the car and gone. It had been an unfortunate alignment, that was all. Mercury in retrograde, perhaps.

My life continued to move along the path I'd foreseen—New York apartment, marriage, career, and dog, in roughly that order, with kids the next item on the checklist. Throughout this time, D. showed up now and then, with infrequent regularity. There were a handful of e-mails, phone calls, lunches when he happened to come to town. I'd pick up the phone and hear his low voice on the other end and my toes jangled with a rush of adrenaline. I always agreed to meet, relishing the chance to bask in dangerous possibility.

But D. was unfailingly, almost disappointingly, proper. The Thing That Had Happened was never mentioned, and though I dreaded these lunches initially, I came to enjoy our occasional hour of conversation. D. was amusing and smart, and his smug yet self-deprecating schtick worked far better on me than it had any right to. And so I gradually worked these appearances into my personal cosmology. Viewed through the superior lens of my life as a happily married woman, these potentially destructive events could be reevaluated as mysterious but ultimately benign blips on my radar. Eric even joined us one night for dinner, and aside from D. and I exchanging an uncomfortable smirk across the table when he was in the bathroom, all went smoothly. An hour with D. was no more risky to the life Eric and I had built than an hour spent watching a meteor shower.

*   *   *

By the time Eric and I had been married for five years, sex—once important, if never the center of our relationship—had become a constant struggle. I continued to cultivate my wild-woman image: My porn library had acquired respectable depth. I had a box full of vibrators, blindfolds, and cuffs. I even owned a black leather paddle, lined with real rabbit fur on one side, that Eric had given me one Valentine's Day. But after an initial kick of the tires, it was pretty much permanently retired to my toy box under the bed. I wasn't sure why, but all of the sex dreams that glistened so beckoningly in my mind felt fake, forced, when we tried to enact them in real life. Maybe fantasies simply don't work, I thought. So nearly all of my gear languished in the box beneath the bed, save for my favorite vibrator, which came in handy when I was between temp jobs and home alone all day.

Eric and I talked the problem to death. I told him I wanted him to initiate more. He countered that when he did, I pulled away. We discussed strategies, read books, pulled out a whole spice rack's worth of tricks. But there was no getting around the fact that our sex life, once robust enough and even a little kinky at times, was guttering like a candle burned down to the wick.

This is just life and the immutable law of marital inertia, I told myself. If I seemed unhappy and frustrated in the last couple of years, if I found myself snapping at Eric, cringing when he touched me, crying for no reason, there was a logical explanation. I just hadn't found it yet. It wasn't about sex, it wasn't about Eric—it was something knocked out of place in me, some gravitational pull I hadn't yet fathomed.

Nothing scared me more or inspired me to ever greater heights of rationalization than feeling that I'd hurt Eric. This wasn't your usual fear of causing a loved one pain. This was the stark terror a moon-walking astronaut has of smashing his face mask, cutting off his air supply, floating off the lunar surface. Eric made my world work. It wasn't simply that he got my jokes and made the same quirky kinds of observations about life. It wasn't simply that he took care of me—listened to me, comforted me—or that taking care of him was pretty much the only thing I did well. Eric, in a very real sense, *was* me; we shared every story, every feeling, every ambition. If I couldn't comprehend the universe without my marriage, it must therefore be the one true thing.

I attributed my nagging unhappiness, my tendency to chafe in Eric's presence, to the fact that he kept me safe from the bad girl I knew I was capable of being. If I didn't have him to come home to, I liked to say, my life would go completely off the rails. I liked to imagine this alternative life, always rich with perversely reassuring melodrama: me, careening in zero gravity, lost in space, a wandering, crack-addicted nymphomaniac. If I felt as if I was choking in my current situation, then maybe I simply needed an outlet, some sort of leap-year clause to trick myself back into certainty. And then D. moved to New York, looking a lot like an extra day in February.

*   *   *

One afternoon was all it took to convert me to a new belief system, the absolute laws of physical attraction. D. and I lingered over our curry. I laughed on cue at his carefully crafted, sourly witty stories about the unique flavor of depression in L.A. and movie stars he'd shared ketchup with over lunch counters. I wondered if I was imagining the shimmery new version of the old thing between us. When we were out of pappadum and excuses to keep us there, he asked if I wanted to stop at the Cedar Tavern for a beer, in the same carefully unsuggestive tone he'd used back when he'd asked if I'd ever heard Al Green's cover of "So Lonesome I Could Cry." It took another hour and a half for him to get me into his bed.

After that, we fucked once or twice a week, for as many hours as I could plausibly cover for with tales of coffeehouse work sessions and trips to the movies. At the beginning, there was no hitting, no kinky power games. Perhaps the occasional love bite. Mostly, though, there were hours-long slots of abandonment, times I didn't have to be a wife or worry about hurting Eric with my hurt. I didn't have to plot ways to hide my sadness from him and lose myself in taking care. D. was utterly without needs (well, except for the obvious, and those I was more than happy to take care of). He was the fortuitous adjustment I needed to knock my life back into whack, like a weekly trip to the chiropractor with the added bonus of fabulous cunnilingus. I could work the kinks out, then go home, walk the dog, and make dinner, wrapped once again in blissful certainty. I felt happy, almost giddy. Eric and I started having a little more sex, even.

There were practical concerns, of course: the invention of alibis and explanations for the occasional toothmark bruises that garlanded my neck. But mostly I thought I'd managed to solve the puzzle of my unhappiness, that my affair with D. was actually saving my marriage, saving it from my dissatisfaction.

But, well, shit. That theory didn't quite work, either.

It wasn't so much Eric finding out about the affair. There are only so many sordid text messages and e-mails two people can pass back and forth before one is intercepted. It was more what happened when I decided to break things off with D., the tearful "I love you" that slipped out of my mouth as I was trying to do it. That was unexpected. I'd only been marveling at how much trouble I was having letting him go. At why this small cog suddenly seemed so essential. And the words just came.

It seemed a small thing at first, a minor misstatement that made D.'s face do a funny wavering thing for a moment, like I was seeing him through a haze of petroleum fumes. But it led to a terrible weakening of my carefully constructed planetary system. I loved D. I said it. He started saying it. Together we made it something close to fact. A trite phrase had led to a profound shift in my understanding of the universe. Three months with D. and my head was littered with circles and cosines and stubbornly sticking cogs. I didn't know what was supposed to be orbiting what anymore.

Eric didn't leave. We'd been married seven years, together our entire adult lives. He no more knew who he was without our marriage than I did. So we tried to make things right again, drinking too much, fighting, throwing things, sobbing in each other's arms. Some mornings I thought I was making progress, wrenching everything back into balance without benefit of afternoons with D. But it was no good. D. and I climbed on the wagon and off with metronomic regularity. Finally, some inner spring popped loose. Eric and I suddenly found ourselves separated. I found myself alone.

For a long time, D. seemed the obvious necessary spindle around which to center my new orbit. But after a while, his murmurs of "I love you" mirrored mine with suspicious symmetry, doubly suspicious because an increased rate of exchange seemed inversely correlated to the frequency with which he made his bed available to me. I had been Eric's necessary spindle, essential to the entire system. D. needed nothing from me and wanted me to need nothing from him. Before, that had been his chief asset, a relief from the burdens of caregiving. Now it was oppressive. Without a person who needed me, I felt lost. I didn't think I could abide a world in which I wasn't the center, in which there seemed to be no center at all.

The only relief I got from this feeling of rudderless panic was when D. was fucking me. Or taking me, to speak more precisely. Because as D. became more distant outside the bedroom, our sex grew steadily rougher. D. was a perceptive lover, perceptive enough to know before I did that I wanted him to hit me, control me, hurt me. He saw how delighted I was with the first dark bruise on my ass, how I peered at myself in the mirror. He could not give me what I wanted, couldn't make himself need me or allow me into his orbit, but he could place his hand around my throat like a pearl choker, apply a slap to my cheek like expensive rouge. It was not his anger or his sadism. It was his gift, the only one he was capable of bestowing.

I don't think D. understood that these gifts made me feel alive and owned, marked, and thus—briefly—wanted. When Eric and I had tried our fleece cuffs and paddles, it had felt as if we were children playing a game in a padded nursery, safe—too safe. With D. it was utterly different. When he was holding me down, yanking my hair, calling me names, making me crawl, he was taking something from me, which must mean he needed something. Which must mean that I was alive, that I had feelings. If he needed something, my world seemed, briefly, not so senseless. This was my last wild theory, the final eccentric deferent I tried.

Except that D. also began withholding his brutality, perhaps unnerved by what he'd unleashed, perhaps simply bored. The less aggressive he grew, the more I was sure that our violent moments, the only ones in which I felt peace, held the secret to my restored universe. It was a crackpot theory, building the mechanics of my existence on the joys of getting slapped around. But when the logic you cling to begins falling apart and desperation sets in, you'll do all kinds of things to make the math come out right.

I took to begging for sex, conniving for it, whining and bribing for it. I made fancy duck dinners, planned trips I couldn't afford, bought $75 pairs of men's underwear. The last time we had sex was in an $800 room in the W Hotel. The sheets were lovely, but he arrived late, fucked me almost perfunctorily, and hit me only once.

It happened after we drifted off to sleep. I bobbed up toward consciousness at some predawn hour, felt the pull of him, and curled up against his chest. Still asleep, he flung out an arm to push me away, his forearm whacking me hard across the cheekbone. I spent the rest of the night crying on the fancy tiles of the bathroom floor.

It wasn't until three torturous months later that we finally broke up for good, but that blow across my cheek was the beginning of the end of my untenably complex and confused D.-centric theory of the universe. It wasn't a matter of my finally smartening up, either. Ptolemy had all the brains in the world. It's simply that eventually a person discovers that there's a limit to how many hard truths and contradictions her heart can accept.

D. never hit me in anger. The first time I saw him angry was when I met him to plead one last time: *Please love me or fuck me or at least talk to me. Please forgive me, though I don't know what for. Please give me my center back.* The sight of me disgusted him. He dismissed me with cold finality in the middle of New York City's Union Square on a day in late November, then went on to the Whole Foods to pick up a sushi lunch. The only shred of dignity I managed to retain was in not dropping to the ground in a pile of broken bits right in front of him. I managed to wait until I walked around the corner to the garden with the Gandhi statue, where I sobbed, gasping, there on the sidewalk. I gathered them up, the bits. But they didn't fit together; I couldn't see how they ever had.

*   *   *

I want you to spank your clit ten times. Count out for me so I can hear.

I wasn't seeing D. anymore. Eric and I had moved back in together, for comfort or love or out of a failure of imagination—it wasn't yet clear. Dizzy with pain from D.'s absence, I desperately sought a new fix. If D. himself wasn't the answer, perhaps the rough sex he had taught me to crave was. So I found Peter in a chat room shortly after D. stopped speaking to me. Peter claimed to be an architect, live in London, and to have a thing for clothespins, dog collars, and wooden spoons. We chatted online, then moved to the phone. For a short time I tried to convince myself that these harmless sessions could fulfill me. But the best part of our exchanges occurred before we got to the name-calling and husky commands. The best part was when he answered the phone and said "Hello." He sounded, for a moment, just like D.

Listening to you suffer makes my dick hard.

Remember how when you were a kid and you'd go to the toy store and ogle those giant Lego sets—castles built of Legos, spaceships built of Legos? You'd think that if only you had all the Legos in the world, anything would be possible. And maybe you got lucky and did get all those Legos, or at least a lot of them, and for a time it did seem that anything was possible. Then one morning you take out your giant box of Legos and they're just a bunch of little plastic bits of crap that you're always losing and that hurt when you step on them.

You there? I can't hear you.

I'm sorry. I don't want to do this anymore.

*   *   *

After D. left me there in Union Square, a young man came up to me and stood beside me. I was sobbing, my face buried in my hands, curled as closely into a ball as I could manage, but I felt his presence.

"Are you okay?"

He was carrying a Staples shopping bag. I was crying too hard to see what he looked like, but his voice was kind. I sobbed some more, wiped my face, managed a little nod. But the man didn't go away. He didn't sit down either. He didn't pat my shoulder, or say another word. He just stood there while I cried as much as I needed to, which wound up being not quite as much as I'd have thought. And then he walked away.

*   *   *

Losing your certainty has a sort of cleanness to it, like a deep cut, like the horrible but pure ache in your gut when you're dreaming of falling. I often look at things now and don't know quite what I'm seeing. My husband loves me despite everything, as I do him. He still sleeps beside me, quietly and maybe a little sadly, every night, still gets my jokes like no one else. But for me, there's the lingering hole of D.'s absence. Now that I know that neither one is the center of my existence, the reason for my being, I sometimes get a vertiginous feeling. Then I think about that man with the Staples bag, about how he wandered into my orbit and out again. I think of my life with Eric, the oblivion of sex, of how right it felt when D. slapped me. I'm beginning to see how benighted was my assumption that a center, any center, had kept my world turning, how harmful my need to believe that anything outside myself could be the body I am circling around.

My own body confuses me with all its contradictory urges, to care for and to be free, to fuck and be hurt and finally get some rest. It's unnerving to feel that none of these things means what I thought they did, that they don't fit together neatly in an inevitable, infinite orbit. It's like starting from scratch, really. I feel as if I'm staring at a neat, vast array of gears and springs and screws that must come together and make something, but I can't remember what it is.

But I also feel sort of invigorated. I don't have to base my actions upon arcane speculations. I don't have to act at all. I'm not looking to get slapped anymore, though I sometimes pine for it. I've come to the conclusion that sometimes, maybe, it's better to do without sex altogether, at least until I know I don't have to be hit to feel serene. Or maybe I won't ever feel serene, not anymore. Maybe we are all simply drifting, falling in and out of one another's gravitational pull, coming together to fuck or to hurt one another or to love as best we can.

The difference is that it's my own gravitational pull that's leading me, whatever bed I fall into or lover I lose or husband I keep. I know now that there's no elaborate system of gears to explain why things happen the way they do. I felt such reassurance when I was being slapped hard across the face. It was a floaty feeling, like hyperventilating, but somehow also like the earth beneath my feet. I knew who I was when I was being hit, I knew what I needed and what the person who hit me needed from me.

Yet I also know that it's better to see my husband as a man I love rather than the essential spindle of my existence, to see D. as a man who didn't want me the way I wanted him instead of as a looming black hole. It's better to be able to look up and, sometimes, to see the stars as merely stars.

Out of Reach

MARTHA SOUTHGATE

Longing, we say, because
desire is full of endless distances...
—Robert Hass, "Meditation at Lagunitas"

When I was nine, I fell in love with Jermaine Jackson, lead guitar in the Jackson Five. I spent hours lying on my bed imagining what it would be like just to take his hand. Later, he was replaced in my affections by Mikhail Baryshnikov, then Peter Frampton, then a host of others. As I got older, these fantasy men gave way to a desperate desire for boys I knew, for snowy walks through starlit woods, for sweet kisses that lasted for days. The boys I imagined kissing often didn't know I was alive. But that didn't matter. I loved them anyway. I tended to pick guys who wouldn't pick me. As a shy, middle-class black girl on scholarship at a wealthy, mostly white prep school, that wasn't hard to do.

As time has gone by and I've had real sex with real men who cared for me, that longing for longing has remained. I love sex—I'm uninhibited and cheerful and noisy. But once I *have* my partner, it's hard for me to stay interested, stay focused. I need someone to want.

*　*　*

Ten years ago, in my mid-thirties, I was on my first stay at an artists' colony, the married mother of a two-year-old boy. I was there to work on my first novel for adults, about the only black man at a boys' prep school. I was thrilled to be there, but I was also very, very nervous. Though I'd published a book the year before, I still didn't feel like a genuine writer, much less an artist.

On my first day there, I met a man I'll call Henry. He was a painter, he told me, and he had a very open, kind face and a nice mouth. That evening, when the colonists gathered for dinner, it was quickly apparent to me that everyone wanted to sit with him. He was smart and antic and extremely funny. By the end of the next day, I had that feeling you get in the pit of your stomach when you're going to fall for someone. By the end of my two-week stay, my fall was complete. I thought about Henry constantly, his hands, his light-colored eyes. He was staying in the room next to mine and I would listen for him stirring. When we were in the same room, I always knew exactly where he was in relation to me, to my body. I could feel it on my skin.

It was summer—the air was like lead, thick and overheated. Sometimes Henry and I took long walks; he always wore the top two buttons of his shirts open and I'd sneak looks at his slightly sweaty chest. He was a big talker. I'd listen to his voice as if it was going to save me from something—I don't think I actually said very much. But sometimes I'd come home and write down what Henry had said, how he'd reassured me that my novel was going to be a "real novel" and that I must finish it. How art and being true to one's art was the only important thing. He told me about poets whose work he loved. One night, a group of us went out to a noisy country bar and drank beer and then came home and lay on the ground and looked up at the stars. I wasn't able to angle myself into position next to him that night—first he was at the other end of the table, then we were separated by a couple of people as we lay on the ground. But oh, how I wanted to touch him. I could feel his hand across the space between us.

It wasn't all in my head. Henry was a big flirt, and he did his share of flirting with me. He was about to move to New York City, where I lived, and at one point said with a sweet smile, "Maybe we could be friends there." At the risk of sounding like a thirteen-year-old, I thought I'd die. I really did.

Finally, I felt I had to, simply *had* to tell him how I was feeling. Again, kind of like a thirteen-year-old, I wrote down what I wanted to say: how much this time together had meant to me, how if I wasn't married, I'd be all over him—something like that. Then I wrote him a note asking him to come to my room after dinner and I slid it under his door. He knocked shyly, then entered and sat on the edge of the bed. I was shaking so hard I could barely speak. After I finished talking, checking my notes a few times along the way, he told me he was flattered. He admitted that he was attracted to me, too. He made a joke about a parallel universe in which we might get together. But for now . . . He had a girlfriend. I was married. There was a child involved. We didn't even kiss. We hugged and vowed friendship.

Once back home, we talked on the phone often. I met his girlfriend, reluctantly. She could tell what I wanted. I'll never forget driving somewhere in his aging van, the three of us squeezed into the front bench seat, her with her arm around him, looking unflinchingly at me. The look said *Don't you dare*. Henry and I kept seeing each other—always in the open, never anything dicey. The dicey stuff was all in my head. Then I got pregnant with my second child, a girl, and after that, I stopped calling—my mind was elsewhere, finally. He didn't call me. We didn't see each other for nearly two years.

After 9/11, overcome with sentiment, I picked up the phone. We had lunch. We had lunch again. He had left the girlfriend who had given me the dirty look. He was dating around but mostly alone—he'd recently ended a tempestuous relationship with a different woman. We kept seeing each other. I never lied to my husband about where I was going. To Henry's studio. To dinner. To lunch. Our behavior was innocent—but, once again, my thoughts weren't. I imagined kissing the base of his throat. I thought about us in some imaginary bed with smooth white sheets. Sometimes we touched in that accidental way that isn't entirely accidental, the same thrilling but momentary contact my husband and I had sometimes shared before we'd ever made love.

Within a month, we were talking nearly every day. We saw each other every other week or so. It was a romance— no doubt about it. He told me his dreams, he played the guitar, he read me poetry and cooked beautiful dinners for us in his small, pristine bachelor apartment. His cats padded around silently and sometimes climbed onto my lap as though I belonged there. Those quiet evenings were wildly romantic, the dates I'd always dreamed of but had never experienced. They didn't end with kisses and fumbled-with buttons but with an ache of desire that pierced me through. I would walk home in the dark, my heart pounding, shaking my head. What was I doing? What on earth were we doing?

I began to question everything about the life I had chosen: whether I should have married, had children. I'd introduced Henry to my husband early in our friendship, hoping to defuse the tension. It didn't work. I was, as they say, in the grip of something larger than myself. My husband (I'll call him Michael), remarkable man that he is, did not forbid me to see Henry. And I didn't stop myself. I stayed out into the evening with another man. I came quietly into my bedroom in the dark, ridiculously late. Michael would ask where I'd been, his voice pained. I'd say, honestly, that I'd been at Henry's, or out to dinner with Henry. We both knew I wasn't saying everything. Michael would stare at the ceiling and say, "What were you doing all this time? It's late." I knew I was hurting my husband. I knew I shouldn't cause him pain. But I couldn't stop.

Henry, for his part, never asked me to leave my family; indeed, the prospect alarmed him. He cared for me, he found me attractive, and he was deeply involved with me in his own way and for his own reasons—but he didn't want me to run off with him. That didn't deter my desire. I kept asking myself *How can I want someone this badly and still stay married?*

*   *   *

A writer friend once said that for him, the onset of a book is usually a mixture of ambition, ideas about what to write, and longing. "Without one of those three," he explained, "I can't do it... it's a feeling like wanting to take out a girl, and she's sort of unavailable, and so I write a book instead." That's true of me, too; longing fuels my deepest work as a writer. More than that, it's a crucial part of my sexuality. That desire for someone out of reach, whether Jermaine Jackson or a real person, keeps passion alive in me.

My husband and I have been together for twenty-two years. We met at a summer publishing course, sixty women and twenty men, all of us living in dorms for six weeks. Michael caught my eye because he was funny and always asked smart questions. He made me laugh at the meals we all shared. Plus, he loved books, and whenever he came running into class late, his hair stuck up in a way I found endearing. As we slowly began to notice each other that summer, I found something new to want.

But I didn't have to want for long. We were both free to fall into bed after only a few weeks of shy circling. I still remember the way he played gently with my ear the first time we kissed, the sweetness of it. I remember our trying to squinch up together in the narrow dorm-room singles, our bodies tightly entangled. I remember the pleasure of learning our way around each other. And I remember feeling a tiny bit relieved when, after those first few nights of togetherness, we slept apart so we could both get some rest. For if I already had him, how would it stay enticing? There was no way to wish for what I had already been granted.

Even on our wedding day, I felt uncertain that I wanted what I'd chosen. I had a great time at the party, we both did, but I was scared of what would follow: Never having sex with anyone else, never the thrill of touching new flesh? Making love with each other exclusively until we died? Suddenly, life seemed very long.

They say it's the man who struggles most with commitment and fidelity. But I've had a much harder time with both than my husband has. I am unwilling to close the door to my heart, to let no one but Michael live there. How could I not crave the touch of someone new at some time? How could anyone not? I wanted to get married but the idea of marriage also made me profoundly uncomfortable. I kept trying to think of ways to get out of it—mostly through fixating on how we were different from each other or thinking that there might be someone else out there better suited for me. Yet I chose to do it.

Michael, God bless him, has stayed with me through all of my searching and struggling and thinking about leaving. Through all the periods when we couldn't stop touching each other and all the periods when I couldn't bear to have him touch me. My husband is kind and giving and patient in bed—our bodies are like warm, well-known countries to one another. Sometimes, when I see him cleaning up the kitchen or talking with our children or when I hear him laugh, my heart contracts with affection. When I embrace him, the familiar feeling of his body is a comfort.

And yet we are fundamentally different. I am impulsive, somewhat disorganized, and emotionally extravagant. He is orderly, methodical, precise, and rigorous. We were drawn to each other because of these differences, but inevitably, the disparities extend to our ideas about lust and romance—and longing. When our children were little, which is when I met Henry, our differences felt particularly stinging to me. I was deep into the dailyness that is marriage with young children—the strollering, the walking, the never-ending what-chore-is-nexting. When I was with Henry, I didn't know what would happen next. It wasn't enough that I had a wonderful, loving, strong partner. I desired someone who would carry on and ravage me inside and out, who would sweep me away.

This wanting made me feel more alive as a sexual being. Having? Not nearly as sexy.

My husband is many things but he is not, like Henry, a little crazy, noisy, and outrageous. He does not spend half his year at artist colonies making exuberant pronouncements on love and literature and the other half of the year traveling the world. Hell, I didn't just want Henry. I wanted to *be* him.

One night, when Michael was out of town, I went to see Henry at his studio. By this time, I'd endured a year or two of sweet torture. Henry wasn't wooing me much anymore and my desperate devotion was starting to feel confining and unhealthy to me. But I wasn't ready to let go entirely. Occasionally, maybe out of pride, I'd poke at the embers of our former passion to see if I could get a response. So on this particular night, as we sat talking, him working away on the computer, I said something about "Back when we were all crazy about each other..." I was trying to be light and offhand, but it came from the deepest part of my heart. "Well, that's over," Henry said. He didn't look away from the screen for a second.

Somehow, I got myself out of his studio—I could tell by his solicitous manner as I left that he knew he had hurt me. But Henry couldn't help me now. I stumbled to the subway station, crouched in a filthy corner, and sobbed as people rushed past. After a while, I pulled myself together enough to get on the train, get home, pay the babysitter without crying, and crawl under the covers, where I spent most of the night sobbing harshly, alone in my marital bed.

That wasn't the end. But it was the beginning of the end. Now Henry and I have a drink or dinner together every few months and talk on the phone occasionally. I still think he's attractive but he's not eating me alive anymore. What I feel for him is a wistful affection mixed with some gratitude. After all, I learned a lot from my passion for him. I learned to treasure good poetry. I began to respect myself as an artist. He also forced me to examine my sexuality, my desire, my life choices down to their very core so I could, finally, begin to understand and embrace them, dark and light. I never meant as much to him as he did to me. But that doesn't bother me anymore. Much.

I know now that if I had left my husband under the engine of my desire for Henry, it would have been the biggest mistake of my life. Anyone might wonder, and rightly so, why my husband would put up with my behavior. I know, from painful conversations we have had since, that there were times he was consumed with anger, times he wanted to grab Henry and punch him. I know there were times he was just as angry with me. There was a ruthlessness to my actions that I'm not proud of. I took Michael for granted. On occasion, I have pushed him to the point where he has thought about leaving me. It hurt him to have to wonder what I was doing with Henry. But he refused to hem me in, and by letting my passion run its course and trusting me to stay within certain boundaries, he allowed it to burn out. That he chose to do that, that he was capable of doing that, makes me love and respect him more. If Michael had forbade me to see Henry, odds are I would have bridled and run to a place that isn't, wasn't ever, the place I belonged—away from my husband, away from my family.

I have a good marriage, and I am more committed to my husband now because I was forced to deeply examine whether marriage and sexual fidelity are what I want, whether they're possible for me. But I've also realized in some fundamental way that I am not going to change. What I have to learn now—as we all do—is how to fully accept and manage the person I am and the feelings I have. My desire for Henry, my love for him, my longing for him, helped keep a part of me alive that I've learned to treasure, not fear or push away. From living through that hunger, I've learned that marriage isn't everything, though I married a man I love very much, a man I've made a life with, a man who, through his generosity and patience, has guided me to a good life with him. We've chosen to have a monogamous relationship. Since I have been married, I have not made love with anyone else. But my husband is not the only man for me. I have deeply loved and desired other men—for there have been others besides Henry. Some might think that means there is something gravely wrong with our bond. That doesn't happen to be true.

For me, marriage is a terrifying choice, one I have to make over and over. I've also discovered that I can let a new partnership into my life without destroying the love I already have. I can love and want someone profoundly and not *have* to make love with him. Or live with him. Or marry him. Though sometimes it hurts not to touch that new body, setting that boundary doesn't mean I have to turn away from what's good in my longing *or* in my marriage. Like having more than one friendship, having more than one love is a gift. The hard truth is, when it comes to love and desire, the greatest gifts are sometimes the most difficult to accept.

Toys in the Bedroom

SUZANNE PAOLA

An act of sex made my son. I wasn't there at the time—he's adopted—but I am still very aware of this fact, and so I'm aware of the paradox that follows: Sex makes children, then children do all they can to unmake sex. In my experience, life with a curious, active, occasionally trying-to-get-you-back kid does not feel conducive to lovemaking, at least on the surface. Kids refuse to go to sleep when you want them to. They wake up if you make too much noise and so you try to prevent each other from doing so—leading to an act I think of as Anti-Erotic Asphyxiation. If you try to use sex toys, they find them. When my son, Jin, was four, my husband, Bruce, spilled the contents of his suitcase and this plastic thingy designed for intercourse rolled across the floor. Jin found it and decided it had once been one of his "binkies." And just a few months ago, Jin, now nine, emerged from a time-out in my bedroom dangling a sex toy called a "tongue vibrator" from his finger. The tongue vibrator, an odd-looking contraption, consists of a ring to slip over the tongue with a small vibrator attached to it. "I know what this is! I know what this is!" Jin sang, doing a triumphant little jig while I nearly negated any use for the tongue vibrator by swallowing my own.

"Uh, what?" came out of me in some form.

"It's a joy buzzer!" Jin said, as if he'd been prospecting through our bedroom and found the Hope diamond. He's a big fan of joke-store gadgets, particularly joy buzzers.

"Yes!" I confirmed, my body flushing with relief, and, though I have built my relationship with my child on the basis of never lying about anything, I started embroidering upon that lie immediately. "It's Daddy's special joy buzzer. He really likes that joy buzzer. Where did you find it?"

"On the floor. Can I take it to school?"

*   *   *

We talked him out of taking it to school. Even in our supremely liberal community, where kids named Bliss and Karma learn to meditate as soon as they can speak, sex aids for show-and-tell would not be cool. Indeed, I found my liberal self unglued by this experience and began hiding all my sex-related accoutrements in places I suspect I'll never remember myself. I also practice what I would say if Jin managed to find this contraband: When I come across a purple tube of lubricant wrapped inside a torn panty in the back of my underwear drawer, my inner liar starts saying, *Hand lotion. Hand lotion.*

A few days ago, after Bruce finished reading to our son, he came to our room grinning. "Jin certainly had a lot of questions about sex." Part of me thought, *Good, that's healthy.* But part of me, surprisingly, wanted to take a big fat pillow and stick it over my head. I felt like a kid again myself. We all remember, I think, the moment in our young lives when we found birth control pills in a nightstand drawer, or another kid told us what parents actually do together in the dark, or, worst of all, we overheard our parents doing it together in the dark. The moment when we realized our parents really did have sex. We didn't care that they liked it, or that sex bonded them and provided a better environment for us. We just thought, *Ick! They put what where? Gross.* We wanted them to cut it out.

"What questions?"

"He wanted to know what vaginas look like and how big they are. He asked me again if you really put your penis in one to have sex."

Cute, I think. *At least it's clear he's not misusing the Internet.*

"He asked me if we have sex. I said of course we do."

No one told me that old, squeamish feeling would extend to knowing my own kid knows I have sex. I'm afraid my husband's next casual revelation will be that Jin figured out the tongue vibrator. I can practically hear Bruce delivering the news with a satisfied little guffaw: *What a boy. He goes from trying to picture a vagina to figuring out what vibrators do in a ten-minute conversation.* But no. I am thankful Jin is not there yet.

*   *   *

When our son came along, my husband and I had already been married fifteen years—years of graduate school and no money, first jobs as editorial assistants, then more graduate school and no money, miscarriage and convalescence—all of which ultimately meant we ended up coming to parenthood later than most, with firmly established patterns in place, including sexual patterns. I had friends who planned sex, and the idea seemed bizarre to me, like a writer who lives alone, then travels to a writers' colony to duplicate her solitude in order to write. Though we planned romantic evenings, drank wine, and ate lovely dinners of crisp-roasted chicken or fresh pasta and chocolate, more often than not we fell asleep afterward. We may have breathed some memorable I-love-yous between bites, but we proved very bad at drawing the different elements of romance together. When it came to sex, we'd always lacked foresight. Instead, we had now's-as-good-a-time-as-any sex. Back then, time was our friend, a sometimes rushed friend but one willing to stand still for the bit it took to withdraw to the bedroom, pull the blinds, and so forth. No one watched us; we necked in the kitchen and developed a habit, not yet broken, of goosing each other on a whim.

Eventually, we got real work and became tenured professors. That's when our undergraduates started comparing us to their parents. I think Bruce and I both wanted to feel cool again, so we went through phases of trying to be more adventurous, to feel sexually brave. Plus, the ease with which my students discussed their "toys" had gotten a little spooky. These men and women looked so young to me. The first student to broach the subject did it so blithely and confidently— "Well, everyone has their toy drawer, don't they?" she said in a conference—that I assumed she meant Barbies and other childhood leftovers. It took me a few days to realize that she'd been talking about strap-ons and other things I wasn't even sure I'd heard of.

I saw a younger cousin of mine after she'd been to one of those modern-day Tupperware parties, where the host offers up appetizers and various products to sell—jewelry, makeup, snack items. "Caroline's doing a lot of these things these days," she told me. "A couple of weeks ago it was toys. I spent a lot of money at that one." I used to babysit this cousin. Now she was purchasing overly pink, jelly-ish plastic penises with motors inside as easily as dry dip mix. *Et tu, cuz?*

When Bruce and I decided to buy a few gadgets of our own, the first place we tried was not a friend's cozy house full of onion dip. We went to a sex shop, an establishment with an unassuming pink sign—the Love Pantry—easy to miss amidst the other strip-mall stores. The place felt comfortable and bland, snugged against a Denny's. On our first Pantry sortie, we stuck with the simple stuff: massage oil, edible panties. We both felt a little shy, especially me, and things like dildos seemed like too much of a statement, a declaration that every orifice needed diddling, that we were insatiable. In contrast, the oil and panties seemed safe; they could be shower presents, gag gifts.

As we opened the door, I took in a wall of frilly pink and black teddies and sex dolls. Only for an instant, though, because the person behind the counter looked sickeningly familiar.

"I'm leaving," I whisper-hissed to my husband, tugging at his arm and walking backward toward the door.

Bruce does not always respond well to my not-so-subtle cues.

"WHY? WE JUST GOT HERE. WHAT'S WRONG?"

"That's my student over there." I got both more whispery and more hissy. She was not only a student, which was embarrassing enough, but a student unhappy about her grade, a student with chutzpah. Her head now swiveled in the direction of the noisy new customers, and seeing me, she stretched her torso across a glass counter of orgasm-inducing items and started calling out my name.

"Ms. Paola? Ms. Paola? Can we talk about my final grade?" I'd had this student in a women's studies class, where we'd dissected the finer points of feminism, the objectification of women. Now we faced off amidst crotchless teddies and vibrators with names like the Spine-Tingler and G-Force. I imagine I could have said something about women empowering themselves by taking control of their orgasms rather than fleeing the store. But fleeing involved less thought.

"Come to my office hours!" I said over my shoulder as I hurried in the opposite direction.

So then, of course, Bruce and I came around to sexual positions. We tended toward a few tried-and-true ways of doing it, and in our adventure-seeking mode, I started reading *Cosmopolitan* and learned about positions like the Piston and the Roller Coaster and the Rock-and-Roll, the elaborate descriptions accompanied by cautionary notes on how overenthusiastic thrusts could lead to twisted penises. The caveat emptors weaned me off the *Cosmo* diagrams, fun as they seemed; that was one trip to the emergency room I didn't want to make.

I do recall, however, a long car ride Bruce and I took from northern Ohio to Atlanta, to see his very ill grandfather. At a rest stop somewhere along the way, Bruce came out of the men's room with a pamphlet he'd bought in a vending machine, a small handbook of unusual sexual positions. We were in the middle of nowhere, and we found the existence of the pamphlet strange—a vending machine of condoms we could see, but who was on the road in rural Ohio seeking out new ways to have sex? It felt like a cross between something that would happen on *The Twilight Zone* and the Playboy Channel. ("These people have used the missionary position far too often," sneers Rod Sterling. "Now they're entering—") Anyway, we stowed it away, not in the mood to think about lovemaking then.

Once back home, we decided we would try all the positions in the pamphlet in a single night, one after another. It was small, like a very large matchbook, with simple line drawings illustrating each move. Like our sex toy experiments, everything was much more difficult than it sounded. My clearest recollection is of a position called the Wheelbarrow, in which Bruce was supposed to hold my legs around his hips while I walked around the room on my hands. The skill or technology or Krazy Glue it would take to stay inserted through all this boggled us, not to mention that we ran into what I think of as the Exotic Sexual Position Paradox: The focus it takes to stay in the position and walk on hands diverts attention from the, um, other stuff. Bruce dropped me over and over, and while we found it all beyond funny, we hardly achieved eros.

When we learned of our son Jin's imminent arrival, the world around us suddenly seemed full of foreboding signals, as if our sex life now had a PREPARE TO MEET THY DOOM sign over it. "Get ready for some big changes," people told us with snarky laughs. Where children are concerned, I've noticed, parents get gleeful about telling you all kinds of awful stuff: You'll never sleep again, you'll become co-parents rather than lovers. Our own investigations didn't help: If you Google "sex after parenthood," you get about three hundred hits implying there isn't any, led by a *Boston Globe* article titled "For Many, No Sex After Parenthood." I worried that we'd sold our chances at some kind of good sex life down a river of mashed peas and formula.

And for the first months after Jin arrived, the predicted

sexual withering did indeed occur, for the usual reasons. Our baby woke up at all hours or teethed and fussed; we were exhausted and sleep moved to the top of our priority list. We also found ourselves so obsessed with him, so in love with him and his every mouthful of avocado, that nothing else seemed real.

As our first year as parents drew to a close, however, I began to miss what Bruce and I were lacking—the loss of our life together as sensual adults. This didn't feel like a great thing for anyone, even our extraordinarily sweet, belly-laughing, and beatific baby, who needed us to have some commerce with one another. So I revived the concept of at-home dates. On date nights, whichever parent put the baby to bed spent about an hour reading, rocking, singing. During that time, the other party in our life duet cooked—seriously cooked as we never did otherwise. I made Bruce steak with truffled mushrooms. He made me lobster salad with endive. No matter what our other obligations, whether laundry or filling up the little ice-cube trays with homemade baby food, we did this. We'd talk about our menu for days beforehand, which became a way to muscle some obsession about ourselves into our lives.

Our radical innovation to prevent falling asleep before sex? Sex before dessert rather than after. Of course, some nights Jin simply wouldn't go to sleep and we gave up. In late spring and early summer especially, our far northern, endless dwindling of the light tended to keep all kids in the vicinity awake, so we began keeping Spanish time, diving into dinner at ten-thirty, famished, then diving into each other in our bedroom, which I'd deliberately freed of Tickle Me Elmo dolls and building blocks to create a space for us, adults with bodies, focused, for the moment, on one another.

At this midpoint moment in my life, I discovered something surprising. Not only did we begin having a sex life again, but the sex was good. Great, even. Better than before. We used sex toys occasionally, putting them aside when we no longer wanted them. We rolled each other around with our feet, being silly, and we told each other frankly what we wanted. As an older woman and a mother, someone not culturally expected to be much of a sexual being, I've discovered a wonderful new sensuality, more playful, more risqué, my climaxes full of intensity.

*   *   *

We still sometimes have our old kind of sex, the spontaneous kind. Given the sheer animal motivation it takes to accomplish that with kids around (true, we only have one, but he tends to draw a billow of others in his wake), I appreciate those encounters. But I'm now a firm believer in foresight sex. I even get why you would go away to a writers' colony when you live alone. At home, instead of writing at your desk, you could call a friend, pull a weed, knock down cobwebs. Away, in a bucolic, artistic setting, when you set up your laptop on a desk identical to the one you already have at home, you know exactly what you're supposed to be doing. The brain—root of lust—is an interesting organ, both bossy and bossable. Tell it that it's in a particular place for a particular reason, and it's likely to believe you.

Anticipation, in other words, is a virtue. I remember a board game I used to play with a boyfriend, an adult version of spin-the-bottle or strip poker. What the game accomplished wasn't so much getting our clothes off—we could have figured that out on our own. Rather, rolling the dice and moving around the board served as a cue for us to get started, providing a certain pacing that kept the whole delightful enterprise from being over with too quickly.

Now that Jin is nine, Bruce and I can't have those wonderful dinners anymore. Unlike a younger child, he doesn't sleep through noise, and he feels very put out if we try to eat without him. But we still plan. "Are we going to get out the Pocket Rocket tonight?" one of us might mention discreetly while setting the table. Then whichever parent is on bedtime duty knows what he or she has to do. There's no saying "Sure, kid, read yourself to sleep," because then Jin might be up for hours if the book is good. No, if we want sex, one of us has to say "Let me sing you 'Froggie Went a-Courtin' a few more times." So what if it's a little boring? It's also soporific. It does the trick.

Once Jin's asleep and Bruce and I finally hit the mattress, we're cued, anticipation pointing our bodies the way we want to go. Often we stop and lift our heads to listen for the flutter of our son's footsteps or his cry, making each act of sex a dozen little acts. The hand over the mouth becomes a new and different kind of sex play. All this eagerness, this stopping and starting, feels naughty, transgressive, full of curses for those cawing bedsprings. I've never been one for thrill seeking, but I imagine it's the kind of frisson some women get from sex in public: dipping down under restaurant tables, cramming into bathrooms, just to set up a situation that, however uncomfortable, feels like breaking out of a defined experience into another, strictly for pleasure.

At fifty, I have a wonderful life, more riches at my feet than I ever expected. My days consist of being a parent and of my work—teaching, writing, volunteering. I tend my garden and cook for my family. I help Jin with his homework and sympathize over teeny scrapes and prepare to lose him one day when he realizes he doesn't need me for any of this, really. A male friend of mine tells me that men want much younger women, women who are beautiful and sexy. I'm all paring-knife cuts and dirt under the nails, neither young nor beautiful. On date days I know someone wants me, is waiting to put his body to mine. My body readies itself in turn and I am a sexual woman again.

I would be horrified if my son experienced our sex—even caught a note of it—but I love taking on my adult, sensual self so aggressively. After hours of being Jin's mom, I become this being with breasts and an open, feeling body. I cross a line, and good sex is about crossing many. My blood flows in a different direction. I have an eager partner and gadgets that hum and buzz when I want them, even if I don't always use them well, even if I have to resort to keeping them in a strongbox with a good lock.

The Overnight

SUSANNA SONNENBERG

I never tell this story.

My well-dressed boyfriend of a year had asked me to move out, and I was still unpacking in my new studio apartment when I had to leave to go to a family party. This meant I had to stop crying. Humiliation washed over me in surges as I sorted through my skirts, as I tried to harden myself to not being wanted. I arrived at my aunt's massive apartment for her usual Thanksgiving gathering, which always promised a wide assortment of guests. As I took off my coat, friends hugged me because they knew about my raw heart, my fresh wounds. Everyone knew.

"I never understood what you saw in him."

"You'll love living on your own."

I looked around for a conquest. Sex. I was quite obsessed with sex, which maybe was natural for a twentysomething woman and maybe wasn't. I was not introspective. My heart had been shattered, but my physical appeal still counted; my body could feed its hunger. Tonight, I decided, I'd make sure the loss of love changed none of that.

In the few weeks since my boyfriend had dumped me, I'd been haunted by our sexual history, the punctuation of sex at every stage of our relationship. We'd started up quickly, attraction igniting at a drinks party, our subsequent dinner date nothing but a marvelous prelude. We didn't finish the meal. We moved in together. It all happened fast, the great sex our insurance. Through the year we talked less, did less, but made love all the time, telling ourselves that with sex like that, we must be destined for each other. Sometimes, as we slept after lovemaking, I came in my dreams, his imaginary body all over me again. In the mornings, as he dressed for work, I'd lie in bed swooning about his handsome pressed cuffs, the drape of his three-button jacket.

Then, one night, on our exquisite cotton sheets, he was coming in my mouth. He raised his hands back against the headboard as I tightened my fingers into his hips. I murmured for the vibration, for the thrill of offering it and loving it, and he came hard.

I wiped my lips along his thigh, then rested my cheek there, watching his rib cage rise and collapse and rise.

"I don't love you anymore," he said.

*   *   *

Days of crying, numb packing, and then it was the morning the movers wedged open the front door, coming and going, unraveling our domestic arrangement. When I hugged my boyfriend goodbye, his hands rose up along my back and down again, outlining me. I looked for the tiniest impulse on his part, the regret, but he was signaling the end. That was his finishing touch.

At my aunt's crowded apartment my cousins and sisters stood and talked. People were arrayed on pretty upholstery, grouped around the grand piano and seated on embroidered footstools before the hearth with its bright brass andirons. One man sat alone. He was looking at women. He was, I guessed, thirty years my senior and attractive in a faded époque way, like Peter O'Toole. Silver hair swept back from his temples. Lustrous brown shoes, gray trousers with crisp creases.

"An old friend of the family," someone said. "You've never met?"

I settled next to him on the sofa.

"Susanna," I said.

"Terrence."

He talked about London in the sixties, his plate balanced on his knee. A way with a knife and fork. He mentioned Damascus. His accent bore traces of travel and too much drink. He intended to be seductive, and I intended to be seduced.

"I just came in for your aunt's party."

A lovely hostess, we agreed. He set his glass on one of her silver coasters, and the lush vapor of good cologne revealed itself, clove and lemon. Silent waiters swam through the rooms with wine bottles on polished trays. Candles stood in pewter holders that rested on the mantel. The gleaming dining table had been set with crystal decanters, short columns of china plates, roast meats. It was a very nice place to be on a night that was gray and chilly, the damp streets below unpopulated except for empty cabs.

Later, Terrence took a fountain pen from the breast

pocket of his cashmere coat and wrote down his number and the name of his town, a couple of hours into the country by train.

"You should come."

It was understood we were talking about going to bed.

I went home to the open boxes in my studio, and when I woke in the morning I dialed his number, and he was pleased.

"Should I come?" I asked. "Next weekend?"

I called a friend. She was married, expecting a baby. My life was a guilty pleasure to her, like trashy magazines. She loved my history of love affairs, my bawdy efforts, all the delicious sex. She was the one who tried to soothe me after the breakup, telling me that everybody gets left sometime. "Even you," she'd said. When I recited the event of the night and my golden prospect, she laughed with glee.

Terrence sent postcards, fragments of Donne and Homer and no signature, just the postmark. How simple and sexy, and I was delighted to be wooed.

The following Saturday I gave myself two hours of preparation, drawing the bath just so. As I shaved my legs, I treated my hair with a precious formula saved for celebrations. I got out of the tub, my feet pressing into the clean bath mat. I saturated my skin with lotion, my elbows, inner thighs. I had butterflies, about to go to bed with a much older man, a first for me, as heartbreak was a first for me. Two careful coats of mascara. Perfume between my breasts. I'd bought a bottle of Barolo I intended to give him, an occasion for excess. I was courting again.

Terrence would bed this impeccable woman, revel in her subtlest scent, lavish her with his talents. He'd see nothing of her pieces and fragments. I raked expensive gel through my curls and dressed. Silk for the mood, boots for courage. I took the subway to Grand Central, holding his slip of paper in my gloved fingers, the velvet lines of black ink. Anticipation fueled me.

When I arrived at the country station, a man waited on the platform, and I didn't recognize him at first. I was lonely stepping off the train, into the empty air. I should have been home, snug.

Terrence wore a down vest, denim shirtsleeves exposed. His hands squirmed in his pockets. He had the thick hair I remembered, but he looked fifteen years older, daylight forcing the truth.

"You're much more beautiful than I remembered. And much younger, God help me."

I tried to summon the mood of our earlier meeting, but with my face turned to avoid the fumes of hot smoke and rubber from the departing train, cold cement under my feet, I couldn't. His car looked horribly orange, the button to his glove compartment missing, the covering to the gearshift gone, as if vandals had gotten to it in a parking lot. He revved the engine and drove away from the station, chattering on random subjects, changing them, zipping over railroad crossings and into curves. We pretended a fascination with the quaint tourism of nearby towns. "There's this little place with country music. Will it impress you, I wonder?"

He had to lean forward to peer through the layer of frost on the windshield. He didn't seem to know where to stop, and mile and then mile revealed only brambled trees. *Let's get to the sex,* I thought, *that was promised the week before.* That had been us, hadn't it? Or, at least, me. For me, sex was easier than this small talk, easier than meals or wise decisions. How good I was, my expert tongue, the best blow jobs, the best everything. Once Terrence had me in his bed, I could feel queenly. *Just you wait,* I thought. Except the more he talked, the less willing to go to bed I felt, so I wished he'd be quiet. He wasn't asking about me. I wished he'd stop speeding. I could feel black ice under the tires. I worried about deer and kept an eye out.

"Do you know how many books I've written?"

I said yes to appear polite.

Under a heavy sky, that time of afternoon when the day darkens and you give up on the things that haven't already happened, Terrence pulled up to an aluminum-sided building and parked on the gravel. A few lights were strung over the entrance, poorly matched colors to suggest Christmas, green, yellow, white, orange. He held the door open, making a flourish with one arm. A few people were singing along with an accordion player, a halting carol. Terrence nudged me toward a booth in the back, and we sat with the table between us. The waitress walked over.

"We've come for something to eat, weary travelers at the inn." In his accent it sounded like "something tweet." He was peering at me, and, purposely avoiding his gaze, I kept my eyes on the waitress. I had the Metro-North schedule tucked in my bag. Six-fifty-five? Eight-something?

"Kitchen's closed. You want drinks?" He ordered a beer, and I had club soda.

He'd lived in Japan, Nairobi, had grown children. This was boring me, like countless dates. Men talking about themselves, asking nothing.

"Right," I said. "Do you want to know about me, what I do?"

He reached across the table and slipped his hand under my arm, fingertips against my breast as he pulled back.

"Cashmere. A sensuous girl. I should have guessed."

In spite of myself and in spite of regretting his juvenile gesture, I felt the soothing warmth of lust travel from my breast to the pit of my stomach. The waitress presented the bill on a Post-it. He tapped on the edge of his empty glass. "Shall we?" When we stood up, he flicked his tongue over my lips, leaving a warm, tinny taste of beer, which canceled his earlier effect. Yet I still wanted to go to bed, to get to the best part of the story I was going to tell. I still thought there was a possibility that we could get it over with and I could make the train. We returned to the car and he drove us farther away from commerce and the train station.

"When's the train?" I said. "Do you know?"

"Don't you want to see the house? You've come all this way, no?"

I did want to, available beds my calling. I needed to know that I was the sexy adventure girl, recent heartbreak be damned. One person didn't want me, but others did, lots of others. The crackle between us could be revived. As his head-lights streaked over the trees close to the road, I couldn't tell where we were. He stopped finally, and we staggered across rutted ice toward a cabin, anxious barking already in full swing from within. Maybe the house had been intended for ancient summers, then added on to in poorly planned shifts. A woodpile leaned against one side as if to shoulder it up.

I followed him into a mudroom, then another room, crowded and small. I didn't want to look at this hopeless refuge. Open cans stood in the sink, silverware poking up from them. Newspapers teetered in stacks against available wall space. Wooden pallets filled a corner, piled with giant bags of dog food and rows of canned tomatoes. A huge dog sulked against him until he pushed it out of the way with his leg.

"Do get off, Jasper." He didn't mention a drink, and we

still hadn't eaten. There was no heat, and it occurred to me that he couldn't afford to take me to dinner. Of course, one wouldn't mention one's income, drinking wine in an Upper East Side apartment; nor had he mentioned personal details, the way he lived, except for "the country," and we had been among people whose reference to the country meant a luxurious choice. He took my coat, but I took it back because it was terribly cold.

"That's a lot of tomatoes," I said.

"You can buy them in bulk. However, there's nowhere to store them in your small city flats." He gestured to a dark room. "Madame?" It contained his bed, a rug for the dog, a window double-sheeted with heavy plastic. He had no light in the bedroom, having recently run out of bulbs, he said.

"You can't read in bed," I said.

"I read on the couch. Come, sweet." He was nervous, which annoyed me. I'd taken a train to a mysterious town; he was supposed to handle things from there. He wasn't holding up his end of the bargain.

"I promise not to look if you promise," he said, turning his back and shedding his denim shirt. I did look, and his skin sagged, dips and shadows highlighted by the remaining light from the living room. We sat on the bed and kissed, me trying to use the power of the kiss to turn the kiss into a better kiss.

I never tell this story. If I did, I would have to tell why, at that moment, I continued to plan on sex, to move toward it. I didn't want to sleep with him anymore, but sex bossed me around, ignored me. It would have been good for me to leave, but I didn't leave. It would have been good for me never to have come. Having sex, though, meant there was less to examine or reveal.

He was semihard as I undid his jeans, and my touch

wilted him a bit. I made my touch lighter until I could feel the throb against my palm. It took longer than I was used to, and I was thinking *So, this is age.* My other hand on his biceps, I felt his stringy muscles. Dry patches. I was glad I couldn't see, and I felt myself lush and ripe and a force that he wanted, if only to ignite the air and ward off the night and soothe the dog and wipe clean his circumstance. I was the new furnace.

He lumbered onto me and my knees widened, a reflex. Easier to go through with it than to stop. His shoulder pressed into my clavicle.

"Birth control," I said.

"Right, that finishes me." He rolled off abruptly. One of my legs glided against the other, the payoff of the smooth shave.

"Aren't you glad I'm thinking of it?" I said.

"No. Is that what women say these days? What a thing. It's been ages. I mean, I never expected..." He trailed off, his mute irritation palpable, a sigh withheld. "Do you even *like* sex?"

I didn't answer. Who was he to blame me for the chill and fumbling? It wasn't my fault that he was out here in the dark, buying bulk goods and heaping his bed with a random collection of worn blankets, eating cold suppers.

"Yet, you. *Here.*" His voice gave way, broke apart almost. "I can't remember how long. Susanna, Susanna." He slowed down: "Susanna." The dog came to the side of the bed, as if called. They had an understanding. I tried to determine the time. The last train had left.

"There's a train at six in the morning," I said.

"I'll wake you, then, won't I?"

I turned and presented him with the curve of me for sleeping, making it obvious I was closed down.

* * *

I woke past six. Terrence slept, and I was still here, deciphering the noises of someone else's dog and belongings, ice cracking in the bare trees. My bones ached from staying at the edge of the bed.

"Please, take me to the station." We were dressing. The minutes grew tighter, worse. "Please." I had no idea where we were, the destination I'd told my friend three towns away. I began to sense the grave reality of my situation. In sorrow I'd been reckless with myself.

"We have time." He handed me a mug of hot water with a tea bag in it. "Sorry there's no toast or jam. No milk, sorry." He wanted to show me old articles. His desk was invisible beneath piles of paper, rafts of loose pages. A couple of postcards lay writing side up, poems filling the white space. They were already addressed to me. As if we'd made love, as if we'd adored it. A letter from a publisher was tacked to an exposed beam by his desk, its date absurdly old.

"It's almost finished, the new book."

"What time is it now?" I asked again.

He became a little cruel. "She simply can't wait to get away, can she?"

I had the feeling that the walls of newspaper and dog food and tomatoes might grab me, so I picked up my things and went out and down the steps and stood in the deserted open, pulling my scarf up under my chin. I glimpsed the wine bottle in my bag next to my wallet and zipped up the bag.

He was empty and beaten, like me. I was furious for not having seen it before. I'd looked at his shoes and his haircut, conjuring glamour, thinking that my gall and fire would match up with his dashing image, replace the worn facts of my recent history. But he was simply making his daily way from breakfast to dinner like everybody, hoping for someone to sit next to him at a party.

He scraped the windshield and drove me to the station.

"You can drop me here."

But he looked for a parking space and pulled in. I kissed his cheek in the car to signal he shouldn't get out. All the same, it was a kiss, and he had the right to think I cared something for him. What I cared about most, though, was his vision of me. Let me be the kiss at the train station, not the woman dumped and hunting, the one with the dashed hopes. I still wanted to think of myself as the best thing that had happened to him in a long while.

"Shall I make sure you find a seat?"

No. The train was coming, and I was going. *Hurry,* I willed it, as I watched its lazy approach. I said goodbye and sat down next to a scratched window smeared with age, and the train delivered me back to the city.

*   *   *

Later that morning, the episode showered off, my overnight clothes out of sight in the hamper, I pressed play on the answering machine, hoping for my ex-boyfriend. *Come back,* he'd say. *It was a mistake.*

It was Terrence, calling while I'd been on the train.

"You'll come back, won't you? Susanna, Susanna, Susanna? Jasper's been asking. Jasper's missing you."

I called my pregnant friend.

"That dump! That dog! He had postcards already addressed to me sitting on his desk. He had plans for us."

"Creepy."

"He was wearing a puffy down vest."

"What about the cashmere coat?"

"I don't know."

"And the sex? How was he?"

"He was..." How little it mattered.

"But he was still dashing? And that accent?"

"Oh, yes." Maybe she'd picture us like an old movie, grays and blacks and shadows on the train platform.

* * *

Hopeful in my aunt's apartment, we'd felt the flash of desire right before the chocolate torte was set out in slices. He invited me and I accepted, bolting onto a train to some little country town for the adventure of it, the anecdote. But we failed to connect and I was impatient with failure. I couldn't see that he was a person caring for himself alone—and what did I know of being alone? I wanted things to turn out just so, match up. The next day, unable to help myself, I sent a thank-you note to close the story with good manners.

Confessions of a Former Sex Geek

ABIOLA ABRAMS

To say that until a couple of years ago my life was devoid of sexual experience is like saying that the United States and Iraq are in a tiff. It's not that I never had sex. I just never equated sex with having fun. I've always been an over-achiever and I made a decision early on that I would be the nicest of nice girls. As a teenager, I was one of the so-called lonely-onlies—the nickname for the black kids in my mostly white school. I was told by my family, by the older black kids, and by teachers, in various ways, that I was an ambassador for my race, that we lonely-onlies would have to be exceptional simply to be acceptable. Other than the domestics in their Park Avenue homes, I was one of the only black people visible to my classmates on a regular basis. Even at eleven, I knew they'd be bound to make some rudimentary assumptions about African Americans based on my behavior. Like their parents, most believed that black people were loud and lascivious, the bearers of trouble and good times. I wanted to prove we were more than that, as if by being chaste and good I could somehow elevate the general opinion of my race.

If this seems like a tremendous burden for a preteen, trust me, it was. But when you visit friends' apartments and are routinely directed to the service entrance because a doorman—black or white—assumes you are a babysitter or housekeeper's daughter, you can't help wanting to make adjustments to people's thinking.

Still, I envied the bad girls. They seemed to have more fun, seemed somehow freer in their skin. I was anything but free in mine. When my parents decided to send me at age eleven to an elite all-girls school on Manhattan's Upper East Side, kooky things were happening with my body—the lumps and hair and smells, oh my!—that no amount of showering could get rid of. In my less-than-tony New York City neighborhood, the old men who used to watch over me protectively now leered as I walked by, their eyes pricking my changing shape with laserlike precision. The young men were more forward, jabbing at my flesh with their words. *Juicy ass. Sweetness.* My body was betraying me, developing before I was ready for the attention, and I hunched to hide my budding breasts, covering my butt with my slack backpack as I rushed to the bus stop.

*   *   *

My mother is a nice Catholic girl from Guyana, the British Caribbean colony where Jim Jones and nine hundred or so of his followers drank the Kool-Aid and died of cyanide poisoning. Growing up, she never once uttered the three-letter word s-e-x in my presence. We never had "the talk." Instead, as I turned fourteen and entered high school, I scoured the pages of *Our Bodies, Ourselves* and began to realize that my sex education had been sadly limited. There were lessons in school, bestowed by a wacky counselor waving a condom-covered banana and screaming about AIDS; it was the late eighties, after all. There was also the informal kind of instruction—like the afternoon my friend Emma and I procured a badly hidden skin flick from her parents' bedroom or, another time, spent a few hours poring over her brother's dirty magazines. I was most shocked by the women—bouncing, blow-up Barbies with flaxen hair, voluminous breasts, and flat butts that looked nothing like mine.

One day in ninth-grade homeroom, Mollie Ann Kaplan announced that we girls were finally going to get a life and stop whining about being sex geeks. Her idea, she told us, was to create a dating club with a neighboring boys' school, similar to something she'd watched on MTV. We quickly came up with forms and dashed off profiles describing our looks, likes, and dislikes. I remember being unsure whether to indicate that I was black, then deciding to write that I had ebony skin and straightened hair. The other girls described their ideal mate using Madonna's lyrics; I wrote about *Midsummer Night's Dream*, my favorite play, and Robert Browning's "My Last Duchess," my favorite poem, which was about a duke whose wife "had a smile too easily made glad." One girl told me to be sure to include that I had dimples "since this was my greatest asset," and we were not including photos.

At fencing practice the next day, Mollie Ann handed the forms to the boys' team, who, photos or not, knew who we all were anyway—New York City's eight posh prep schools are a very small community. Up to this point, I hadn't exactly been popular with the opposite sex. Back in grade school, my hair a colorful configuration of barrettes and bows, I was subject to some teasing; one afternoon, a classmate serenaded me in the cafeteria with his own version of Michael Jackson's pop song "Pretty Young Thing," which he dubbed "Ugly Young Thing," complete with backup singers. I wanted to crawl under the table and barricade myself against the laughter with my Hello Kitty lunch box.

When I latchkeyed myself home that afternoon, I had a new image of myself to consider: me as ugly or, not *just* ugly, but gross, undesirable, one who deserved to be publicly scorned. How could I not have realized this before? With our odd names, colorful clothing, exotic foods, bare feet, ebony complexions, and sharp accents, my family had never fit into our surroundings. But I'd always been able to brush off that sense of not belonging, of being out of step; after all, though my parents were Guyanese, *I* was technically American, or desperately wanted to be. Having an entire cafeteria sing about my ugliness was a different kind of humiliation altogether.

After that, I accepted that I was ugly to boys and moved forward, careful never to draw attention to myself. I begged my parents to call me Abby instead of Abiola; invisibility, I decided, would be my shield. Yet by ninth grade, I still stuck out in the rarified environment of my private high school. I lived in a lesser zip code (defined as anywhere other than the Upper East Side). Compared to my classmates, I was considered underprivileged, even with a father who'd attended an Ivy League university and was a renowned expert in precious metals.

Nonetheless, I excitedly tore open the large manila envelope containing our dating profiles along with Mollie Ann and the others, eager to see what the boys had written. "Lemme see yours, Abby," Mollie Ann called out. *This is great,* I remember thinking. *I'm finally in!*

When I found my rumpled loose-leaf page, the comments on the front were sweet. "I like dimples," one boy wrote. "Smart is for geeks," another had scrawled, making me smile. Then we discovered more writing on the back, the boys' final assessment of me: "Big hips, lips, and ass. Nobody wants to see brown nipples." Brown nipples? No one at school had ever overtly mentioned my race, much less my breasts. At first, I was confused, but as the words registered, I crossed my arms over my uniform and rushed from the room.

Technically, I knew I was different from my mostly white classmates, but in those superficially politically correct times, I'd never once considered that my blackness might be distasteful to some of the boys. If they'd written that brown skin was ugly, I could have had a good cry and moved on. After all, the media and most African Americans themselves concurred that blackness was ugly. My mother's *Ebony* and *Essence* magazines were filled with ads for skin bleaches and hair relaxers, the only way to be both dark *and* lovely. But I had to admit that the boys were right about my "big hips, lips, and ass." They must, I decided, be right about my nipples, too. Speaking too white for the black kids or dressing too black for the white kids could be improved upon. Brown nipples could not.

* * *

The girls dropped me from the dating club, Mollie Ann declaring semiapologetically, "Since none of the boys really like you, Abby, there's no point in your staying on." I understood. I was a liability. Boys were new to them, too. Adolescence was hard enough without having someone with the wrong color nipples in their midst.

So when cinnamon-skinned Mark Rose asked me out on my first date at sixteen, I was shocked—and thrilled. Mark had a summer job on the Good Humor truck that rolled past my parents' house and he introduced himself one afternoon as I purchased a fudge bar. When he asked me to the movies, I said yes, with my parents' approval, and just like that we were a couple. Looking back, I don't think I much considered if we had anything in common or if I even liked him. None of that mattered. Mark liked me and I was grateful. With him as my boyfriend, I could avoid school dances, the rough-and-tumble of high school dating, further taunts about brown nipples.

I remember once after I'd been with Mark for six months, my mother said, "I hope there isn't anything going on I wouldn't approve of." I told her, truthfully, that we had not had even a first kiss. "Good, keep it that way," she said. She needn't have worried. Sex, when I thought about it, seemed scary and forbidden. My friends and I weren't like the popular girls, the ones my mother considered to be fast. The thought of disappointing her, disappointing either one of my parents, was somehow terrifying. They had left their families and their continent to make a better life for me. I didn't want to screw that up.

So I clung to my identity as the annoying kid other parents held up as a good example. I made Mark wait almost two years to see my brown nipples. As we finally, awkwardly, fondled each other in the backseat of his mother's Volvo, I told myself I was in love, but honestly, the most thrilling thing about our make-out sessions was their clandestine nature. Nothing is more fun for a good girl than sneaking around.

I did eventually gift Mark with my virginity on an utterly forgettable and unspectacular afternoon a few weeks before I left for college. I don't remember much about it except that we were fully clothed and in his grandmother's house. That was as bad as I was willing to get. I was more concerned with avoiding pregnancy than pursuing pleasure, which was a good thing since it was pretty much over before it started.

Soon after, I went off to Sarah Lawrence, a liberal arts college where the majority of students were women. Of my six African American male schoolmates, only three were straight. Of those three, none had any interest in women of color. But I wasn't too worried. I'd pledged to love my ice cream sweetheart Mark forever. Except now that I was free from the confines of my parents' curfews, there was no reason to sneak around simply to have boring, fast sex. To make matters worse, once Mark went to trade school to learn how to fix air conditioners and I began to meet more people like me—smart, artistic oddballs from around the world—it suddenly struck me that we were nothing alike. So I dumped Mark and, in a flash of unexpected coolness, discovered that I loved clubs, dancing, and music. I was known as the drug-free girl who, weirdly, didn't even spark up a doobie, but I sure enjoyed a party. Dancing felt reckless, reckless felt fun, and fun felt like freedom. Finally.

One night, while out dancing with some friends, a man approached me and asked for my number. He was, it turned out, ten years older and lived three hours from my college. That was inconvenient, but his family was in the music business, which thrilled me. Here was a man of the world—and he wanted me! I never thought to question why he still lived with his mother. I was eighteen. He seemed decent and was keen on me—that was enough.

My girlfriends told me to brace myself for sexual lessons from an older guy. None were forthcoming. Our sex life was almost nonexistent but I didn't know enough to want or demand more. Besides, with twenty-page papers due every week, who had time? So I kept on dirty dancing with guys at clubs, always countering any requests for more with the fact that I had a boyfriend. I was there to have fun with my friends, I insisted, merely masquerading as a bad girl on the weekends. As for my so-called boyfriend, the mere fact that someone so much older liked me gave me a shot of self-confidence. That is, until he left me for someone even younger. Friends tried to soothe me by sharing rumors that my ex was gay, but that only made me feel worse; no wonder he never wanted to touch me.

So when I moved to New York City after graduation and connected with an African American guy who'd gone to a neighboring private school, I was so relieved that he was paying attention to me that I had sex with him on our second date. So soon! Later, I tried to explain to him that I never did that sort of thing as he nodded knowingly and dropped me back on campus with a wink. This was awful. I liked him but now he thought I was a slut. What if he told our mutual friends? So I kept on dating him until he became my boyfriend. I didn't want to be a bad girl.

We stayed together during my twenties, dating for ten years until I convinced him we should be married. Or, rather, until everyone around me insisted that his not proposing after all this time was humiliating and disrespectful. No one thought to ask me if *I* wanted to be married; I didn't think of that myself. It was assumed that I did, that my job was to snare this man. Besides, we had a good sex life; we'd even done it on a balcony once. And I was determined to establish myself as an actress, an unstable career proposition at best. Marriage seemed like a necessary anchor. Around our thirtieth birthdays, we jumped the broom and tied the knot in a lavish island ceremony.

Less than three months later, I discovered my new husband was cheating; when I confronted him, he confessed that he could be happy only if we had an open relationship. Devastated, I moved out faster than a Hollywood starlet can say DUI, then cried for weeks, blaming myself for not being smarter, stronger, and more appealing. Then I picked myself up and began to learn things about men, women, dating, and sex that might seem obvious to the average postmillennial fourteen-year-old:

1. Showing your new, gorgeous underwear to a group of women on your way to your first lesbian club might be a bad idea unless you're interested in said women.
2. If you invite a man who likes you to your apartment at 2:00 A.M., he most likely expects sex.
3. Men sometimes lie. This is considered "game."
4. Inappropriate men are completely appropriate for *some* things.

My ex got custody of our married friends and I connected with a group of single girlfriends who filled my head with delightful yet scary stories of trysts and illicit affairs. I loved going out with them and dancing on tables; it made me feel like a wild child, though at heart I was still naive. I quickly learned, for instance, that my whole way of operating gave people the wrong idea. I am a huggy, touchy-feely girly-girl, the kind who runs her hand up your arm unconsciously while talking to you. I was used to hanging out with other couples; paired off, no one overtly reacted to my behavior. When I was single, however, I discovered that men expected some kind of sexual payoff from a woman who comported herself this way. I was on the market and apparently everything, including me, was up for grabs.

One night, I ran into a crush at a swanky bar at 1:00 A.M. After talking on a velvet sofa, he mentioned that he'd like to come back to my apartment "to hang out." I invited my best girlfriend along for security because he made me giggly and nervous. As we settled in and I browsed through my movie collection and popped corn, the disgruntled suitor revealed that he expected a threesome or, at the very least, sex. Highly offended, I kicked him to the curb.

Another night, at a business event, I met a man who, after a brief conversation, looked intently into my eyes and said, "I never thought I could love again after my last relationship, but speaking to you makes me feel open." My heart soared and I wanted to love him until I caught up with a friend in the bathroom and learned that he'd said the same thing to her an hour ago. "So what?" she said, laughing. "That's the game. Men lie."

Friends advised me to get out there and date. "Re-lose your virginity," said one. "Get your numbers up and then you can judge who's worth it and who's not." But the misunderstandings and snafus continued, guys I considered platonic friends confessing that they were dying to kiss me, then sulking if I didn't comply. From the age of eleven, I had gone to school with mostly women; I had never been single as an adult. I didn't know what I was doing, felt as vulnerable and awkward as any teenage boy.

But I had also never felt so free. *Freeeeee!* And desirable.

One night, at a party, I fell into an unexpected sexual encounter with a man I'd once worked with. His skin was a delicious dark chocolate, even darker than mine, and his body was ripped. This time, there were no mixed signals. I knew what I wanted; I wanted him. Okay, perhaps it was a little ninth-grade to have a friend go and check on his level of interest, but once that was out of the way, I liked feeling as if I was on the prowl, the one doing the choosing rather than the other way around.

We sealed the deal at my place, devouring each other's body in spectacular fashion. Bad boys, I discovered, could be fun to play with, and I didn't actually have to settle down with one simply because we'd had sex. As time went on, I began to love that this man was *not* "the one" (he had too many kids for my comfort and an on-again, off-again fiancée). Yet I enjoyed his desire, even more so because I now knew I didn't need it, that there would be others who wanted me.

I am still the same woman who felt she had to settle. Big hips, lips, and ass, and, yes, brown nipples. But these days, I please myself—no more pleasing others. I do not want a relationship. Yet. Recently, when my new friend with benefits fell asleep in my bed, I realized I did not want him to spend the night; I had to wake up early. So I woke *him* up and he left, then I called and left a spicy message on his cell phone about all the ways I would let him have me when we saw each other next.

As a recovering good girl, it feels so good to be bad.

Mommy Lust

LORI GOTTLIEB

Two months after my son was born, I was sitting in my Mommy and Me group daydreaming about a torrid affair when suddenly something seemed terribly wrong. I knew, of course, that I was different from the other moms—the regular ones, the ones with husbands, the ones who'd conceived their babies by making love instead of buying sperm from a bank and having it shot into their uterus by a medical professional.

But that's not so much what set us apart. However we'd gotten pregnant, each one of us was sleep-deprived, overwhelmed, and hopelessly in love with our newborns. What made me different was that these moms were trying to avoid sex—and I was dying of sexual frustration.

The group topic that day was "Intimacy," and I watched as one woman broke into tears—tears!—over the burden of dealing with her husband's massages, which had become a bit too amorous.

"I pretend to be asleep," she confessed. "Or I say it still hurts."

The others nodded empathetically.

"It's normal for your sex drive to disappear after giving birth," the group's leader, a mother of two, reassured her. "Actually," she confided, her voice lowered conspiratorially, "it will never be the same again."

Oh yeah? Then how to explain me?

*   *   *

When I decided to have a baby alone at age thirty-eight, sex wasn't even on my radar screen of concerns. I was worried about money and work and child care, but I figured I'd meet a guy eventually. After all, I'd always had boyfriends; I simply hadn't found one I'd wanted to marry yet. Meanwhile, I'd heard dozens of stories of single moms who'd met their soul mate—some, incredibly, while pregnant. Male friends told me they'd find it refreshing to meet a woman in her thirties who'd already had a kid on her own, someone calmly looking for true connection instead of frantically searching for the father of her future children.

I also assumed sex wouldn't interest me, at least for a while. New mothers dodging sex isn't merely fodder for TV sitcoms; the pregnancy and parenting books I read devoted entire chapters to the hormonal changes that make a woman's sex drive plummet postpartum. So imagine my surprise when, soon after I gave birth, my sex drive went in the opposite direction. I felt like a sex-crazed teenager. Except that I was middle-aged, with a newborn, and without a partner.

It wasn't just odd. It was downright problematic.

I couldn't understand why my sex drive skyrocketed. It's not like I'd ever been the forward femme fatale or the lusty librarian type. I wasn't into anything particularly kinky, and while there was often a lot of heat at the beginning of a new relationship, by the one-year mark, the nights of sleeping with each other versus simply falling asleep tended to be about even.

At first, I attributed my mysterious sexual appetite to my new, postbaby physique. My whole life I'd been scrawny, with the boyish body of an eleven-year-old, but pregnancy had given me the voluptuous figure I'd always longed for: full breasts, curvy hips, shapely thighs. I rarely brushed my teeth or showered, but I felt sexy in a primal "I am woman!" way. Actually, I felt more than sexy, more than that giddy sense of physical attractiveness that comes from something as simple as a fabulous new haircut paired with a low-cut camisole and body-hugging jeans. I felt *sexual.*

Every few hours, my son's cries woke me from dreams so erotic that, even in the haze of middle-of-the-night feedings and poopy diaper changes, I couldn't erase images of writhing naked bodies from my mind. I didn't get out much, but every man I encountered—the cashier at Whole Foods (who accidentally brushed my arm when offering me a pen), the FedEx guy (whose hand I'd purposely touch during the package exchange), the mailman (who wore shorts during the winter)—filled me with a dizzying desire.

Did I mention that I had utterly no outlet for my raging libido? Nor could I discuss my feelings with other new moms, one of whom was so busy evading her husband's advances that when I finally got up the courage to mention my dilemma, her deadly silence on the other end of the line made me feel like a pervert.

I shouldn't have been surprised. With an infant clinging to various body parts all the time, most new moms I knew needed their physical space—there was simply no room for anyone else. I, too, relished the intense closeness with my son. The skin-to-skin naps, the velvety softness of his body cradled in a sling as I carried him on my chest, and even the spit-up stains on my shoulders spoke to our boundaryless melding as one. I wore his bodily fluids as if they were my own. His cheek pressed against mine as we danced in the moonlight, the lavender scent of his nearly bald head after a bath, the sound of his heartbeat while he slept next to me—it was just too much to bear.

Emotionally, that is.

Physically, it wasn't enough. A friend who went on Prozac during maternity leave, then promptly went off it after she returned to work, told me that not saying a word to another adult all day drove her to despair. "I'd strike up conversations with strangers in Target just to hear myself speak in an adult voice," she confessed. "I couldn't stand not interacting with anybody over the age of one."

I couldn't stand not being touched by anybody over the age of one. If the married moms I knew craved adult conversation, I craved adult contact. So at three months into motherhood, when a friend gave me a gift certificate for a massage ("Thought you might like some pampering," the card read—little did she know), I instantly made an appointment.

"Would you like a male or female therapist?" the spa's receptionist asked, and I eagerly replied, "Male!" Generally, I prefer a female masseuse—I like the smaller hands, the level of comfort—but this time my muscles needed a special kind of rubbing.

I hadn't anticipated that those strong male hands would

only make things worse. Rob, my handsome masseur, would slowly work warm oil up my belly, make an abrupt turn just under my breasts, gently stroke his way down my belly, and make an abrupt turn just above my pelvis. This went on for a good ten minutes. The entire massage felt like a tease, what I imagine a college freshman must experience when he's making out with a half-naked girl who won't go all the way. I left the spa more frustrated than ever. By the time my son was four months old, my formerly scrawny, boyish physique had returned, but my sexless state continued to feel as dire as oxygen or food deprivation. I remembered that oft-cited statistic that men think about sex every ten seconds. The irony wasn't lost on me: Motherhood, that intrinsically female enterprise, seemed to have turned me into a man.

Years earlier, a boyfriend and I had gotten into a conversation about the longest we'd ever gone without sex. (Like the talk about how many sexual partners you've had, no good can come of this discussion.) My boyfriend said that he could last about two months before he'd find someone to sleep with. At the time, I was astounded. "You can't control your urges for more than sixty days?" I said. Now, if he still lived in town, I would have invited him over. I didn't know where else to turn.

You'd think it would be easy for a decent-looking (and, more important, willing) woman to get some action, but as a new mom, I rarely left my house. If I wasn't parked in a rocking chair feeding my son every three hours, I sat at my computer working to support my little family. I didn't have time for online dating. Besides, even if I got a date, how would I go on one? I hadn't thought through these kinds of logistics when I decided to hold out for Mr. Right instead of marrying Mr. Wrong. I'd been so focused on saving myself for "true love" that I hadn't considered the purely practical benefits of having a husband: Not only could he contribute financially, take out the trash, and share in the child care, but as his wife, I wouldn't have to shave my legs, blow-dry my hair, find a puke-free outfit, apply lipstick, drive to a restaurant, and sit through a tedious two-hour meal for the mere possibility of some heavy petting while the babysitter meter is tick-tick-ticking away. With a husband, I wouldn't have to follow up with flirtatious e-mails or engage in time-consuming court-ship rituals. I wouldn't even have to make conversation. With absolutely no effort on my part, a man would be right where I wanted him: in my bed.

Perhaps naively, I also hadn't realized how few unmarried men I'd encounter as I approached forty. By the time I had my baby, the dating pool had dwindled dramatically and it seemed to me as if all the eligible bachelors had been spoken for. Even worse, the few available guys I encountered seemed never to have heard of the pop culture acronym MILF (mothers I'd like to fuck). As one male friend explained it, "Guys feel creepy sleeping with the mother of an infant because she's so . . . mother-like. It feels almost like a fetish. But don't worry," he added. "That changes completely as the kids get older."

"How much older?" I asked.

He shrugged. "Maybe around five?"

Five?

So while my son kicked on his play mat and cooed at his mobile, I was confined to looking at men on the street—men dressed in business suits or tight T-shirts or low-slung jeans. At the playground, I secretly ogled young dads pushing their kids on swings. (I'm not sure who loved going to the park more—me or my son.) I found it exciting to be around the husband of a good friend because I knew (from his wife) precisely how long it had been since they'd had sex (twice in eight months), and I felt covertly bonded to him because of this. *He knows what it's like to be this frustrated.* I wasn't especially attracted to him, but the one time he came over to fix my shower, I imagined ripping off his damp clothes and jumping in there with him. I knew, of course, that if we were married, I'd feel differently; like his wife, I'd probably find his torn-up T-shirt ratty rather than hot. I knew, too, that the fatigue, the nightly negotiations over who was doing more dishes or changing more diapers, would make him seem far less attractive than he now appeared from my comfortable distance.

But I continued to idealize my married friends' access, perhaps because it's human nature to focus on what you can't have. I was aware that the married moms I knew, for whom sex was overly available, felt its presence the way I felt its absence: as a burden, something to feel guilty about. Of course, we all had the typical mommy guilt about breast-feeding versus bottle-feeding, working versus staying at home, and rocking your child to sleep versus letting him cry it out. But while they felt guilty about denying their sex-starved husbands, I felt guilty about obsessing over sex.

For starters, I didn't know how to be sexual, single, and a mom all at the same time. Before I had a baby, being single meant occasionally having sex with people I wasn't officially in a committed relationship with. Now that I was a mother, albeit a single one, sleeping with someone I wasn't in a relationship with felt irresponsible, if not sordid. In the back of my mind loomed this calculus: If I got a babysitter to have a quickie with a guy I didn't see a future with, did that make me empowered because I was taking care of my sexual needs or did that simply make me a slutty mom?

The guilt was debilitating. But so was the need.

Meanwhile, my married friends seemed to be making a natural shift from wife to mother, from lover to caretaker, from sexual partner to co-parent. They often gushed that they loved their babies more than their husbands, and I, too, loved my child more intensely than I'd ever loved a man. But wasn't that a different kind of love? And wasn't there room for both?

I wasn't sure. The first date I had after my son was born, when he was five months old, highlighted this ambivalence. A thoughtful guy I'd met at a bookstore brought both a book for the baby and wine for me. Oddly, I was simultaneously charmed and creeped out by this gesture, which I'd somehow boiled down to this: *I give her kid* Goodnight Moon, *she gives me head.* Irrational? Absolutely. But despite my desperation, I bailed at the end of the night.

The summer's hot, humid air and men walking around in tank tops did little to dampen my desire. I'd take walks at sunset with my six-month-old strapped to me in his Baby Bjorn, the serenity and sense of completeness kicking me into maternal overdrive. Then, just as quickly, I'd run into a male neighbor, we'd exchange a casual hug, and I'd be reminded of how much I was craving a man's touch. Sometimes, when all I wanted was a little release before bed, I'd feel resentful about my single state and think, *Do I have to do* everything *for myself?* In a way, I experienced the same dynamic as married couples: Sleep or sex, choose one. Except I never had the option of simply lying back and enjoying it. And during those first six months, I was too tired to do any extra work, even to help myself. So I'd feel frustrated, then I'd feel frustrated about being frustrated. It was a vicious cycle.

One afternoon, at a rare restaurant lunch with some married mom friends, talk of purees and pacifiers and falling under the magical spell of a baby's belly laugh inevitably turned to talk of marriage and sex—or the lack thereof. One friend revealed that she'd never liked giving blow jobs; another admitted she'd never liked sex much either. Both felt relieved to have an excuse to skip it now (too tired, baby kept me up all night). One mom said she didn't mind having sex because it was a twofer, pleasing her husband and also allowing her free time to make a list of baby to-dos in her head: clean bottles, fold burp cloths, buy detergent. I laughed, but she said she wasn't kidding. For her, listing chores made sex, well, less of a chore. Something in me snapped.

"Do you have any idea how lucky you are?" I said. "Someone touches you who's not *you*! Your husband makes you coffee *and* makes you come! And you're multitasking?"

All four of them stared at me silently until one signaled the waiter for a check. But voicing my frustration felt invigorating. Lately, I'd been feeling invisible, like I was disappearing into oblivion. *If a woman lies in a bed and nobody touches her, is she really there?* My biggest fear, in fact, was no longer that I might never marry. It was that I would forget what it was like to feel sexual. Which came first, I wondered: You stop having sex and no longer feel sexual, or you stop feeling sexual and no longer have sex?

*   *   *

A month after my lunchtime outburst, a friend introduced me to J., a thirty-nine-year-old divorced dad with a young son. They were only work acquaintances, but he said that J. was smart, kind, and accomplished. I asked my friend what J. looked like, and he said, "I don't know, he's good-looking," but when pressed for details, he couldn't describe a single feature other than to say "He has a nice smile." ("Kiss of death," a female friend said when I relayed the comment.)

A week later, I sat at a corner table in a restaurant as a strikingly handsome man walked in, spoke to the maître d', and made his way toward my table. I thought there must have been a mistake. J. was six feet tall with wavy, longish dark hair, a strong jaw, penetrating green eyes, and a chiseled body. His smile wasn't simply nice, it made me woozy.

I found our two-hour dinner thrilling, despite the mundane conversation. ("How's the salmon?" "Wonderful, and the veal?") There was no witty banter, no engaging repartee, no easy back-and-forth, but I chalked this up to blind-date awkwardness. Besides, I was too distracted by J.'s beauty to care. When he excused himself to go to the men's room, I could hardly wait to watch him walk across the room so I could check him out from behind.

J. didn't kiss me that night, but he did ask if he could see me again. "Again" turned out to be the following evening, when his son was at his ex's house and I found a last-minute babysitter. We went to see a local band, danced in the aisles, and, having exchanged few words all night, ended up back at his house where, finally, I was touched by somebody who wasn't me.

I had waited so long for my first postbaby encounter that I knew it would be hot (heck, at that point, merely bumping into a short, bald guy exiting an elevator seemed hot), but even now, a year later, I can still remember the way my skin tingled, the way the hairs stood up on my arms. It was like being in an incredibly sexy movie, except that it was my movie, so I was able to do more than gaze at the beautiful, stylized images. I could taste and smell and feel them. I was one of them. The intense chemistry that seemed so absent from our stilted conversations ignited in bed. But once our clothes were on, we shifted back into the tedious void. ("Wow, it's cold." "I know, it's unusually chilly for July.")

Over the next couple of months, I viewed our lackluster dinners or hikes or walks on the beach as the cost of admission to his bedroom; engaging in these decorous activities felt like the parentally appropriate veneer we had to place over what was essentially a string of fabulous booty calls. At least, that's how I saw it, and I assumed J. had similar feelings. To me, it seemed obvious that our natural connection in bed didn't translate to the real world, where we struggled to make small talk over a meal, where he'd answer the question "Why?" with "Why not?" (every time) and find that hilarious while I found it annoying. We had completely different sensibilities. Other than exceptional sex, we had absolutely nothing in common.

"Really?" J. said when I brought this up, hoping to dispense with the "dating" portion of the evening and proceed directly to bed so that I could spend more time with my son and save on what had become an exorbitant babysitting tab. At first I thought he was joking (consistent with his "Why not?" sense of humor), but when I saw that he was genuinely confused, it dawned on me: Of course he wasn't joking. This was simply another example of how differently we perceived things.

Unwilling to relinquish the sex, I backpedaled and let the subject drop. But soon my irritation with J. went beyond our dull dinners. I felt so disconnected from him out of bed that I began having trouble getting turned on in bed. And yet, essentially, nothing had changed. Or had it? The fact that we didn't get each other wasn't a revelation to me. I was more surprised by my inability to pretend it didn't matter. After all, wasn't I getting exactly what I'd daydreamed about—great sex?

Increasingly, I felt myself going through the motions in the bedroom, trying to muster up some fire despite the fact that the pilot light had gone out. Sometimes my mind would drift during sex and I'd start thinking about lists of baby supplies to buy, photo albums to order, doctor appointments to make—the same things that popped into my friend's mind. But she was in love with him; I would never be in love with J. What I thought I'd envied in my friends—access to a warm body—turned out to be an illusion.

I can't say the physical urgency went away, but what I needed even more than a wet tongue, it turns out, was the minutiae of a shared daily routine that happened to include sex. I craved the sensation of being tightly wrapped around a man's naked body, but also the profound closeness that can spring from a happy domesticity. I'd confused the two, maybe because sex is easier to attain than those other, more subtle forms of intimacy. In a sense, I was dealing with my loneliness in the most clichéd of ways, by seeking solace in sex.

I stopped seeing J. a few weeks later, with less reluctance than relief. Partly, I admit, I'd gotten what I'd hoped for—the opportunity to feel sexual again. But I wanted more than a physically hot, emotionally vacant relationship. I wanted something even sexier than sex: to be truly known, *seen*—both with and without my clothes on—within the private context of a marriage.

When I think about what I now call my "seven-month itch," I see how impossible it is to neatly separate longing from loneliness, love from lust, affection from companionship. My married friends say I'm lucky to be able to pull on some baggy flannel PJs, curl up with a book, and turn out the light whenever I feel like it; I say they're lucky to have an audience for a negligee. But I know it's more complicated than that. Recently, a friend told me that although she and her husband rarely have sex, she has never felt sexier. Parenthood has brought them closer, she said, which is a turn-on of a qualitatively different sort. Other friends have also confided that they're enjoying a new kind of bond with their husbands, one that's much deeper, if not very sexual. They talk, laugh, plan for the future. They hold hands, kiss, give and get massages. The sex, well... They tend to drift off here, leaving this sentence unfinished.

Here's how I might finish it: The sex, well... it can make me feel alive and connected on a purely physical level, but what I crave just as much from a bedmate is pillow talk, with a baby co-sleeping on the pillow between us.

Looking for Mr. Snickers

JENNY LEE

Even though I'm the one who walked out on my husband, I will say that failing in a marriage basically fucks with your self-esteem. On the scale of bad unions, mine wasn't even all that wretched. The breakdown of my marital contract simply came down to the fact that while my husband loved and adored me, his priorities were pretty much his career as a scientist, the Italian subs at Pinocchio's in Harvard Square (which were quite tasty, so I'm not harboring a grudge about that one), and then me. At least, that's how I saw it.

So I left my husband and moved back to New York City, my first true love. Though the rational side of my brain knew there was nothing more I could have done to save things between us (I'm not the cry-me-a-river, poor-lonely-wife type; if you snooze, you lose when it comes to having someone like me for a spouse), the irrational side of my brain, which has a much louder voice, couldn't help wondering if a skinnier/sexier/prettier/better version of me would have been able to convince my ex to spend a weekend at home instead of in his lab, oohing and aahing over blue yeast cells. It's one thing, after all, to get left in the dust for a supermodel; it's another thing entirely to get trumped by a single-cell organism.

In the past, when I'd needed a mood boost, I'd get a new haircut, a fabulous pair of shoes, or doughnuts. Lately, none of these were working, so my friends took matters into their own hands and dragged me out to a dark, swanky, noisy Manhattan bar to enlighten me.

"Jenny, you need a one-night stand."

I forget who actually said the words, but suddenly I felt as if everyone in our vicinity was nodding emphatically and empathetically in my direction, a Greek chorus of tsk-tsking.

I was confused. I couldn't quite understand what a new nightstand was going to do for my self-esteem. Then it dawned on me, and I nodded conspiratorially. "Oh, you mean I need a *nightstand*. One that maybe has a *drawer*?" Wink wink, nod nod. I had pretty much left all the furniture with my ex, so my current nightstand was a moving box with a lamp and a few books perched on top.

I sighed. "C'mon, guys, the you-can-do-it-alone vibrator movement is so late nineties." Now my friends looked confused. We did a quick exchange of "What are you talking about?" "What do you think we are talking about?" "You go first." "No, you go first." "You're drunk." "I'm not drunk, maybe you're drunk." "Fuck, maybe we're not drunk enough." "Hey, I've got a little pick-me-up in my purse. Maybe we could all excuse ourselves to go to the ladies' room?"

And with that, the three of us squeezed ourselves into a stall to talk about sex over powdered-sugar doughnuts—

something that was probably happening in ladies' rooms across the country, minus the doughnuts, of course. Lately, I'd taken to keeping an emergency six-pack sleeve in my purse. That's when I discovered they hadn't said "night-stand" at all, but "one-night stand."

I'd always relished talking about my sex life with my closest friends, but owning up to having actual needs and desires with no prospects of fulfilling them made me feel a tad self-protective. For one thing, I'm not in the habit of admitting I want something I can't have—when I'm low on funds, you'll never see my face pressed up against the glass at Bergdorf's. And while I'd done a pretty good job of convincing myself that a smart, independent woman didn't need to settle down in a traditional domestic role with a man, it was suddenly clear that I'd forgotten to take my future sex life into account, or rather, my lack thereof.

I shook my head. "No. It's too late for me. I'm too old and far too neurotic to even consider a one-night stand. No way. No how. I have no interest in looking for Mr. Goodbar. The only thing I'd be remotely interested in is looking for Mr. I'm-Gonna-Bring-You-a-Snickers-Bar, or Mr. How-About-We-Go-Get-Lattes-and-Talk-About-the-*New-York-Times-Sunday-Book-Review*-and-then-I'll-Buy-You-a-Snickers-Bar."

After all, I went to college in the late eighties, at the height of the AIDS crisis. No one was sleeping around back then, trust me. Plus, while married guys have *Fatal Attraction* as their cautionary tale, my personal touchstone had always been *Looking for Mr. Goodbar*. I mean, getting walloped by a lamp is bad enough, but Diane Keaton was then stabbed over and over and over. Whenever the idea of a fling even crossed my mind, I'd find myself asking the guy in question what sort of kitchen knives he favored, which naturally prompted him to go off in search of the men's room, never to be seen again. I also married at twenty-nine, after a series of long-term boyfriends, so improbable as it might seem, it really wasn't so odd that I'd missed out on the whole one-night-stand experience.

I gently reminded my friends that as a woman who'd actually hid the one vibrator she'd ever owned in a Ziploc bag in a shoe in a shoebox under her bed in case she happened to die in a freak accident and her mother ended up going through her stuff, I was absolutely not the type of person to bring home a stranger and enjoy carefree sex.

I'm no shrinking violet, mind you. I even slutted around in high school; I lost my virginity at the relatively early age of fifteen. (I grew up in small-town Tennessee, so it was either that or cruise grocery store parking lots.) Still, that was then. Now, in order for me to unleash my inner sex goddess (not that I was convinced I had one in me, but a girl can dream, right?), I explained that I needed to be in a very secure and trusting relationship (or, evidently, in the back of a pickup truck in Tennessee). Besides, if ever there was anyone whose very first one-night stand would end up being secretly video-taped and blasted around on YouTube, it was me.

My friends conceded that point yet would not be deterred. Both of them were married with kids, and if they were going to live vicariously through anyone, I was their best shot. Wasn't I feeling anxious of late? Couldn't that be because I needed to get laid? Wasn't it about time I embraced the optimistic possibility that a wild and crazy one-night stand could be exactly what I needed?

I pride myself on being ridiculously nonjudgmental when it comes to my friends, so much so that I've sometimes wondered if I'm an enabler. (Just do it! So what if you're breaking, like, every commandment? Seriously, live a little. It'll be fine. The worst that will happen is that you could end up in a Mexican prison, but think how skinny you'll get, and you know we'll road-trip across the border to come bail you out.) When it comes to my own behavior, however, I've always had trouble giving myself permission to act out. (Thanks, Mom.) So when it suddenly dawned on me that my friends weren't merely pitching this idea as something to consider but wanted me to go after it that very evening, I panicked. "Now?" I said, gesturing to my black silk off-the-shoulder top, now covered in powdered sugar. "Look at me! With my luck, the only guy interested will be someone who happens to be hypoglycemic."

"Stop making excuses," my friend Trina countered.

"I'm not!" I protested. "But I'm not wearing a thong, and I know that's been the thing for years, but I missed it completely. The panties I've got on probably appeared in cave drawings. And the Brazilian-waxing-south-of-the-equator thing? I missed that, too. If I'm having issues with some strange guy getting in there, do you think I'd let an Eastern European woman go at me with a Popsicle stick and a bowl of hot wax?"

I'd always dreamed of having a life so ridiculously exciting that my best friends would feel compelled to come up with some surprise intervention to get me back on track. And I'd deny, deny, deny, then have a mini-breakdown, lock myself in my apartment, and finally realize the error of my ways. (Think Demi Moore in *St. Elmo's Fire*, which—when you're fifteen and not allowed to wear makeup or high heels or watch more than an hour of TV a day—is not a bad life plan for your adult years, right?) This was, I realized, my best-friends-having-to-intervene moment. Except my best friends were intervening because my life was so damn boring, as opposed to the opposite. How disappointing.

"Fine. I'll do it on one condition." My friends nodded simultaneously, and I felt a bit better, because I realized that sure, maybe my life wasn't exactly how I thought it would be, but it's not as if they weren't right there with me when it came to less-than-glamorous Friday nights. My one condition: The seduction scenario had to take place in my friend Peter's bathroom.

In unison, again, they reacted: "You want to do it in Peter's bathroom? Ew!" No, I explained patiently, I didn't want to do it in Peter's bathroom. I just wanted to figure out a way to get Mr. One-Night Stand in there before we did the deed.

They still didn't get it.

"I look great in Peter's bathroom." That was the damn truth. You know how there are certain department store dressing rooms with perfect lighting and perfect mirrors and you can try on almost anything and look great in it? Well, there was something about my friend Peter's bathroom that made me look amazing. Seriously, I have never been better-looking than when I've been in there. I don't know if it is the lighting, or the color of the walls, or if it happens to be located the perfect number of miles from the sun. Whatever the reason, it works for me, and, well, I told myself I deserved a little extra help in the bravery department. If I wasn't going to get the warm fuzzy feeling of, oh, actually knowing a guy's last name or whom he went to prom with his senior year in high school, I sure as hell needed to know that at least my skin had a rosy glow.

"The woman in Peter's bathroom is sexy. That woman could have a really great one-night stand. Whereas this woman"—I pointed to my powder-dusted chest—"is going home alone to watch TiVo."

Peter traveled frequently for business, and I was the one he entrusted with a spare set of his keys (probably because he knew I was the one least likely to use his home as a wanton pleasure palace). So I called him, and as luck would have it, he was out of town and actually bought my whole stupid fake story about how I had some annoying neighbor who was painting her apartment and leaving her door open, thereby causing noxious fumes to leak into my apartment and make me feel ill.

The plan was hatched: I would take Mr. One-Night Stand to Peter's place on the premise that my own was being painted. I'd figure out a way to lure the guy into the bathroom with me, and then *whammo!*, he'd immediately realize that I was ravishing and I would get ravished.

Of course, I added, if I ended up getting murdered in Peter's apartment, my friends would have a lot of explaining to do. They said they were willing to take the risk, so we proceeded to spend the next hour checking out all the possibilities in our vicinity.

The whole selection process was pretty much like shopping, except I was trying to please not merely myself but also my two friends. The guy at the end of the bar was too skinny, and would make me feel fat in comparison. His friend was also a no-go, as he was just too slouchy and his clothes were wrinkled, which made me feel that it'd be hard to get him to leave afterward. That fellow at the other end of the bar should know better than to wear a backward baseball cap over the age of twenty-one. Another possibility had weird-looking hands. And one looked like he'd already killed a bunch of other girls. "That guy looks too cocky," I said of a recent arrival.

Trina stopped me there and explained that it was very important for me to understand that the night's mission wasn't about searching for love, it was to get laid. "Too cocky might be exactly what you need. In fact, it's reasonable to assume that a dumb, hot, overconfident guy might be pretty experienced in such endeavors, which could make things easier. That way, it won't totally be the blind leading the blind."

"So is this the part where we're trying to build up my confidence? Sheesh!"

Ava ignored me, pointing out, in case I hadn't understood, that the goal was not to get a phone number or to make some big romantic connection. The goal was to find a guy who made me feel sexy, who made me feel wanted. (It would also be helpful to find a guy who might not take offense when I started laughing hysterically, which is something I'm prone to do in times of high stress. Yes, I am an inappropriate laugher.) Pretty soon we were all nodding in agreement and I was getting elbowed from both sides that it was time for me to make my move.

Like any good neurotic, this is when I chose to have my breakdown. Sure, I was a little gun-shy about love and romance, but was it truly necessary that I go for broke? I hadn't started buying hats with stuffed birds on them, nor was I collecting stray cats from the neighborhood, was I? Using their best soothing-yet-stern mother voices, my friends explained that I was overthinking things. The point was for me to simply have some good, fun sex.

"But what if I can't have good sex without being...uh, I

mean to get naked in front of a guy requires, uh...I think
that maybe an emotional connection would be..." I trailed
off. The three of us stared at one another. What no one mentioned is that my divorce was particularly sad to me and my
friends because my marriage had seemed especially promis-
ing. My husband and I were *that* couple, the one with the
chick-flick cinematic beginning, where you meet the super-
cute guy but you already have a boyfriend so you fix him up
with all your friends and he gamely goes along so you'll continue to call him. The couple who, when they finally get together, think it's going to be a big surprise to everyone, then
learn everyone so totally knew it was going to happen. The
couple that make everyone sick because of the way he looks
at her and the way her voice goes up an octave whenever she
talks about him. We were them, so seemingly destined for the
happily-ever-after that when things started to go south, it
didn't merely make me question everything I'd ever believed
about love, it made some of the people closest to me wonder,
too. I can't tell you how many times the news of my divorce
was met with stunned silence or lots of "But, but, but..." To
which I replied, "I know. I don't understand it myself."

It wasn't that I still believed my ex and I could have
worked things out. Love, I'd learned, is not enough to save a
marriage. But now that I'd had sex and love together, could I
really settle for simply sex? Did my friends honestly think a
random hook-up with some overly big-toothed dude was going to make me feel better?

Another moment passed. Then we all burst out laughing.
Okay, fine, maybe I was taking things a bit too seriously.
They knew it and I knew it (sort of). Life. Love. Marriage
vows before God. Their point was that I had somehow lost

perspective, that lately my every date had been fraught with will-this-be the-next-love-of-my-life anxieties.

No one in the history of the world has ever called me shy (mainly because I'm loud), so it was an odd revelation that perhaps I was indeed a bit shy when it came to sex. I was aghast at the idea that I might be a prude or, worse, an uptight woman who didn't even realize she was uptight. Like any normal person faced with what may or may not be the truth about herself, my instinct was to deny it. Who, me? It wasn't possible I was a sheep in wannabe wolf's clothing. I owned every Madonna album, damn it!

Of course, I was raised by conservative Korean parents, which means from a very young age, I was trained how to be a good daughter (by making straight A's, always having a clean room, and knowing it was my job to refill my father's water glass without being asked during dinner, in case you are interested). I also learned how to be a good girl, which, in my mom's eyes, meant not talking too loudly, not laughing too much, and always having well-behaved hair. As for sex, I was taught that it came with rules (not surprising, since everything pretty much came with rules in my house). When we had "the talk," my mother told me that it was a special, private thing between two married people who loved each other.

Kids with superstrict parents seem to do one of two things: fall in line or rebel like hell. I did both, meaning that to my parents, I appeared to have fallen in line quite nicely, but behind their back I was sneaking out and dabbling in everything I had been warned against. The only time I ever got busted was at Harvard summer school, when I mentioned to my mother that I'd gotten my first UTI and she informed me that UTIs were a married person thing (aka usually resulting from sex). I started talking fast and managed to convince her that my experience was a fluke, sort of like the immaculate UTI conception.

I'm not saying that it's my mom's fault I had sex early. But back then, sex had very little to do with sex and everything to do with defying my parents in every way possible without getting caught. It's not that I wanted more attention; if anything, I wanted less. Now that I look back at it, perhaps it wasn't even about teenage rebellion as much as it was about not being quite comfortable with the person they expected me to be.

I suppose my last true act of teenage defiance (or my first true act as an adult) was deciding to be a writer even though my father considered that the same thing as being unemployed. This first victory started me on the road to understanding and accepting a few things about myself, like the fact that I will never speak in a well-modulated, ladylike voice, I will never tamp down my subversive sense of humor, and I will never care if people find my competitive nature off-putting.

Like most women, though, I'm nothing if not complicated. I now answer only to myself (best exemplified by my decision to divorce despite my mother informing me that she would rather see me unhappily married than not married at all), which made it even more surprising that my shyness about sex was still very much intact.

Not that I've ever been one for putting my own sexuality out there. I refuse to wear those tiny, sheer tops with sparkles on them (for some reason such tops make me feel like a hood ornament). I have always thought of myself as the ironic, fast-talking, smart-ass sidekick rather than the sexy main attraction. But these days, when women aren't merely embracing their sexuality but flaunting it (and I now live in L.A., where you've never seen such flaunting), why *shouldn't* I feel free to take ownership of my sexuality? Why not declare (while my mom is still alive and able to get on a plane and fly to where I live and give me that I-did-not-raise-you-this-way look) that not only have I had sex, but that I like it? There—I've said it: I. Like. Sex.

Yet while I know that sex can be pretty damn great when it's dirty, lusty, and forbidden, I will also say that the best sex of my life has been when I've been madly in love. I will not go so far as to say that I regret having done it at such a young age, but I remember thinking after having sex for the first time "in love" that I'd sure been wasting my time before.

I did eventually go up to the cocky-looking guy at the bar. I made him laugh. I let it be known that I was smart and witty and available. He let it be known, after we talked some more, that he was interested if I was. I considered it for a good five seconds, but ultimately, I passed. The whole thing, as it happens, is a tricky little bitch. But I've figured out that while sexy may be a state of mind, to my mind, sex is a commitment, even if it's only for a night.

Procreational Sex

BRETT PAESEL

At its worst, sex had been companionable. Floppy, why-not?, kind of sex. At its best, sex had been intense. Fierce, desperate, slammed-against-a-wall kind of sex. Which is to say that through twelve years of marriage, the sex had been good. Very good. And when we decided to make a baby, it got even better. I was thirty-eight. Relieved of the rituals and devices that prevent pregnancy, we slopped around in a decadent stew of sticky afternoons, crumbly food in bed, skipped work, wine, and hope ("Want to make a baby? Let's make a baby"), to be followed by languid, sweat-soaked cuddles ("Do you think we made a baby? What if she gets your nose and my hair?"). And when we became pregnant after five months of such paint-peeling, all-encompassing sex, we considered it the natural result of our devotion to the sport.

I was forty-two when we tried again. This time, there

were no lost afternoons floating on wine and hope. This time, there was a toddler to chase, feed, and bathe. It took a year to get pregnant, and when I miscarried, we were hit with the kind of grim reality that dampens any romantic venture. A couple of months later, when we'd recovered enough to try again, it seemed the heart had gone out of it. In the months that followed, nothing lined up right. Somehow, Pat and I kept missing that perfect moment when our biology and our hearts and the mysterious workings of the universe merged to create our longed-for baby. Worse, sex, always so easy throughout our relationship, became a thing to be calculated, negotiated, withheld.

*   *   *

I lie on the bed, my legs propped up against the wall, imagining Pat's sperm swimming upstream. Pat stands, looking down at me. He's been sweet. He's been tender. He wants this baby, too. But his gaze is weary. And I know that the clinical scheduling of sex is beginning to wear him down.

"Wanna watch the end of *Frontline?*" he asks.

"Nope. No noise. I have to imagine the sperm penetrating the egg."

"How long are you going to lie like that?"

"Shhh. Your sperm just made it to an egg and it's sniffing around."

"Well," says Pat, "tell me when the sperm worms his way in. I'm making a grilled cheese and watching the show."

"Stay. Snuggle."

"It wouldn't be snuggling," he says. "Snuggling is done lying on your side."

"That's not true. You could lie on your back with your arm under my head."

"I'm getting a grilled cheese and watching the end of the show you made me miss."

"Why didn't you record it?"

"I didn't think we'd take that long."

"We're making a baby. I wanted it to be romantic."

Pat looks toward the living room and exhales.

"It's not romantic," he says.

The statement lands and *whomp,* my stomach contracts and my knees drop to my chest. Why did I push the snuggling? I should have just taken the sperm and been happy. Now we have to talk about it. We have to talk about six months of my saying "We've got to do it now" and him gallumphing after me like the hired hand. "Yeah," he says. "It's not romantic when you pull on my arm and say, 'It has to happen today and I'm getting too tired to wait till bedtime.' It's not romantic."

My eyes start to sting, so I rub them with the heels of my palms.

"I'm sorry," I say quietly.

"It's not romantic," he says, "because the only reason you wanted to have sex just now was because you wanted my sperm, not because you actually wanted me."

He stands still and I lie with my knees to my chest. I wish I could say that I had wanted him when I pulled on his arm— because he smelled good or because I couldn't stand not having him another minute. But he's right. All I wanted was his sperm.

"And it's definitely not romantic when you tell me to slow down and be romantic because we're making a baby, right after you've pulled me into the bedroom so we can have sex before you get too tired." He pauses. "I really resent..."

The rest of the sentence hangs in the air and I pull my knees tighter to my chest.

"I'm sorry," I say.

I don't say that I resent, too. I resent that it's only me who is counting the days in my date book and looking for sticky discharge. It's only me who waits each month feeling every imagined symptom of pregnancy, only to experience the heaviness of our failure when I stain my underwear.

"Well," he says, "I hope this one works."

The silence that follows is a truce. Domestic truces are fashioned by what we choose to leave unsaid.

"Wanna carry me into the living room like this, so I can watch with you?" I ask.

Pat looks at me curled into a ball. He smiles, leans down, and slips his hands under me. Our progress to the couch in the living room takes a good ten minutes, as Pat has to stop after each unbalanced and heavy step. My head bashes against the door frame and my foot scrapes against the wall. When we get there, Pat hurls me onto the couch and plops down beside me. Gasping, he reaches for the clicker and we settle in to watch the credits roll.

*   *   *

I lie next to Pat, listening to the rhythm of his breathing. Most of his breaths come in regular tempo, but then he'll stop and hang on to one. I wonder if these moments are connected to his dreams or are simply tiny physical reflexes, suspended seconds when he teeters on the edge of nothing.

The line on the ovulation stick means that Pat and I are most likely to conceive in the next twelve hours. My best bet is to wake him now. Our son, Spence, will be up by five-thirty, and shortly after that, Pat will run to work. If we don't have sex now, we may miss the whole month. Another barren month.

Pat's breath catches and I hold my own. What is he dreaming of? Is he standing on some cliff, looking down at crashing waves, contemplating a jump or flight? Is he looking at a beautiful woman who is not me?

He exhales. I slide my arm next to his, which does not move in response. He's distracted. Maybe he's talking to the woman who isn't me. Fuck that. Maybe he's making love to the woman who isn't me. Normally, I'm not the jealous type. But the thought of this unknown woman getting my husband's sperm makes my pulse speed up.

I roll onto my side and look at his profile and at his chest going up and down. I've always loved his chest, though not for the reasons Pat thinks I do. He thinks I love the hair on his chest, and he wears his shirts with the second button undone to display it. This makes him look like his father, who did exactly the same thing. The hair's okay, but that's not why I love his chest. In fact, the open button makes his shoulders look rounder, and I'm forever reaching over to fasten it, a gesture Pat finds motherly and therefore infuriating. No. I love his chest because I like putting my head on it. I like hearing his heart. I like thinking of all the years I'll have to rest my head there.

I lift up and scoot over to put my head right where it fits, perfectly. Then I slide my hand down the length of his body. I don't care if he makes love to the woman in his dream, because I'm the one who gets his chest and the rest.

*   *   *

I lie on the examining table as Dr. Sammy gently manipulates the ultrasound wand inside me. Though Pat and I have de-

cided to forgo heroic and expensive baby-making efforts, the
doctor is helping us figure out the best time for us to have sex.
I've been seeing him monthly while Pat is at work. Along
with the ultrasound, I hand him a chart of my temperature to
analyze. These visits are part science, part guesswork.

Dr. Sammy looks at the monitor. "There's the follicle,"
he says, adjusting the wand. Dr. S. has become an unwitting
third in my sex life, issuing orders to which Pat and I submit.
It occurs to me that if I were more creative, I could make this
out to be sexy as hell. But so far, it's been a dry hump of an arrangement.

"I don't want you to have sex until the egg has dropped,"
he says. "And, of course, Pat shouldn't either." I take this to
mean that Pat shouldn't ejaculate (with or without me) until
Dr. Sammy says he can. He has told me before that if Pat re-
sists releasing his sperm for a few days, it will come charging
out of him with more force than it would if he had been releasing it all over the place in a happy but regrettably unfocused fashion. Since Pat is a happy but unfocused guy, this is
an order I dread delivering. If I simply announce it out of the
blue over dinner, I know Pat will give me one of his "Where
did all the passion go?" looks that makes me feel like a complete shit. I consider other ways to tell him. I could write him
a note. Or I could casually bring it up as a passing thing I
heard on the radio. ("Honey, I heard that skipping sex and
masturbation for a few days can liven things up.") Or I could
claim exhaustion tonight and, before going to bed, turn to
him and sweetly say, "And remember to save up all that
sperm just for me."

"Come back tomorrow," Dr. Sammy says, snapping off
his gloves. I pull my legs together and inch my ass along the
crinkly paper until I'm sitting. "If the egg drops, I'm going to

want you to have sex tomorrow night and the next morning." Dr. Sammy turns to write in my chart, and I think about the best way to convey this latest edict to my husband. Not that we mind the sex part. Even with the baby-making pressure, Pat and I both think that sex, as they say, is like pizza: When it's bad it's still pretty damn good. It's the pussyfooting-around part that enervates me. Fatigue seeps through my body like black dye. I don't want to pussyfoot around my husband anymore. I'm tired of thinking about sperm and charts and eggs that drop in the night. Maybe we should stop doing this, I think. Maybe I should go home and say to Pat, "Hold on to your sperm until the moment is right, then blast me like it's the last time and let's call it a day."

"See if the receptionist can fit you in around ten," Dr. Sammy says.

*   *   *

I lie on the couch and pop another dark chocolate truffle into my mouth. On the television, Tim Russert introduces Secretary of Defense Donald Rumsfeld. I taste the bittersweet ooze of the truffle as I contemplate the newsman's trademark smile. Pat leans forward, grabs the bong from the coffee table, and fires up. I've never been much of a smoker, but after months of good prepregnancy behavior, the pot feels pleasantly subversive. Spence is snug in bed, and Pat and I are watching an evening rerun of *Meet the Press*. For half a year, our lives have been consumed with making a baby. Emotionally depleted, we've decided to take at least a month off, and possibly give up the enterprise altogether. I've called a moratorium on ovulation sticks, Dr. Sammy, and despair. Pat's called a moratorium on resentment. Life is good and we both love Tim Russert.

"But to get back to the question," Russert says.

Pat jumps up from his chair.

"That's it. Don't let Rumsfeld get away with that. He didn't answer the fucking question," he yells at the TV.

When Pat gets mad like this, his whole body comes alive. There isn't a part of him that isn't activated; even in stillness he's like a runner on starting blocks.

Pat hates Donald Rumsfeld. He hates Rumsfeld so much that if he had to choose between hating Rumsfeld and loving me, he might pick Rumsfeld.

"Yeah," I pipe in. "This is what Rumsfeld always does. He brings it around to what he wants to say, no matter what the question is."

"Fuck, yeah," says Pat.

He plops down on the edge of the couch, next to me. When I bought the cashmere throw that's covering my legs, I'd envisioned nights like these—my feet wrapped in its softness and pressing against Pat's back, my mouth full of chocolate, and an adversary somewhere out there, banding us together in righteous indignation. I also imagined us both snuggled under the throw, watching *NOVA*, another favorite activity. Maybe we'll do that after *Meet the Press*, I think.

Pat absently lays a hand on my shin, his attention fixed on the TV. I slide my leg back and forth a bit to remind him I'm here. Somewhere through the fog of my high, I'm aware that I'm smack dab in the middle of my cycle. A day I would be circling if I were still circling days. That isn't, however, why I press my feet a little harder against Pat's back. I press them harder because he's so goddamned attractive to me right now.

"What about Guantánamo?" Pat says at the TV, his back tensing away from my feet.

Pat has aged well, I think. His face is still open and boyish. It's true that his shoulders look a bit stooped. But if he learned to button that one button, his shirts wouldn't slip down, creating that schlumpy effect. I look at Pat's body, energy zipping through it, as he raises a fist at the TV. "FUCKER! YOU AREN'T GOING TO SAY A GODDAMNED THING!" He jumps up from the couch and paces in front of me. He's like an animal, I think—a pissed-off panther. Under the throw, I slide a hand between my legs. Tim Russert says, "Mr. Rumsfeld, here's what you said just two months ago."

Pat stops his furious pacing and stands, his legs apart, right in front of the television. His ass, defined by the digital glow of the screen, looks hard.

I sit up. "This bra is digging into me," I say, removing it through the armholes of my shirt. Pat turns, his eyes trained on my swaying breasts. He takes two steps, then launches himself into the air, landing on top of me. No ramp-up. We are there in seconds. I shift under him as *Meet the Press* goes to commercial break.

*   *   *

Three weeks later, when the fuzzy line on the pregnancy test appears to indicate that I am pregnant, I take another test. When that yields the same result, I am humbled by the unknowable, infinite intricacies that shape our existence. How could Pat and I have so randomly hit the perfect moment shortly after my egg dropped? Without sticks and doctors, how could the universe have lined up so precisely as to produce our second boy nine months later? Scientists say it is extremely unlikely that mankind should have come into being in the first place. They wonder, how did this little planet get the right atmosphere, the right balance of elements, just enough distance from the sun, and the cosmic luck not to be destroyed by colossal bodies of rock and ice whizzing around in space? All of which combined to create creatures who walk the earth, build cities, and live in apartments where they make love on couches without a thought about a particular sperm finding one egg that will attach itself to the uterine wall and produce all of the matter necessary to create another human being.

Hours after my son is born, I hold him in my arms. Science tells me that his existence is extremely unlikely. But as I uncurl his fingers to look at the palm of his impossibly tiny hand, I believe it to be inevitable.

Do Not Enter

BETSY STEPHENS

I'm sitting in a dark brown Barcalounger on the first floor of my doctor's office, with a plastic sensor inside my vagina. A putty-colored wire snakes between my legs, peeking out from beneath the black and white swirls of my skirt. It connects to a computer across the room, which tracks and projects the muscular activity of my vagina onto an eight-foot screen in front of me. Each time I contract and relax, squiggly lines creep and jerk across the wall, reminding me of the seismograph charts used to track earthquakes. My doctor and my husband of three years, Dean, cheer me on as they watch the spikes pulse higher up the Richter scale. I squeeze again, creating a spike I imagine could wipe out the city of Los Angeles. "All right, good one," they say encouragingly. I squeeze once more. The squiggly line jumps. *There goes San Francisco,* I think.

* * *

Of course, San Francisco is still standing. I am the one who is falling apart. Eight months into my marriage, I developed what I thought was a run-of-the-mill yeast infection. After two months, it was still with me and I worried I'd never be able to have sex again. After two years, I worried it might end my marriage and land me in a mental institution.

Even before my need for seismic gynecology, my relationship with sex had been shaky. From the time I was old enough to sit up in church, I knew that the act, if done before marriage, was a sin, just as surely as I knew the name of my grandfather's church was Marvin United Methodist.

My family never made the five-hour drive to my grandparents' home in Tyler, Texas, without packing clothes for church. In the sanctuary, I always sat next to my cousin Chrissy. Perched on the velvet cushions of the pew directly in front of my grandmother, Chrissy and I scrawled notes to each other on offering envelopes, the musty carpet smell mixed with the faint scent of lilies. My grandmother accompanied hymns on the piano and the congregation read aloud from the Bible: *"Put to death therefore whatever belongs to your earthly nature, sexual immorality, impurity, lust, evil desires and greed, which is idolatry. Because of these, the wrath of God is coming."*

Chrissy and I always put our pencils away when my grandfather stepped up to deliver his sermon. His voice boomed with stories that moved us to tears, about sin and how it separated us from God and about the joys of having a personal relationship with Jesus. My favorite moments were when he mentioned me from the pulpit—sometimes by name and other times simply as his youngest granddaughter. I beamed, loving the feeling of all eyes in the sanctuary on me.

The summer before my freshman year in high school, my family moved from Houston to the tiny Texas town of Dripping Springs. I brought an armload of stuffed animals and the knowledge of right and wrong I'd gleaned from regular visits to my grandfather's church. The population in Dripping Springs hovered around eight hundred and the former springs, hidden beneath a patch of foliage near the post office, were no longer dripping. Gossip, however, flowed like a river, easily spread by the town's unique phone system, which required dialing only four digits to make a call within city limits.

One Sunday after church, sitting in our house on a two-acre lot south of the blinking yellow traffic light in the town center, my mother told my sister and me a story of her own, about a doctor's appointment she'd had before she married my father. She didn't discuss the details of the exam, but recalled how the doctor had turned to the nurse and said: "Now, that's the flat stomach of a virgin."

"He knew you were a virgin just by looking at your stomach?" I asked, wide-eyed, never stopping to consider that my mom might have been making the whole thing up to impress the virtues of virginity upon her two almost-teenage daughters. What I gleaned was that sex could make your belly bulge; for years afterward, I'd assess strangers' sexual status by scoping out their stomachs—anyone who had eaten more than her fair share of bean burritos had done the dirty, as far as I was concerned. Of course, I couldn't help noticing that despite my own lack of experience, my belly bulged, and I worried I'd be labeled a sinner.

A few short months later, that's what I became, along with my then-boyfriend, Spence, a native of Dripping Springs. We had been dating for close to a year and though we'd never talked about having sex, I knew it was on his mind, mostly because we'd begun shedding more clothing whenever we were alone.

My grandfather had passed away earlier that summer, and my belly already bulged no matter how hard I sucked it in. But I still secretly hoped to get out of having sex with Spence. I also didn't want him to break up with me, so one sticky-hot summer day, when we were swimming in his pool and his mom left to run some errands, I found myself following Spence down the hall to his parents' bedroom. Underneath their cornflower blue comforter framed in Holly Hobby lace, he pressed his body against mine and pulled at my bathing suit bottom, which stubbornly clung to my legs with the heavy scent of chlorine. My eyes were shut tighter than they'd ever been when I prayed; there was a lot of thrusting on Spence's part, and a lot of me saying: "Maybe we shouldn't be doing this," which is as close as I could get to saying no. Despite my halfhearted objections, Spence continued driving his hips; he still hadn't managed to enter me entirely when we heard the sound of his mom's car pulling into the driveway.

That night over dinner at a local chain restaurant, Spence beamed at me from across the table. "Do you think the waiter can tell we're not virgins anymore?" he asked.

"I don't want to talk about it," I said, but later I did.

"Spence and I had sex," I breezily told my best friend, Samantha, trying on my new nonvirgin personality. The words sounded clunky coming out of my mouth, as if I'd just sung an off-key note in the middle of the sanctuary on Sunday morning.

By then, the population in Dripping Springs was threatening to break a thousand, and making a local call now required all seven digits. The three additional numbers didn't slow the news of my recently acquired sexual status. My friend told my sister, who may have mentioned it to my mother, who came to my bedside later that night with her Bible.

"Is there something you want to talk to me about?" she asked, looking strangely childlike, sitting on the floor of my bedroom with her knees drawn up to her chin.

"No," I said, warily eyeing her Bible.

"Am I to understand that you and Spence had sex?" she asked.

"What are you talking about?" I hissed, glaring at her as my heart pounded beneath my white eyelet coverlet.

"I heard—" she started.

"Well, you heard wrong," I snapped.

"I just want you to know that I'm here for you if you need to talk."

Tears welled up in my eyes and I was glad for the darkness; the two of us sat in silence until finally my mother left with her Bible.

Wait! I wanted to cry out. *I've done something horrible. Can you help me take it back?*

But there was no going back, only forward into the darkness of the night where I tossed and turned, holding fistfuls of white eyelet, worrying about what hell was going to be like. My scalp tingled and I felt as if I could hardly breathe. I didn't want to go to hell, especially because I knew I'd be there alone—my mom and sister would surely be in heaven with my grandfather.

The fact that my mostly failed attempt at fornication took place after my grandfather's death was no coincidence. And neither, I suspect, was my parents' starting divorce proceedings only months after the funeral. Now that our family's anchor and moral compass was gone, my father began spending his Sunday mornings sleeping in with his twenty-seven-year-old girlfriend. My mother spent hers decorating her new apartment, trying to make it feel more like a home. My sister and I went off to college, where I accumulated my share of drunken close calls with various boys. Why not? I figured. I was already going to hell. I didn't bother to join a church.

Then I met Jake, a chemistry major whose family had immigrated to Texas from Greece. He told me he wanted to get married in a Greek Orthodox church. "Do you know how hard it is to get a divorce in a Greek church?" he asked rhetorically. "Almost fucking impossible." Jake, I decided, promised stability. On the heels of my parents' divorce, it was just the type of salvation I was looking for.

Whenever I hooked up with a guy, whether it was short- or long-term, my initial plan was always to abstain from sex. So I told Jake I wouldn't be sleeping with him. "Okay," he responded. "I don't want to make you do anything you don't want to do. I just want to be around you."

Over the next three or four months, we spent most of our time in his windowless room, tangled in a mass of sheets and blankets on his bed watching the never-ending loop of CNN. Mikhail Gorbachev was elected as president of the Soviet Union. Jake kissed me. Latvia declared its independence. He pulled me close and I felt safe snuggling into his muscular frame. Somewhere between the news of Bush signing a peace treaty with Gorbachev and breaking his vow of no new taxes, Jake's hand wandered up my shirt. "Does that feel good?" he asked. I nodded. His hand continued wandering and I continued nodding, eyes open this time, taking everything in—his hand on my breast, then on his penis, guiding it into me.

Jake drove me home in his red Isuzu pickup truck, and when we pulled in front of my building, he turned to kiss me. "I'm really glad we did that," he said.

"Me too," I answered honestly.

It wasn't until I was alone in my bed that the guilt washed over me. I tried to comfort myself with the thought that if Jake and I married one day, I might be redeemed retroactively. Besides, I knew other girls who were having sex. They sometimes worried about getting pregnant or whether a boyfriend was cheating, but I was the only one, it seemed, who worried about going to hell. With a toss of my Texas-sized hairdo, I tried hard to feign that cavalier attitude toward sex. On the days it didn't work, I prayed to my grandfather's God for forgiveness.

When it turned out Jake's offer of stability didn't include monogamy, I decided not to marry him. I met the man who would become my husband soon after. Dean and I had both landed jobs out of college as reporters at a local West Texas paper. He was the quietest reporter on the news desk, and dating him meant I was allowed to see inside his private world. One lazy Saturday not too long after we'd started dating, in the middle of a morning of kissing and tickling each other, I blurted out, "I love you!" We were both startled.

"I mean *this*. I love this," I said hurriedly. Dean didn't say anything, merely rolled over and kissed me. Driving back to my apartment that afternoon, I realized I did love him. I also wanted to have sex with him if I could be sure it wouldn't add to the list of things keeping me up at night. So I told Dean I needed to wait, and we did—six months—long enough for me to determine I wanted to marry him. After that, I (guiltily) began to fornicate to my heart's content.

I eventually moved to New York City for a job and a few

years later Dean followed with an engagement ring in hand. After our wedding, I couldn't wait to have all the sex I wanted, comfortable in the knowledge that God wouldn't smite me for it.

One night early into our marriage, I rolled over and asked Dean if he wanted to sleep naked. We pressed our bare chests together. "This is my favorite feeling in the whole world," I said, and within seconds we were making love. After that, "Do you want to sleep naked?" became code for "Wanna have sex?" Yet sometimes, our bare chests and hips pressed together, I felt the familiar guilt, so closely inter-twined with sex in my mind. I'd squelch it by gazing at my left hand, pressed into the flesh of Dean's right butt cheek, the sparkle of the diamond on my finger rocking with our hips, a reminder that I was allowed to be doing what I was doing. We slept naked in the loft bed of our nine-by-ten bedroom, and in the bathroom, the living room, the kitchen. We laughed that when we were out of rooms, we'd have to go up to the rooftop.

But before Dean and I could make the giddy ascent, our God-sanctioned spree was cut short by a persistent itch be-tween my legs. For six months, my doctor prescribed creams that I slathered on the raw skin of my vagina. When those didn't work, I saw a new doctor who prescribed more creams and a giant pink horse pill called Diflucan, for what we all as-sumed was a yeast infection. After each round of treatment, Dean and I tested the waters, always hopeful. *I'm actually feeling a little better,* I'd think as he lay on top of me, when the truth is I was slowly forgetting what "better" felt like. I was becoming so accustomed to the burning sensation between my legs that it was beginning to feel almost normal. Except when Dean entered me; then it felt as if he'd exchanged his penis for a bottle brush with razor blades for bristles. I held my breath, hoping it would end soon, finally yelling, "Stop!"

"I'm sorry, but that was hurting me a little. Maybe we shouldn't go so fast since we haven't done this in a while," I said. We started up again, slower. If I held my breath, I could almost block out the stabbing pain, and Dean seemed not to notice my silence. Afterward, he asked me if something was wrong. "Not at all," I lied. "I'm just a little sore." Dean got up to go to the bathroom and I lay in the loft, silently crying. I'd begun to worry that the itch was God's way of punishing me for my earlier sexual transgressions.

Returning, Dean brushed a tear off my cheek and tentatively asked if I thought the pain could be psychosomatic. A week later, I sat in my doctor's office reading that question off a list Dean had prepared for me, tears trickling down my cheeks. My gynecologist normally chatted through office visits the way a waitress at a truck stop chats through a shift, but now he stopped cold. He spoke slowly as he said to me: "When I examined you, you were red and inflamed. That's not in your mind." Even if his prescriptions didn't help, his words were a reprieve, freeing me from any responsibility I felt about my shortcomings as a wife. For his part, Dean began to show concern instead of frustration when we couldn't have sex. Both of us continued to hope things would get better, even as they seemed to be getting worse.

Because we were having sex less and less, seeing each other less and less. Slowly, despite our good intentions, Dean began evicting me from the quiet world he'd invited me into when we'd first met. He was working nights in a new job, scouting locations for a popular TV series. I suspected he was secretly relieved that his schedule prevented us from seeing each other much.

I was relieved, too. As much as I didn't want to lose Dean, his presence was a physical reminder of the problems I couldn't seem to fix: my vagina, my sex life, my marriage. Besides, being alone gave me an opportunity to sit, quite unladylike, with a bag of frozen peas on my crotch. If I kept them there long enough, the stinging sensation became so faint I'd almost swear it was gone.

Six months after the first itch, my doctor announced that the balance of yeast and bacteria between my legs—which he'd deemed the cause of my problems—had at last been restored. I was completely depressed by the news. There was nothing wrong with me, nothing left to fix, yet I was still in pain. My doctor looked a little confused when I burst into tears, then he prescribed another cream. Dean and I moped around our apartment—the bedroom, the bathroom, the living room, the kitchen—I even went up to the roof to mope. We tried to have sex, I cried, I bled, and we both moped some more. The mental distance between point A (sex) and point B (pain) became so abbreviated, so certain, that merely brushing my skin against my husband's stirred a not-at-all-pleasant tingling down below that I knew would lead to stabbing pain. So I began inflicting pain on Dean, lashing out at him whenever I could. After all, if Dean left me, I wouldn't have to deal with his pressing urge for sex.

When I told my mother about the itch I thought would ruin my marriage, she tried to help by recruiting God, the very being I blamed for my trouble. She told her prayer group to ask Him to help me have sex. Aside from contributing to my complete mortification, her prayer requests had little effect. The skin in my vagina continued to itch, growing so thin that it tore upon the slightest touch—like panty hose running, one of my doctors remarked. I almost grew used to the bright red spots of blood on the toilet paper and the constant stinging, as if I had several hundred paper cuts down there. Wearing jeans or sitting for long periods became impossible; sex was out of the question. One night, climbing down the ladder of our loft bed to go to the bathroom, I saw Dean, illuminated by the blue glow of the television. He was masturbating. I couldn't blame him. I jiggled the handle on the toilet to stop it from running, but he didn't seem to hear me, the rhythmic movement of his hand continuing as if I wasn't there. I climbed back into bed and wept for the loss of intimacy our closeness of breath and shared sweat had once fostered.

By this time, I'd consulted two different doctors in my quest to rid myself of the burning and itching between my legs. After the second doctor tried, unsuccessfully, to determine the cause of my pain, I sought out a third. This one proceeded to poke different parts of my inflamed vagina with a Q-tip until I was shouting: "Ouch!" at the top of my lungs. All was forgiven when, afterward, he announced that he knew exactly what my problem was: vulvar vestibulitis, a little-known condition that I would soon learn is even harder to treat than it is to diagnose. He went on to explain that vestibulitis referred to inflammation and pain at the vestibule, or entryway, of the vagina, then referred me to another doctor for treatment. The word *vestibule* made me think of the entrance to my grandfather's church. Though I could hardly call my vagina holy territory, I was becoming more certain that this was some sort of punishment from God.

Diagnosis in hand, I next made my way to doc number four, who tried to cure me with biofeedback, then doc number five, who prescribed more drugs than all my others combined, followed by doc number six, who told me my problem was a two-centimeter-by-two-centimeter swath of skin in an unfortunate spot.

"Location, location, location," he said. "If this was on your arm, it wouldn't bother you nearly as much." He recommended surgery to remove the skin, followed by months of physical therapy to stretch the area enough to make sexual penetration possible. As I considered this drastic measure, Dean and I began to discuss another.

I didn't want to be married anymore, and I told Dean as much—regularly. He'd quit his TV job to try his hand at film editing, working for no pay on an independent flick bankrolled by the father of the twenty-five-year-old director. This didn't thrill me—we'd just signed a mortgage for a prewar apartment in Brooklyn. Most days, I'd come home from my low-paying job as an assistant magazine editor to find him in front of the TV, unshaven and in his pajamas, surrounded by stacks of empty Pepsi cans. "Getting a lot of work done?" I'd ask as Dean glared at me. I didn't want to go to work and I didn't want to go out with friends. What I wanted to do was knock Dean off the couch, then curl up myself and stay there forever with my bag of frozen peas between my legs.

A few years earlier, when the itch had first begun, Dean told me that I was his wife no matter what—sex or no sex. "My sister wouldn't stop being my sister if she were sick," he reasoned. But along with the skin in my vagina, Dean's resistance to my frequent pleas to put an end to our marriage was weakening. "Do you just want to get a divorce?" he asked one Saturday afternoon as we stood glumly on a subway platform. It was the first time he'd been the one to suggest divorce, and it sounded at once like a tragedy and a relief—the first because I didn't want our marriage to end, the second because it couldn't continue the way it had been. I'd had the itch for six years; sex had become a distant memory. Dean and I moved through our new apartment as if alone, him watching television while I cooked extravagant meals he showed little interest in eating. I'd given up on us, on me. Two of my doctors were at odds about whether I was a good candidate for surgery, so I did nothing.

But when Dean mentioned divorce, I added a new doctor to my list—a couples therapist. Every Tuesday at six o'clock, Dean and I sat on a sticky leather couch next to an air conditioner that sounded like a jet airplane. I vented my anger, frustration, and feelings of abandonment while Dean silently stewed, but, surprisingly, the visits seemed to give us something we needed—time together during which neither one of us could hide. In truth, the healing began on the subway platform when Dean uttered the word *divorce* and I realized that wasn't what I wanted after all.

And so, after a few months on the couch, the mood in our Brooklyn apartment shifted, ever so slightly, from despair to cautious hopefulness. Dean still spent a lot of time in front of the TV, but now he also spent some time in the kitchen talking to me as I cooked. I felt that he was beginning to let me back in, which made me think we might want to have sex again someday, which sent me in search of a new doctor near Boston named Elizabeth Stewart. She had written a book that included three or four pages on vestibulitis— the most I'd seen written about the subject aside from on the Internet. I made an appointment and booked a hotel room. Dean sat next to me while Dr. Stewart examined me, her sweater set and pearls reminding me of any number of women I'd seen in attendance at Marvin United Methodist.

"Hmm," she said, over and over, as she, too, prodded

me with a Q-tip. I curled my toes and dutifully reported where I felt pain, which was just about everywhere. She left the room to look at samples under the microscope and when she returned, said she thought she could help me. I left her office clutching a fistful of prescriptions, my free hand nestled safely in my husband's. On my third trip to Massachusetts in as many months, the doctor inspected the skin between my legs and said, "Much better." I wasn't surprised. I'd noticed the burning had eased, but what she said next shocked me: "You can try to have sex whenever you're ready." I called Dean, who was back at home, and gave him the full report as I munched on a hamburger and fries. "She said I look much better," I told him, pulling a big swig of Coke through the red-and-white-striped straw. "Yeah, she wants me to keep taking everything and come back in December." I scooped up ketchup with a soggy fry, unwittingly leaving out the most important bit of good news.

Back in New York, Dean and I resumed the weekly meetings with our therapist as if nothing had changed. Then, one Saturday morning, I turned off the stove, walked back to the bedroom, and put on a black lace teddy. Without a word, I walked into the living room and stood between Dean and the TV.

"Wow," he said. I smiled, feeling giddy, embarrassed, and fearful.

"Is it okay?" he asked. I shrugged, then giggled and felt my face turn red. Couples who have sex consistently fall into a rhythm; it seemed we'd lost ours. We'd been married for seven years, and it had been nearly six since we'd had sex with any regularity. I climbed onto his lap and kissed him with the awkwardness of a teenager. We moved to the floor and Dean thrust his head forward to kiss me, our teeth colliding. But when he began to move his penis inside me, we were so sharply focused on the same goal—avoiding pain and failure at all costs—that our bodies somehow fell into synch. Dean cautiously pressed himself into me and I felt the distinct sting of skin tearing and caught my breath. As I lay motionless, I felt my muscles relaxing, allowing him to inch his way farther in. "Okay. I think it's okay," I whispered. Slowly, he pressed. This new rhythm of ours continued until Dean was all the way inside. "Don't move," I said, partly because I was afraid of the pain that might follow, but also because I wanted the feeling of Dean inside me to stick in my memory—I couldn't be sure I'd ever experience it again. Soon, a different rhythm returned, halting yet familiar.

Afterward, as we lay in each other's arms, I knew I'd never again be the young girl who thrilled to the idea of having sex with her husband on a New York City rooftop. I'd miss her eagerness, her innocence, her ignorance of the pain or tears sex can bring. But gone, too, was the girl who couldn't separate guilt and fear from the wonder of sex. In her place stands a woman who, when she is joined with her husband, knows she is entitled to these moments of passion without judgment or shame. A woman who can let go of her childhood preconceptions and let herself be swallowed up by joy, sadness, close connection, and, ultimately, a deeper understanding of her husband, her marriage, and herself.

My Not-So-Kinky Sex Life

M. P. DUNLEAVEY

Let me tell you about the time I met a guy, fell in love, and decided to pretend that I was kinkier than I was.

I am not the kinky type. I have been fighting my earnest, Ivory Girl, Laura Ingalls braids-on-the-prairie aura my whole goddamn life. Plus, I was born and raised Irish Catholic. I'm not sure if that means there is a chromosomal predisposition to be somewhat sexually guilt-ridden, or if two thousand years of Church doctrine (sexual pleasure bad, Virgin birth good) can't help but seep into your psyche.

Despite these hurdles, the ace up my little calico sleeve has always been this: I love sex. It has always come naturally to me, pun intended. I've often wondered if Irish people are really horny but are forced to repress it, or if the repression makes us all secretly more horny. In any case, although it has been a struggle for me to achieve a modicum of cool in other areas—even a thin veneer for social emergencies—I've always been confident in my abilities in bed. I may not be much of a risk taker (pot yes, coke no), but I've never shied away from sexual adventure. I did it on top of a mountain once. Very rocky. I don't recommend it.

So the one thing I was counting on as I got older was that my innate friskiness and sexual confidence would continue to shine even as the sun went down on my thirties. But when I found myself single again at age thirty-six, after a devastating breakup followed by a cross-country move (always a rotten combination), I suddenly felt as if I'd fallen out of step, sexually speaking. One night, a friend happened to mention that he'd been spanked by two women at a party (at an art museum, no less); another friend described her decision to leave another gathering, you know, before the orgy started. And the one I'll never forget: I was hanging out with a few friends at an Indian restaurant, sharing plates of curry, when one woman announced that her new beau had just introduced her to nipple clamps. "It was kind of fun," she said with a giggle. I tried not to gag on my lamb korma as I imagined cold steel on my most tender parts. I wanted to ask her if they hurt—but of course, that would be the point of clamping one's nipples, wouldn't it?—so I decided to keep my questions (was I the only one who had any?) to myself.

Clearly, I was missing something. I did not want to spank or be spanked, clamp or be clamped. Or pee on somebody, if that's what was next. I was really looking forward to getting laid again (soon, I hoped), but these conversations left me uneasy. I read them like tea leaves, as portents of unsettling changes afoot. I'd never thought of sex in terms of trends, but I detected a hipper-than-thou air floating about these discussions, the same sort of tone people fall into when describing their kitchen remodeling projects: *Well, we decided to go with slate for the floor and Sicilian marble for the counters; the contractor said we'd love that lived-in bistro look.*

I have nothing against kink or Sicilian marble, for that matter. But the idea that sex wasn't simply for fun anymore, that there was now some cachet attached to whether you frequented nightclubs with names like the Vault or used a butt plug—now *that* was irritating. Suddenly there I was again, the good girl, the not-quite-cool girl, squeamish about the idea of donning a harness or whatever. I know I sound neurotic, but when I got home after that Indian dinner, I felt compelled to tally up my slightly off-the-beaten-path sexual experiences. The list, as it turns out, was depressingly short:

1. Drugs and sex—limited
2. Blindfolds—once or twice
3. Whips—never
4. Chains, ropes, handcuffs—nope
5. Porn—a little, but you know, the production values are terrible
6. Hot wax—only accidentally, while moving a lit candle from the dinner table to the bedroom, and it did not inspire me whatsoever

My sexual prowess had always been the one thing, my secret thing, that I believed kept me from being a dork. Now that small corner of my confidence felt threatened. (Hey, it was a vulnerable time in my life, and there's nothing like self-doubt to screw up your inner compass.) For many reasons, I now felt I had something to prove sexually—as if I were a fifteen-year-old trying her first cigarette. Who cares if you like it; you want to at least be able to say you tried it. There *had* been a little kink in my last relationship, mainly in the form of occasional anal sex. It wasn't my favorite, but I had added it to my repertoire the way a Girl Scout picks up another merit badge. I felt it gave me some street cred—until my friend's nipple clamp confession, that is.

In the midst of this crisis of sexual confidence, I happened to hook up with a guy who seemed like a safe bet for a nice, simple boink—exactly what I needed to get my groove back or exhale or whatever. Instead, he just added fat to the fire, as my mother used to say. Shortly after we started sleeping together, he launched into a merry story about one of his nights at an S/M club, and repeated with gusto what it had been like to be whipped in front of a small crowd. He was fishing, clearly. And though I wasn't biting (in fact, I bid him a prompt farewell), it seemed to me that the Kama Sutra was on the wall. The whole world was a lot kinkier than I'd thought. It was time to upgrade from Mary Richards to Carrie Bradshaw.

*   *   *

That's where my head was when a friend suggested we organize a dinner party for a few singles we knew, ourselves included. I'd provide the women, he would bring the guys. I arrived armed and ready for anything. Or so I imagined. I spent most of that evening flirting and bumming cigarettes from various people while claiming I didn't smoke, trying to be as swashbuckling and outré as possible. I thought I was Ms. Cutting Edge—or at least that my command performance might make others think so. Dating, especially in New York City, is all smoke and mirrors anyway. That night, fueled by many glasses of wine, I freely opined on masturbation and whether sex with a dildo was better or not. What I cared about most was fitting in.

Meanwhile, there is a moment that lives in my mind as proof that as much as you try to escape yourself, she shows up anyway. I had invited a cousin to this gathering, also single, and both of us had been raised in very much the same Irish Catholic climate. When the aforesaid topic of masturbation came up, I remember noticing that she looked uncomfortable, especially when I plunged in saying God knows what. We didn't speak again for several years after that night, and I always wondered if she was appalled by my insincerity. Or if, on some level, I was.

I started dating a guy I met that evening. With his wavy, slightly unkempt hair and worn motorcycle jacket, he looked every inch the downtown poser, so I was wary. But he was also sweet and well mannered, a thorough listener, and, as I found out, an amazing lover. Appearances, as they say, can be confusing. Despite the rocker-poet garb, he seemed more of a quiet, bookish guy who was finishing writing a novel. I was smitten, but also convinced that the other boot was about to drop. Surely Mr. Downtown Poser Guy had other things on his mind besides standard-issue sex. How many S/M clubs had he been to? How many orgies? Despite our obvious chemistry—most especially our simply being able to talk to each other—I couldn't stop fretting that he would be leagues ahead of me experience-wise, already bored by mere blindfolds and nipple clamps. What if he was a porn-watching, cock-ring-using, golden shower freak?

I can see now that my fixation on kink was mostly a manifestation of all I lacked back then: bravery, confidence, strength, and the gutsiness gained from finally shoring up your life so no one else can wreck it. Then again, Freud once wrote that the fear is the wish. Perhaps beneath my anxiety about kink lurked a desire to cross lines and break taboos. What else could explain this dogged pursuit of something I didn't even want?

One night after we'd made love, I whispered to Mr. Downtown Poser Guy that I was open to, you know, trying different things. "What sorts of things?" he asked.

Well. He had me there. I hoped the darkness would cover the fact that my bluff had just expired, as I struggled to figure out what, exactly, to propose. Handcuffs would sound pathetically junior high. Doing it in a restaurant bathroom might make me sound like a nut. Whips? Well, I wasn't desperate enough to suggest something I'd never actually try. So I mumbled something about "experimenting" and hoped I sounded convincing.

"Okay, we can experiment," he said, snuggling me close. As for me, I could feel the flush of embarrassment crawl through my skin. Here I was, thirty-six and trying to prove I was hip to something that didn't even appeal to me. How stupid was that? Especially since the sex we were having didn't seem to require any embellishment.

Speaking of, I realize that this is an essay about sex, and right about here the reader would be entitled to at least one description of how our lovemaking melted the sheets. Which it did. Despite my offers to tie him up or let him blindfold and spank me (you can tell someone has no knack for kink when her ideas come mostly from comic books), we were generally too lusty to do anything more creative than get our hands on each other and fuck. Mostly in bed. Although I think we tried the sofa once.

Yet even as those early weeks flew by and we both knew we were falling in love, I found myself waiting for him to express his dissatisfaction with our sex life, to admit that for him, two-on-one was the ultimate. Personally, I loathed the idea of a threesome, so of course I became obsessed with the notion that this must be what he craved. Farewell, Mr. Ménage-à-Trois. But I had to know.

So one morning, before we got out of bed, my façade now in shreds, I put my arms around him and asked if he had ever had a threesome. He didn't hesitate. "Nope," he said, with a telltale gleam in his eye that told me he knew more than I was giving him credit for. "What about you?" he asked.

"No," I admitted, so relieved I felt like flying. Almost. I inched out on the last twig of the limb. "Well, I mean, is that something you want?"

"You know, to be honest, it has never really appealed to me," he said. "It just seems pretty messy." Then he clarified that he didn't mean lube on the sheets, but emotionally. "I'm just really jealous. I don't like to share my person with some other person," he said.

But still, I needed to be absolutely sure: Did he want us to be more adventurous?

He said he wouldn't close off the possibility, but our sex life didn't depend on it, no.

Did he want to add a couple of exotic role-playing games or mild bondage to our repertoire?

Not really.

Wouldn't he like it if I wore high-heeled boots and no underwear?

Well, yes, that would be hot, he conceded.

But, my future husband stressed as we lay in our favorite position, limbs entwined, eyes locked, he would rather we took our time getting to know each other and let the experimenting emerge from there.

Six years later, with both our façades now retired (that motorcycle jacket lives in a box under the guest bed), I have to admit that my husband and I are still pretty tepid explorers. After we saw the movie *Secretary*, we tried on some power games for size. That was titillating, and the experience led us to flirt with some role-playing (you won't be surprised to hear that the priest and the ingénue was one, but that was a while ago). Every once in a while, we go nuts and try some variation on a theme, like talking dirty. Or I'll get a bikini wax and things will really heat up. To be honest, now that we've got a toddler running around, we're thrilled that we still have a sex life, unlike some couples we hear about. And we have years to explore what we've always loved best: each other.

Fantasy Man

SUSAN SHAPIRO

Hold me down harder, so you're overpowering me and I can't move. Like *this*." I showed Aaron, trying to pin my hands under his arms as he lay awkwardly on top of me.

"It's uncomfortable," he complained.

"Oh, come on. Now rip off my shirt!" I ordered him. "Can you be more aggressive?"

"Can you be more castrating?" he asked, slipping off my sweater so gently you'd think I was a china doll about to break.

"Now grab my breasts and say something mean," I instructed.

"You're a controlling shrew," he said calmly, obeying me so halfheartedly I didn't know whether to laugh or cry. Maybe friends who'd called me a control freak were right. It appeared that I was now 100 percent in control of my own sexual domination.

My husband refused to act like he was raping me. Nor did he want to tie me up, restrain me, spank me, or force me into any form of submission, except to pick up his dry cleaning, which I was always forgetting.

Aaron was tall, handsome, brilliant, funny—everything I wanted in a lover except reckless. Indeed, the kinkiest thing about him was his luxuriant Jewish boy's 'fro; I loved to run my fingers through his curls. He was raised to be a suburban gentleman in the conservative 1950s and went to college in the liberated 1970s—which may explain why he wasn't so into bitch-slapping me while pretending he was a pimp and I was his hooker, or playing the principal punishing the naughty schoolgirl sent to his office, or acting like a kidnapper tying up his naked, quivering victim. Instead, he put his ardor into his work while making sweet, calm, comfortable love to his wife once every week or two. Or three. Okay, a few years into our marriage, we sometimes went an entire month without even a quickie.

This was a far cry from our lewd long-distance courtship, where I'd fly to L.A. in tight jeans, braless under my T-shirt, and he'd throw me to the carpet as soon as I walked into his apartment, or take me in the hot tub on his roof (where we once got caught by the building's manager). The West Coast earthquakes we lived through were an apt metaphor for how I'd initially felt fooling around with him, as in "Oh, baby, the earth moved." The first year he was aggressive and I was happy to be tamed.

Of course, we couldn't maintain the thrill of our bicoastal relationship forever. Eventually, we got engaged, married, and moved in together. At thirty-five, I was pleasantly shocked that a strong, intense, career-driven woman like me could actually get a great husband. Soon, paying off an expensive mortgage, dealing with infertility, and mourning the death of a few close relatives intruded on our fun escapades. So when the sexual status quo became less than hot and salacious, I cut us some slack.

While my mate was working late and away on business trips, I'd get my rocks off by imagining a mysterious naked couple acting out semiviolent fetishes. I also paged through *Penthouse* and surfed porn sites on the Web. When Aaron got home, I offered to enact any lascivious scenario that might appeal to him: A private wet T-shirt contest with me as the only contestant and him as the judge? Hand job with scented motion lotion? Trying it doggy style? Titty fucking? I even asked if he was interested in giving me a "pearl necklace." To be sure he didn't think I wanted him to buy me jewelry, I explained that the phrase was a euphemism for a man ejaculating onto a woman's neck, something I'd read about online. "Great, now I'm married to a porn addict," he said, going into his den to check e-mail.

Mild, metrosexual men have never done it for me. Maybe it is because my father grew up a Lower East Side street kid who, my mother used to brag, would have been a gangster had she not put him through medical school in the Midwest. Her favorite photograph of him is when he was sixteen, wearing a black leather jacket, smoking an unfiltered cigarette, and looking handsome and menacing. I wondered if she'd cursed me to a life of cads. Then there were my three big, tough brothers, known for yelling "switch to tackle" before landing on top of me in the middle of a touch football game on our lawn. Not surprisingly, I turned into a loudmouth tomboy unafraid to compete with the guys and stick up for myself. When

I introduced my junior high best friend, Claire, to a sweet fellow student who'd asked me out, she whispered, "Are you kidding? You have more testosterone than he does."

Then, at fifteen, I met David, a wife-beater-wearing, Marlboro-smoking, self-styled James Dean. He was obnoxious and aggressive—even anti-romantic—calling me an "old sea hag" with "violent eyes" and "breeder's hips." When we made out, he rubbed his hands all over me and said his father owned a meatpacking plant where he worked in the summertime, so he was used to slinging sides of beef. Bored by polite West Bloomfield boys who'd ask permission before kissing me, I was a goner. The fact that we were at a B'nai B'rith camp convention where I was president of my chapter and he was a straight-A pre-med student from a well-off family was incidental. He correctly surmised that since I was such a powerful type A personality used to being in charge, I needed an arena where I could loosen up and let someone else call the shots. Six turbulent years later it ended in (predictable) disaster after he slept with not one but two of my close girlfriends.

Brad, my first gentile (and thus taboo) bedmate, was also virile and buff; he'd hold me down in bed, talk dirty, and take what he wanted. I assumed all girls went mad for he-men. After all, every bodice-ripping R-rated movie, soap opera, and Harlequin romance showed a John Wayne action hero taming the shrew. I saw myself as just such a tough-talking, chain-smoking femme fatale, albeit from a tony Detroit suburb.

Eventually, I wound up in Manhattan in grad school, where I hung out with a crowd of left-wing, liberal, independent career women. I feared that confessing my craving for being dominated by macho men in bed would mean I'd have to revoke my credentials as a serious, intellectual feminist, so I simply decided to keep quiet about my sexual predilections.

I'd broken off with macho David and Brad because of their insensitivity and infidelity, and I was starting to worry that the Lotharios who stimulated me most in the sack were bound to make me sick when we put our clothes back on. By my thirties, I seriously suspected that there were only two types of men to choose from: bullies who'd bewitch my body, then try to seduce my best gal pals when I wasn't looking, or sensitive souls who'd take me on nice dinner dates but put me to sleep under the sheets.

Then I met Tommy, a kind, good-looking lawyer who treated me well but was also up for a little deviant dance in the dark. Once, after my roommate Emily, a radical documentary filmmaker, overheard some minor smacking and tickling in the bedroom, she asked if Tommy was abusing me. Of course not. We were just having fun, I reassured her. She eyed me skeptically, as if I was exhibiting signs of battered-woman syndrome. But as a big-boned five-foot-seven gutter-mouthed girl with a decent right hook, I knew for certain that if any guy ever really tried to hit or touch me against my will, I would have beat the hell out of him.

Still, as more years passed, I felt increasingly ready to make a trade-off: rambunctious lovers who were into lying, head games, and cheating for an honest, caring spouse I respected. So, at thirty-five, I wound up with a mensch who walked me down the aisle and swore he'd be faithful. That he also happened to be a big, hot, hairy, sardonic, sports-obsessed man's man who easily returned my father's and brothers' male-punch hellos made the decision fairly easy.

Yet only a few years into our blessed union, my spouse seemed to find me too warm-blooded. On Saturday nights he preferred work to body-wrestling me to the floor and taking me where I wanted to go. If I tried to bring it up, he'd get defensive, as if I were insulting him. But I felt too young and frisky to forfeit my physical fervor. I wasn't self-conscious about pleasing myself, but it felt sad not to be sharing my pleasure with the partner I adored.

"You have to insist that your husband fulfill your sexual fantasies," instructed my therapist, who happened to be tall, dashing, and happily married himself. "Try asking him again."

"I tried, and he can't act them out," I said. "It makes him uncomfortable. Which makes me uncomfortable."

"What's wrong with a little discomfort? Fight through it," he advised.

"It's too weird and awkward," I admitted.

"Well, your alternative is to give up. So, do you plan to cheat on Aaron or just be sexually unsatisfied for the rest of your life?" he asked.

"But he's just not into it," I muttered, embarrassed enough that I'd spilled my steamiest X-rated fantasies to my therapist, who actually looked embarrassed hearing them. (Ironically my dreams about Dr. Winters involved being gently embraced by him, not manhandled. Let's analyze that.)

But I took his suggestion, raising the issue of my carnal cravings again. This time, my husband flat-out refused me, leaving me feeling totally, humiliatingly rejected. Deflated, I slunk back to my shrink and tried my old theory on him. "Isn't this the typical marriage compromise—you give up some sizzle for consistency, social acceptance, and security?" I asked.

"No! That's ridiculous!" he countered. "According to the Torah, a man is obligated to please his wife sexually or he is not a good husband."

This from a WASP, who was using my tribe's customs to

argue with me. I went home and looked it up. He was right! A Jewish husband was mandated to make his wife feel fulfilled when she so desired. "Her food, her clothing, and her duty of marriage relations he shall not diminish" (Shmot 21:9). How funny—a Reform Jewess who'd always resented rabbis and all forms of religious authority found the biggest champion of my libido in my own people's ancient laws. If they'd taught me this in Hebrew school—instead of the Holocaust—I might have kept the Sabbath and learned to cook a brisket.

But I wondered how a woman fashioned her man into a passionate brute. You couldn't force your guy to be forceful, could you? My therapist requested some appointments alone with my husband. "Okay, let's try what you want," my mate announced when he came home from a psychotherapy session one night. I knew he was trying to compromise because he loved me. But I could tell he felt uncomfortable, even horrified that his perverted vixen of a wife had strong-armed a shrink into insisting he strong-arm me. Still, I wasn't giving up on my desires and I didn't want to look for sexual fulfillment elsewhere. Plus, I had an apparently Torah-given right to receive pleasure from my partner. So I led Aaron into our bedroom and told him what I wanted. Again. He acquiesced, passively, cracking jokes about castration and decapitation, taking me totally out of the mood.

"Shut up, don't make me laugh," I begged, explaining that he needed to deride me and take me against my will. After several minutes of orchestrating both the physical movements and the dialogue ("I want you to fuck me harder, Tarzan" and "Stop calling me beautiful, you idiot"), the whole thing began to feel too phony to get me off to anywhere. "Let's just forget it," I said, getting out of bed.

"No. Don't you *dare* leave! Get over here," Aaron snapped, grabbing my arm and throwing me back on the bed. He stopped joking and roared, "Okay, you stupid bitch, now you're going to get it." He sounded enraged. I didn't know if he was genuinely pissed off or simply playing the role. But when he ripped off my jeans and slapped me, something happened. I felt nervous. Tingly. Excited. Transported. Rubbing against him, I had a major orgasm before he was even inside me. It was more intense than any "little death" I remembered with those bad-boy idiots I'd gone for in my teens and twenties. Who knew you could be so erotically enraptured by your own spouse?

I was so gratified and grateful afterward that all I wanted to do was please Aaron. So, for our second act, we went all the way, the way I knew he preferred—gentle strokes, sweet nothings whispered in his ear, plenty of "I love you, baby." I wasn't bored this time. I felt so close to my husband, I didn't mind running this half of the show.

Both of us were restless sleepers who usually crashed far apart on our California King bed, but the next morning, I woke with my arms around him, kissing his warm back. Our tryst was so memorable that I made myself come in the middle of the day just thinking about it. Then I sent him an e-mail—"Last night was so hot!"—and when he got home, we did it again! The last time we'd done it twice in twenty-four hours was back when we'd had sex for the first time. Seeing how delighted I was, and how my being sexually satisfied changed our whole dynamic, he became more willing and open.

Five years after taking our wedding vows, I was shocked to find myself falling madly, passionately in lust with my husband again. I'd thought marriage meant making a choice between adoration and ardor, but it turned out both were possible in one package. Okay, it took therapy with a perceptive shrink, figuring out what rang my bell, and asking for it blatantly—several (dozen) times. But when I stopped expecting my mate to read my mind and body and clearly verbalized what I wanted—exactly the way I wanted it—I got it.

After celebrating our twelfth anniversary, Aaron and I still score several times a week. Nowadays he gets into being the dominating bully and stays in character for as long as I want him to. He was recently annoyed with me for throwing out an old ripped T-shirt. He wanted to rip it to shreds himself, he told me, with me still wearing it. (I was happy to offer another with a small hole he could go to town on.) A friend who plays out more brazen bedroom games with her lover told me we needed a safe word, in case it ever gets out of hand. So far "Stop it" works just fine and I only used it once—when my leg was getting a cramp. Meanwhile I've come every single time my husband and I have gone for it in the last six years, which seems quite unbelievable and astounding.

"That's way too much pressure. Stop saying it or you'll jinx it," he warns, and I happily obey.

Kiss Poker

STEPHANIE DOLGOFF

There's an archetype dear to horny teenage boys and horny teenage boys who grow up to be pornographers: the prim librarian who is one bobby pin tug away from hair-down voracious sexuality. The lucky student happens by when she's just reshelved *Lady Chatterley's Lover.* She whips off her thick tortoiseshell glasses and shimmies out of her twin set, splaying herself on a thesis carrel to reveal that she is not, in fact, some buttoned-up maiden aunt but a breathless nympho in crotchless panties just waiting to ravage a fellow with whom she has a deep intellectual connection.

Yes, well, I'm the opposite.

Picture a curvaceous, big-haired, earthy brunette on whom a twin set would look constricting, if not slightly obscene. My body, while not pert or balletic, is sexy in a settled-in kind of way, like a lovingly worn pair of jeans. I don't dress

like hootchie—no over-the-knee stiletto boots and micro-
minis for me—but I don't feel attractive unless my clothing
pays my body a little respect, helps it get its moment in the
sun. That usually means at least one article is plunging, low-
riding, or on the tight side. My grandmother used to describe
certain girls as being "hot in the pants," as if their clitoris was
chronically inflamed, leading them by the crotch to seek relief
in any form. If she didn't adore me so blindly, she would have
seen that the kind of girls she was usually referring to looked,
dressed, and moved a lot like I do.

My personality isn't meant for the library's musty hush,
either. I laugh loudly and often, and rarely censor what I say.
Men often mistake my friendliness and directness as a come-
on. Oh, and did I mention I write about sex for a variety of
women's magazines? I can converse as easily about vaginal
lubrication, penile girth, or the Reverse Cowgirl (see me after
class) as others do about imported versus domestic beer. I've
been on all-women sex retreats to summon my "inner
Aphrodite," during which I danced draped in a scarf to com-
mune with my pelvis. Once, for an article for *Cosmo*, I flew to
Alaska to determine if the favorable men-to-women ratio re-
sulted in an embarrassment of hotties to choose from. It did.

Given my appearance, personality, and profession, guys,
understandably, tend to assume that I will be as expansive and
open in the bedroom as out—if not a wild ride, then at least
an easy one to hitch. I remember one night at a Brooklyn bar
called Mooney's, the kind of place that keeps Christmas lights
up indoors year round. My friends and I were in our early
twenties and generally in the habit of staying out until the wee
hours, flirting and joking, determined to close down whatever place we happened to be in. That particular evening, in
walked Steve, a friend of a friend; we'd been locking eyes

across various smoky rooms for months. He was sexy and inarticulate with a leisurely smile and I sensed his eyes on my hips as I danced alone by the jukebox. (Need I describe how I dance?) I felt both invincible and objectified, a potent combination for me. If I wanted him, I knew I had him, and I relished that feeling.

Eventually, Steve joined me at the jukebox and we moved to a corner, pleased to discover that our instincts had been right, that we liked the way the other kissed. With little conversation we drifted the few blocks to his place and onto his futon. We kissed some more, and after ten minutes or so, his hands searched my back for a bra clasp.

That's when I felt a little click, like a door closing, and my brain began to take over for my body, flooding with thoughts until I couldn't feel anything pleasurable. As we kissed, I found myself observing the action from a distance, like a silent sportscaster narrating a game on a faraway field. *This bra is a front-close,* I thought as Steve's hands tugged. *I wonder how long it'll take him to figure it out.* My mind then jumped to a scene from the seventies sitcom *Happy Days*, in which Fonzie shows Richie how he can unsnap a steel-reinforced 1950s bra with a quick flick of his fingers. *Why am I thinking about the Fonz at a time like this?* I wondered. Steve lifted my sweater, finally freeing my breasts from their constraints. I noticed red marks on my skin from the underwire. *Geez, looks like I need a 36 instead of a 34. Ach, the elbow on the hair! Ouch!* I could barely feel Steve's hands on me, but I was hyperaware that the futon was especially thin in one spot and that the small of my back was rubbing against the wood. I shifted my hips.

"What?" he asked, looking up from where he was settling in to spend some time with my breasts.

"Nothing. I'm fine." I kissed him, hoping the beery bar smell in his hair would bring me back to the moment, or rather, the moment I'd been at twenty minutes earlier. But I knew it was over. The momentum was shot. My mind was roiling with analysis, none of which had to do with sex. I sighed internally. *Here we go again.*

Steve's eyes were half closed, his lips unself-consciously parted, coming in for a kiss. He seemed far, far away, in the zone. *What the hell am I doing here?* I wondered, looking at him. I'd wanted him—I knew I'd wanted him—but I couldn't remember what that wanting had felt like, that rush of heat and attraction. Desire had led me to my current state: topless on his futon. But now that I was here, everything felt wrong. I sat bolt upright, rehooked my bra, and told Steve I was sorry but I had to go.

"Are you sure?" he asked. "C'mon, I mean, we don't have to do anything. We can just sleep."

"Yeah, no, I have to go. Totally not you—I swear." He looked perplexed, but I kissed him and said I was fine. I might have made up a lie about getting over a breakup. I smiled wide like the woman he had so recently been dancing with by the jukebox, the one who seemed so sure of what she wanted and sure to follow through. He got up to walk me home but I didn't let him. I needed to get out of there and I couldn't bear to have to look at him and be reminded of what a freak I was. Who did this kind of thing? By the time I reached my building, the sun was coming up, and as I unlocked my door, I nearly cried in frustration: What was wrong with me? This wasn't how the night was supposed to end.

* * *

I never connected that night to another winter's night nearly a decade earlier. I was a freshman in high school and was hanging out with a bunch of kids in a dive motel in Philadelphia. We were there for a track competition; I was co-manager of our high school track team, along with Maria, the girl I was sharing the room with. It must be said that we went to a highly competitive science high school. The teams that brought us glory were the math team, bio squad, and debate club. Winning at sports, at least through conventional means, seemed unlikely. So together, Maria and I had hatched a plan to keep our local rival high school's star runners awake playing cards all night. The next day, we hoped, they'd be tired and perhaps so mesmerized by our flirting that they'd be off their game, drop the baton, or maybe even sleep through their races altogether. At the very least, they'd be impaired enough not to kick our boys' skinny, dorky, Westinghouse Science Competition–winning asses too badly.

The game we'd proposed was kiss poker. Maria, a year older and in charge as usual, shuffled the deck and spelled out the rules to the four boys assembled and me. The winner of the hand would be entitled to a kiss from whomever he or she chose; each time you won, you could request an upgraded kiss. You might start with a quick peck, then try something a bit more prolonged or openmouthed, and on from there.

Since Maria and I were the only two girls and no high school boy would have kissed another publicly back then, in the very early eighties, I knew I was in for a lot of kissing. That was okay with me. At fourteen, I had practiced at least a half-dozen variations on the basic kiss theme. Things couldn't get too carried away, I figured, so long as no single guy won too many times.

Cards were shuffled, kisses exchanged, Cokes drunk,

and eventually two of the guys went back to their rooms to sleep. Soon we were down to four players, a sprinter I'll call José, another guy, Maria, and me. I didn't know much about the sprinter. English was not his first language, which may have been why I thought he was shy. I also wasn't the best at distinguishing deep and brooding from aloof or simply dumb. In this case, it didn't much matter. José had tight, glossy dark curls, light latte skin, and the kind of sculpted body you don't get from lifting at the gym so much as doing pull-ups on the playground. I didn't mind kissing him one bit.

The two boys spoke to each other in Spanish and laughed, one inching closer to Maria to indicate his proprietary interest. She slapped his knee and laughed but didn't push him away, eventually settling into the crook of his arm. Soon she excused herself and dragged me into the bathroom for a girl chat. "I'm going to lose my virginity tonight," she whispered as soon as she closed the door. I tried to pretend I didn't find this shocking; "Are you sure?" was about as far as I could go without her rolling her eyes like I was a moron. She was sure.

After we emerged from the bathroom, we played a perfunctory hand, then I had to figure out a way to give Maria and her boy some privacy. Once I knew her itinerary for the evening, I had no desire to stick around. Neither, apparently, did José, who took my hand and led me into the bathroom.

The fluorescent light was so bright I needed to squint. I giggled and he smiled at me, a wide, goofy smile, his eyes flat, uninvolved with the rest of his face. I was nervous and excited. I saw us as being in on the same conspiracy, him helping his buddy "get over," as we called sex that year. I concentrated on pretending that these kinds of situations were an everyday occurrence for me.

As soon as the hollow wood door was closed, José began kissing me, pressing my body flat against it. This was fine with me. More of the same and possibly even a trip to "second" were within my comfort zone. I was a well-informed, sophisticated Manhattan girl who had done her share of making out. I assumed José and I understood each other.

Except these kisses were different from the public ones we'd shared; I'd say more ardent, but that connotes emotion and we'd barely said two words to one another. Within seconds, his hand was grabbing at my breast and squeezing hard with a twisting motion, like working an orange half on an old-fashioned juicer. His other hand held my hair at the nape of my neck and pulled just a little too hard. He was over six feet, a good six inches taller than me, and his rock-hard runner's thigh pressed against the zipper of my jeans as he leaned in with his full weight.

I opened my eyes to see his squeezed shut as if he were in pain, the freckles on his nose grotesque in their proximity. I was suddenly so alert that I could have counted his pores. Fight or flight, I suppose, though I thought to do neither. Instead of relaxing into arousal, I was vigilant, a soldier at attention. As he snaked his tongue between my teeth to pry open my mouth, I was aware of the sound of my own hair scraping against the grain of the unfinished door as I tried to turn my head from his mouth's assault. I looked down at my blouse and noticed how his long fingers had thick joints and nail beds. His lean, slouchy torso, sexy to me just minutes earlier, was unyielding as I pushed him away, or tried to.

Still, it took me a few seconds to realize that something was wrong, and even then I didn't know how wrong. I was more shocked than scared. I said no, laughing, taking the sprinter by the biceps and holding him away from me. He opened his eyes and said, "No?" I laughed again and said no, moving his hand off my breast.

Years later I would blame myself for laughing. Did I lead him on? Why did I laugh? I think it was 15 percent awkwardness, 30 percent disbelief that he had crossed the line I'd thought was so clear. The rest, I hate to admit it, was not wanting to hurt his feelings or offend him. I'm white and he was Dominican. A teeny part of me didn't want him to think I didn't like "Spanish" guys.

He paused, briefly, and went back to kissing me. I kissed him back, deliberately. If we kissed and he didn't push it, it meant he had gotten the message, and we could proceed at a slower pace. But almost immediately his hand was back where it had been, on the same breast, leaning into my rib cage, and this time it really hurt. "No!" I said, without laughter. "No?" he asked, smiling. I smiled back weakly. Then the hard, insistent kisses began again, his thigh grinding into my fly.

What I wished more than anything at that moment was for him to stop. What I wished for second most was to feel something even close to desire. If I could want him, it would have meant that what I was beginning to suspect was happening was not. If I could only get into it, I reasoned, if I could match his pace, then our activities that night would be consensual. My mind was already at work whitewashing the scenario. As for my body, it was numb.

The sprinter's hand went down to my pants and he began pulling the button on my jeans. "No!" I insisted. His hand went back up to my breast. That felt safe, if only by comparison. Then the fear welled up again. "No, stop it. I want you to stop," I said. He did.

My mind was a morass of thoughts: Was he slowing

down? Would he reverse course? Would he be angry? I tried to keep up with all the lines that were being crossed, tried to suppress the knowledge that I was losing control of the situation, but I was too embarrassed to scream, to disturb Maria in the next room and reveal what a baby I was. I felt that I had been complicit in the sprinter's expectations. Stupid, idiot me, I must have missed something. The stakes had been raised on our game while, like a kid, I was concerning myself with whether or not the sprinter liked me or *liked me* liked me. How remote that concern suddenly seemed.

His hands were on my fly again, pulling the button undone and reaching down the front of my jeans. This time when I told him to stop, he didn't even pretend to slow down. It was as if he'd run out of patience with what he saw as our little game. I felt his hand on my pubic hair.

That was the moment I abandoned my body completely. I wasn't strong enough to hold him off so I retreated inside my head. His hands were everywhere at once, touching me in a place where, up until that point, I'd only barely touched myself. I couldn't put out the fire, so I had to minimize the damage as much as I could. Full-blown rape, penis cutting through unwelcoming, internal flesh, was beginning to seem inevitable. I didn't particularly prize my virginity, but it was mine, if anything was. The decision to give it over was one I did not want made for me.

So, in my way, I took control. I would end this thing. I could feel him through his jeans, pressing into the exposed triangle of my underwear. His dick was like a bomb, and it was my mission, I reasoned, to defuse it or allow it to detonate safely. I made the decision in an instant, dispassionately, feeling nothing, my mind sharp and impenetrable. I felt safer and stronger than I had since we were playing cards.

I pushed him away from me a few inches, enough to slide his hand out of my jeans. He pulled me to him, filling my mouth with his tongue so I gagged. "No," I said. It was my last no. He seemed to sense that the tide had turned, that I'd seen the futility in fighting. In a way, he was right, but I felt strength in my surrender. I knew it would be over soon.

He used the hand that had been in my jeans to undo his own, freeing himself over his white cotton briefs. Every detail was clear, as if I were filming the action, not actually in the film myself but with a body double standing in for me. José made a soft noise, a cross between a groan and a growl as he stabbed at me with his penis, just for a second, on my belly.

The feeling of him, rubbery against my body, and his look of ecstatic self-involvement spurred me to action. He seemed, for a moment, a bit less in control. I said, "Wait, okay?" He did. He didn't need my cooperation, but he was glad to have it. He stepped back a few inches and I moved away from the door, catching my reflection, green and mussed, in the mirror. I must have paused. "C'mon," he said, and pushed me down so I was seated at the edge of the bathtub.

I'd never given anyone a blow job, but how hard could it be, I thought. I shut my eyes and took him in my mouth, closing my lips around him. I didn't move. Maybe I thought that just holding it in my mouth would be enough, or maybe I froze. Impatient with my tentativeness, the sprinter grabbed the back of my head and started moving it forward and back. I gagged but didn't try to stop him. He knew what he was doing, and the faster he was done, the better. I slipped back off the ledge of the tub from the force of his thrusting, holding onto the sides to keep from falling in. I thought about dinner and whether or not I could keep it down. I pulled back a bit and felt him scrape against the roof of my mouth.

Soon, mercifully soon, he shuddered and I tasted his bitterness. I remember being relieved at how quickly it was over. I stood up and spat into the sink. He chuckled a little to himself, and I saw his reflection behind me; he was smiling, his eyes soft, finally. "Good," he said. "Yes?" I don't remember if I answered. I do remember he reached up to touch my hair, almost tenderly, in thanks. I felt like vomiting.

It was over, the transaction accomplished, the tension diffused. I ran out of the room, past Maria and her boy in the shadow of the bed, to the motel lobby. I collapsed into an old wool-covered wingback by the brochures of local attractions, sobbing hard, yet not quite understanding why. Because, after all, nothing had happened. I went into that bathroom willingly. I hadn't been raped; rape was being forced to have intercourse. We'd simply fooled around. No big deal.

Soon Raymond, a skinny West Indian kid on our school's team, happened by with a friend; when he saw me he shooed the friend away. I don't think he even asked me what was wrong. If he did, he didn't push it. It's hard for me to believe now that a fifteen-year-old boy had the emotional intuition to tread lightly, but he did, and what was left of my shredded instincts told me I could trust him. Raymond took me into his room, put me in his bed, and slept on the floor, no questions asked.

And that was it, the last I thought of the sprinter or the rape until I finally remembered. When I saw José at a track meet a week after that night, I felt angry and physically ill, but I had no idea why. I'd already forgotten.

Although *forgetting* is not the right word. It's too passive, connoting something that slips through the cracks, falls behind the bed, and isn't missed until a once-a-year cleaning unearths it, covered with dust bunnies. Forgetting can be made up for with a conscious effort to pay more attention. Don't forget—raped in February 1981. Not something you'd write on a Post-it and stick on your computer monitor.

No, I forced the memory into submission and went on to spend the rest of my teens and much of my twenties and thirties leaving various men's beds. I'd either bug out in the middle of foreplay, or go through with it and have sex while pondering the stucco on the ceiling. I never told anyone about my problem; after nights like that one with Steve, I let friends draw their own conclusions about what had happened. I wanted to seem normal, after all, like someone who loved having sex, whether or not the hookup turned into anything serious. If they asked what was happening with this guy or that, I insinuated that I couldn't handle being tied down, hinting that the men were somehow lacking. It was complete bullshit, but at least it conformed to what I assumed were people's expectations of me.

As I got older, though, running away at 5:00 A.M. began to feel pathetic. I wanted a partner. So with thirty approaching, I stopped hightailing it home, instead trying to "work through" the discomfort, begging my various boyfriends' forbearance with my sexual skittishness. Not surprisingly, the relationships all ended sooner or later. I blamed the sexual issues on a lack of chemistry or some insurmountable problem with the guy that was preventing me from letting go in bed. I continued to hope that when I met the right person, great sex would simply happen, that this mythic man would cast a magic spell and lure me, finally, out of my head, away from the thoughts that snuffed out my lust. He'd be so skilled that my intense bodily sensations would overpower those distracting thoughts. It was your basic princess fantasy, except my prince would break the evil spell and awaken me from my sexual slumber with cunnilingus.

By the end of my twenties, my prince had not come. But one night at a New York City club, I met or, rather, became reacquainted with Raymond, from high school, a prince of a different sort. I was listening to the band when I spotted him. He was leaning against a banquette with a friend and when I caught his eye, I felt a sudden, intense warmth for him, and ran over to give him a hug. The reason for my reaction would come to me only gradually, in drips and chunks, over the better part of the next decade.

The knowledge of that high school rape was too explosive for my mind to absorb, but my body remembered anytime it was touched by a hand not my own. I wedged the event fixedly into a corner of my mind, where it festered like a tumor, eventually becoming so hulking and malignant that I had no choice but to notice my symptoms, not headaches or seizures but an inability to be close to a man in the physical sense.

Now that I do remember, I have hope that finally, on the cusp of my forties, I can truly begin to forget, or at least move on and learn how not to absent myself during sex. I feel hopeful that I can. After all, my body somehow remembered Raymond and his profound kindness back then, which is why I felt a wave of affection for him at the club, why I've always known that there are men who offer not just physical threat and danger but the possibility of goodness. Perhaps that is why I kept trying to find a man to love, even if my body wasn't ready to fully participate.

These days, once the bedroom door is closed, I still tend to become shy, slowing the progression of passion when I feel it careening out of control. No matter how heady the bar-room banter or what got fondled in the elevator, the urge to decelerate overwhelms any other physical desire I might be feeling and my brain takes over, my roiling thoughts carrying me far, far away. My husband of six years understands this, sometimes better than I do. It is one of the reasons I married him. "Hi, honey," he'll whisper softly when he notices that my mind is wandering. "I'm right here. Are you?" The sound of his familiar voice helps me remember that he is the man I love and trust, the man I choose to be with, fully myself, mind and body merged, naked in every sense.

The Great Pretender

JANE JUSKA

In 1957, I was twenty-four and getting diddled in the back-seat of my Chevy convertible with my boyfriend, Jack, where I orgasmed all over the place, my first time. *Wow! What was that?* It was so thunderingly wonderful I figured I was engaged. And when in the course of human events I let Jack undress me ("Oh gosh, no!") and lay me down on the box springs of his Murphy bed ("What are you doing?") and then have his way with me ("Please, please!"), I figured on a June wedding. In my mind he was no longer Jack; he was now my fiancé, had become so the first time he fumbled with the hooks on my bra, the first time he bent his head to my over-sized, droopy breasts and did not recoil in horror, as I did, every time I saw myself naked in the mirror. My gratitude was boundless.

Alas, in giving myself to Jack, I soured the deal. At least

that's what my mother would have told me had I possessed the courage to confess to her.

Jack and I kissed, he diddled, I came. In the haze induced by my newly awakened sensuality, I told myself that our prenuptial canoodling wasn't wrong; after all, I knew we would marry. All I had to do was glance down at the ring I'd taken to wearing on the third finger of my left hand, in secret, in the dark. It was from a Cracker Jack box and it was turning my finger green. Not long from now, I convinced myself, it would be replaced by a diamond presented to me by Jack on bended knee. It was the beginning of a new era. My future sparkled.

* * *

In the 1950s, boys and girls didn't talk to each other before, during, or after sex. Nor at any time in our two years together did Jack and I discuss marriage, which I considered automatic, or birth control, which I never considered because I didn't know where or how to get it. I never told Jack that every single month I spent five days terrified of being pregnant, the rest of the month relieved I wasn't. We did not discuss the admonition given by all fathers to their sons at that time: "Whatever you do, don't get her pregnant." Instead, we had sex accompanied by unspoken fear, though mine was at least alleviated by my certainty that I was going to get married. Jack, who had almost but not quite mastered the art of early withdrawal, was rightly terrified. And desperate times called for desperate measures.

I walked in on my "fiancé" with another woman, the two of them on the same box springs I considered my marriage bed. When I knocked on the door, I managed to catch a glimpse of her medium-sized, pouty breasts before she had a chance to cover them up. They were nothing like mine and everything I wished for. I'm sure Jack hoped I would get the hell out of his life and leave him to Miss Pouty. Too bad for him: I forgave him and ran after him, on a crusade to make everything right by luring this boy to church where he would stand at the altar, smiling me down the aisle, silently.

I was in love, after all; besides which, fifty years ago, once a woman was deflowered, defiled, and delighted, there was nowhere for her to go but to church. So I chased after a boy who went to great lengths to prove to me that he was not "the one" before he disappeared for good. For many years afterward I repressed the humiliation I had brought upon myself. Repression was big in the fifties.

Still, I'd already lost my innocence in the backseat of a 1956 Chevy; it had been replaced with a lively libido. I was a modern woman. So what was a nice modern girl to do when she got horny? She looked for a husband.

*   *   *

The man I got to marry me, Steven, was a lover ahead of his time. We fell into the backseat of my car the very night I picked him up at Mike's Pool Hall, a beer and burger joint in San Francisco. He turned out to be a lousy kisser—his upper lip seemed to disappear on contact—but the rest of him promised a dark delight; Michelangelo's *David* comes to mind. He seemed to enjoy my outsized breasts, though maybe he didn't; maybe he found them as distasteful as I did. In the absence of conversation and blinded by the light of sheer need, I plunged ahead heedless of convention or common sense or the absolute necessity of birth control.

How could I have been so foolish? Now the answer seems simple to me: I was starving for sex. Jack had given me a hint of its pleasures and mysteries and I wanted more. But in 1964, a woman who had feelings like those was still considered dirty, unnatural, and bad. If I wanted sex and I didn't want to be bad, I had to get married.

Instead, I got pregnant, during a time when legal abortion wasn't even around the corner. The decision was made for me. We got married and I discovered that there is something to be said for marriage, even a minor one, even an unhappy one. Marriage resolves an important problem: celibacy. You get to fuck when you're married. You even get to make love. Or you're supposed to get to do that, though in my case, on my honeymoon, pregnant as I was and spotting, my new husband could barely hide his repulsion at what I had wrought.

For it was my fault, of course, and I knew it. I was the one who should have waited for marriage. And if I simply couldn't wait—bad girl that I was—then at the very least I should have protected my partner from my pregnancy. But in my ignorance, willful or otherwise, I didn't. Instead, I pretended to myself that I was happy. I made myself believe that at last I had found a proper outlet for my forbidden sensuality, that I had not betrayed the man who was doing the right thing by marrying me when he had every reason to kick me out onto the street. That's where women like me belonged.

Though he never said it, my husband thought I was immoral. He was ashamed of me and of my pregnancy and of our baby when he arrived six weeks early. He was ashamed in front of his parents, especially, and in front of his friends, who, I knew, were laughing inwardly at his having gotten caught in an age-old trap. I wasn't laughing. Not me, the Great Pretender. Nor did I feel ashamed or immoral, not on the surface at least. I knew I had been stupid, or, more accurately, too oblivious to insist on condoms, or to have gotten myself fitted for an intrauterine device.

Mostly, though, I was happy. I was married and pregnant, though not in that order. But that was as close to being a proper married woman as I had been able to get; my mother would certainly agree. Only she sided with my husband and apologized to him for my behavior before we went off on our honeymoon. That first night as man and wife, my husband did his joyless duty, lights out all the way, initiating the two of us into a marriage doomed from the start.

Never mind, though, because in the eyes of society, we were legal and therefore subject to a very real and forgiving rule: Once married, a woman is allowed to go about her business without fear of discovery, retribution, or remonstrance from her mother or anyone else, as long as she remains faithful. No cheating, unless maybe the husband wanders, but then again, men do these things.

But the wife? In exchange for her fidelity, marriage provides not only respectability but a certain amount of privacy. Without fear of public opinion, you and your husband can become as one or you can live separate lives; you can beat each other up; you can console each other; you can help each other make the best of a cruel world; you can hide from it. You can, if you do it right, reach a state of grace, the two of you, and no one need know the struggle you've endured and the serenity you've won. Whatever you do, respectability is no longer your problem. Coupled, married, all you are expected to do is make a baby. In that order.

I don't think Steven ever forgave me for screwing up the order. I couldn't be sure, of course, because, like most men and women of our generation, we rarely talked to each other. It would take my husband's eventual refusal to engage in sex at all to drive home his anger. Rather soon, my happy-housewife façade began to crumble. My husband avoided our bed, staying up all night, turning a deaf ear to my pleas for sex. I could no longer pretend to be happy.

He did not, however, refuse to engage in sex with other girls, undoubtedly prettier than I, with perkier breasts. I learned of these affairs near the end of our five years as man and wife. His psychologist told him to confess; it would be good for his recovery. His, maybe, not mine.

I didn't feel the need to share with him the fact that three years into our marriage, I had become an unfaithful wife: I had an honest-to-God affair. His name was Howard. He was married and so was I and he was a prick and so was I, though women can't be pricks so I was a heartless bitch. Of course, I didn't think so when we met in the teachers' lunchroom at the school where we both worked, about as unromantic a locale as one could imagine. But my hunger for sex overcame the cafeteria food; I was starving.

As for Howard, he enjoyed sex, his churchgoing wife didn't, so he was forced to break the rule of fidelity. Since he was also a good Lutheran, he managed to convince himself that as long as he didn't do any actual fucking, he could avail himself of whoever and whatever was being offered ("Thou shalt not penetrate but getting sucked off is okay"). I found this axiom hard to accept, but I kept at it until, by golly, even I had to admit that for Howard our sex was one way (oral) and for one person (him).

So I left them both, my lover and my husband. After Steven's confession, I put my little boy in the backseat of the car and drove off to California, just the two of us. But I did not escape my marriage unscathed. I had spent all my sexuality on men who didn't want it. I was sick of myself, of the little girl with her nose pressed against the window of happiness, certain that marriage would provide pleasure and warmth and company. I have never been as lonely as I was during those married years. But I was a mother now, with no time for self-pity or desire or for finding a new someone who wouldn't want me either. Once again, my feelings went underground.

In the golden state of California, divorced and happy, I was celibate for an uncomplicated twelve years and a single mother to a delightful and rambunctious son. I was closing in on fifty, passionate about my work as a high school English teacher, and contented with my books, my students, my boy. My daily carpool to and from school provided a camaraderie that rivaled the good fellowship of the locker room. Except when there are both men and women in the carpool, as there were in mine, that camaraderie can catch fire before you know it.

One evening, on the way home from work, only two of us in the car, Will, my best friend and colleague, reached over and put his hand on mine. "I love you, you know." It didn't take more than a second for me to say it right back. After ten years of talking and laughing about everything under the sun—books and music, kids and parents, backpacking and swimming, friendships and enmities—we had become close. Now, suddenly, the dam had broken and passion swept over the two of us, drowning common sense and concern for others in a sea of neediness, of long-pent-up desire. Both of us were aware that time was fleeting, that something had passed us by, that now perhaps we could catch up and truly be happy. I was in love with my soul mate. Carpe diem.

Except Will was married, and to a woman unworthy of him. At least that's what I forced myself to pretend—there's that word again. Will never actually said an untoward word about her. But blaming the wife was easy for me, since many years before, my mother had told me: "If a man strays in his marriage, it's the wife's fault. She has failed to adequately perform her wifely duties."

On the surface, I agreed with Will, who said that what we were doing had nothing to do with his wife or his children. Thank my apparently boundless capacity for self-deception; I now know that it had everything to do with his wife and his children. But I wanted to marry this man. He was my best friend. He said he loved me. I almost believed him. How could I turn down his invitation to kiss me and hold me when he smelled so good? It had been so long since I had known any of that; I wanted it to continue for the rest of my life.

The affair lasted six weeks. Will was a wonderful lover before and after sex. During, he wasn't so good; he had premature ejaculation, for which I of course blamed his wife. But at least Will refrained from commenting on my breasts, which had slid even farther south. As always, I was grateful.

During that time, I changed carpools for fear of giving away our secret. At school, Will and I avoided each other. At home, I sat next to the phone waiting for calls that rarely came, writing in my journal and drinking myself to sleep. (A word of advice: Don't keep a journal, because if you do, you will reread it at some future time and want to kick yourself.) I did everything except admit to myself that I might be making another blunder, might be about to take yet another ride into the valley of despair. Too late, when I emerged, I was already bloodied and bowed, sadder and not much wiser, full of guilt and self-hatred, leaving behind my best friend, both of us lonely beyond measure.

*   *   *

This should be the end, shouldn't it? I ought to be able to say that I returned my passion to my teaching, to safety. After all, I hadn't had an orgasm since 1964, not by way of a man, not since Steven performed oral sex with me before our marriage, but not after. Once we wed, nada, not with my husband, not with Howard, not with Will. Men had brought me nothing but heartache, and I was getting a little old to keep looking for passion, for love, even for plain old sex. But then came Ken, and how do you turn down a fantasy come true?

Check this out: The sexiest guy in the band, probably the piano player, comes down off the bandstand, takes your hand, looks deep into your eyes, and says as if he really means it, "I'd like to get to know you. I get off at one."

There ought to be a law, something like truth in advertising, that requires married men to wear wedding rings. Most women, after all, wear their rings, perhaps because it keeps us down on the farm, far from temptation, which is why they are festooned with beautiful diamonds and other precious jewels. We can smile at our rings—they will smile back—instead of at some piano player denuded of rings and free to roam.

Had Ken been wearing his ring that night, I would have scampered back to the safety of the quiet little nest I had built with good faith and common sense. Surely I had learned my lesson. Appearances aside, I did not have a penchant for married men, did not go looking for marriages I could break up or for men who were unavailable or wives I hoped to punish. If, when I met Howard way back in 1965, someone else had come along, someone single, well, I would have been pleased and happy. And my best friend, Will? Oh, gosh, I wish he had been single, but he wasn't, he certainly wasn't. If only some caped, unmarried crusader had rescued me from him and him from me. But he didn't.

So here I was salivating over a naked ring finger. Okay, Ken didn't actually say he'd like to get to know me, just that he got off at one, the implication being that he could get off on me. And he didn't take my hand. He did, however, look deep into my eyes, probably because the hour was late and I was one of the few women left in the joint. We went to the backseat of my car and got it on. The wheels of progress grind exceedingly slow.

If you want a long-term relationship, don't become involved with a musician; if you're lucky, you'll rank right below his instruments, the one he performs on in public and the one he performs on in private, and not only with you. Not that I wanted to marry this man. I would be happy, I told myself, with something that extended beyond a single encounter. I craved ongoing sex with a man who would stay the night and wake up with me in the morning. Was that too much to ask?

It was, after all, 1985, and the rules of the previous decades were in shambles. I was fifty-two years old and I had not had sex, except with myself, since Will, some three years before. Solo sex is preferable to no sex at all, though if, like me, you were born in 1933, you have to get over the shame— first that you're even thinking about sex at your age, and second that you're doing what your best friend in high school told you only dirty boys did to themselves, just look at their warts. But shame, thank God, is usually a short-lived emotion and so it was with me. I did what I needed to do and was grateful. Masturbation is a gift from God, in whom I'd believe if I could be convinced that He invented it and that not believing in Him would result in its disappearance.

Anyway, for fifteen years I had been mostly satisfying myself with a sympathetic washcloth when Ken played his piano into my life. So what if he was married? We both knew what we were after, and Ken was sexy, onstage and off-, dressed or not, standing or lying down, the latter my preference. He was as good as he looked: He could get it up and keep it there forever; a Rock of Ages was Ken. At first I couldn't believe my luck. Fucking the way he did—forever—seemed the answer to my prayers.

Except for one thing: I couldn't have an orgasm. I hadn't been able to climax with Will, either, not being speedy enough to match his three minutes before pop-off. Ken was my chance. As the weeks went by, I tried my very best until I finally faked it. Ken guessed immediately, after which he made himself scarce.

One night, on the promise of feeding him, I inveigled him into coming back to my house. I bet an orgasm that meatloaf, mashed potatoes, and Guinness would be precursors to something even more elemental, and I was right. Soon we found ourselves entangled in damp sheets, a phrase etched indelibly in my imagination by the bodice rippers I'd read in my youth. Ken went to work. Jesus, I was doing it! Or on the way!

But I didn't get there, and eventually, Ken got tired. In the wee, small hours of the morning, he sat down at my piano and played a most melancholy "Memories of You," his way of telling me the obvious, and painful as all get-out. Ah, musicians. With a touch of their fingers they can create joy, sorrow, or in this case an unutterable longing for what would never be: a romance or at least a mutual orgasm.

*   *   *

Pretty dismal, all this. Four men in forty years, one per decade. How pitiful, my romantic history. Gradually, the decades have allowed women to go after whatever it is we think we want—orgasms, companionship, cuddling, conversation. But over the years, I'd given up wanting. I'd had enough of wanting. My desire for a sensual life was once more lodged deep beneath my surface and I was determined to keep it there. I had been a passionate woman whose very passion had been her punishment. It had struck at my courage, my will, injuring me, then leaving me, at the end of each affair, lost and alone. No more. Before it could be the death of me, I buried it.

What I didn't understand is that passion loves the dark; it rests there, gathering strength to rise again or, if thwarted, to tear at the walls of an unjust imprisonment. I did not understand that passion is patient, content to wait for a reentry it knows will come. So, in ignorance verging on the blissful, I lived a reasoned life. I had work and a son I loved; my needs were met. Or so I thought.

Until, nearing sixty, I found myself for the first time exhausted by my teaching, the work that I loved, and unable to recoup my energy on weekends. Perhaps it was that my son was at last off on his own; perhaps it was that a few years earlier my father had died, leaving me lonely and, as the oldest in the family, the next to go. Perhaps it was the idea of only four lousy men. Whatever it was, I could not get myself up off the couch until one day I reached for the phone, called a friend, and the following week lay on a new couch, this one belonging to Freud.

At that time, the late nineties, Freudian analysis undiluted by medication was beginning its fall from favor. Thank God I caught it before it went. In less than a decade on that couch, I gave over self-deception for a clarity I could never have imagined possible or desirable. I learned that my passionate self was not shameful, was not abnormal; it simply was. I admitted that I desired the touch of a man, then forgave myself for it, forgave my mother for leading me to believe that sexual desire in a woman was wrong and my father for having died without counseling me about pregnancy as he had his sons. I forgave a whole lot of my life; I got cleaned out; I got free and came alive. I looked for a man without embarrassment, certainly without shame. I put a personal ad in the papers. I advertised for myself. And I got lucky.

Now, at the age of seventy-five, I find myself up and running, embarking on yet another unpredictable affair. I am in a late stage of life, in no condition to sustain the broken bones that come with a fall. Yet I know I want to live a passionate, full life, and that means readying myself for pain as well as pleasure, despair as well as delight.

So in full possession of the wisdom of age and a mindful awareness of the fragility of my limbs, the unsteadiness of my gait, and, shall we say, my ever lower breasts, I am once more heading out to sea with a man who is almost my age. This is not his first foray into the unknown, though he says it will be his last. Mine, too. I am in my eighth decade, and I love having sex with this man I love, who also loves me. My body, which matches my age, no longer forbids me the pleasure I sought for so much of my life. My mind is clear of plans for the future. The future is now. All I have to do is enjoy it. It's as easy as having an orgasm.

In the Beginning

ALI LIEBEGOTT

Nothing I could think up, no matter how dramatic or
completely horrible, ever made her repent or love me
the way she had at first before she really knew me.
—*Denis Johnson,* Jesus' Son

Who doesn't desire the beginning of a love affair, new like a mop, pretty in all its potential? In the beginning, we're dying to show our best self to each other. Our best self draped around our horrible past. *Tell me the story of that scar. Tell me the story of that disappointment.* We're caught up in smells and idiosyncrasies and the beauty of curving hip bones. When we can't sleep next to our new lovers, we clutch articles of their clothing, curling next to worn T-shirts like puppies searching for their master's scent.

My eight-year marriage died like an old, loved dog, all worn out. One day, those creaky back legs couldn't get up out of their dog bed. My wife and I loved the dog immensely when it was alive. As we watched it die, we petted its head sweetly, then walked away from each other and went looking for our own new puppies.

After my marriage broke up, I started obsessively making lists. Lists of books I'd finished: *Giovanni's Room, The God of Small Things, Death in Venice.* Cities and countries I might want to live in: Rome, Thailand, Montreal. Things I was sure I didn't want from future relationships: monogamy, joint real estate, children. Even kinds of candy I like. I rarely even eat candy, but when I heard another recent divorcée say, "I didn't even know what kind of candy I liked when I was married. I always bought the kind he wanted," I thought indignantly, *Yeah! What kind of candy do I like?* Suddenly, the world seemed filled with candy and the opportunity to find out who I was outside of a partnership.

One list was called "People I Want to Fuck." There were only five people on it and number five didn't really count since it was Angelina Jolie. Numbers one through four were women I'd found attractive over the years but didn't pursue because I was married. After I wrote Angelina Jolie's name down on the list I sat for a long time with my pencil hovering over the possible number six. My newfound freedom was paralyzing. I put down my pencil and promised to add names to my list as they came up.

A few months after my breakup, I was at a birthday party for a friend in a karaoke bar. The minute I saw E. I was attracted to her. "Who's that?" I said. It took about ten minutes for E. and me to start making out, and after we started, we couldn't stop. I managed to pull my mouth off hers long enough only to say in an astounded voice, *"Fuck."* We were practically tearing each other's skin off, pressed up against a Dumpster outside. It was pure chemistry. We made out for hours, dry-humping our way around the perimeter of the parking lot and eventually landing in a grubby bathroom. E. had to go back to Indiana, where she lived, on an early-morning flight, so we said our goodbyes, but it was the kind of make-out session that made me seriously consider flying back to Indiana with her.

At the end of my marriage, my wife and I hardly ever had sex, unless we consciously made a date for it. *And sex was so easy for us in the beginning.* In our first few years together, we reduced each other to a pile of hickeys and bruises. In fact, two weeks into our affair I limped off to my feminist gynecologist because I was so sore from fourteen days of nonstop sex. After examining my well-used parts, the gynecologist put her hand on my arm for emphasis and said, "It's very important that you and your partner take it easy for a while so things down there can get a rest." Even as she was telling me, I could see that she knew her words were useless.

Oh, beautiful blind beginnings, when no one sulkily insists the other brush her teeth before a morning kiss or dares complain about being too tired to do it. Oh, the urgent flights across the country to see one another, the car trips interrupted by numerous roadside trysts, the grace period where your lover doesn't know how flawed and ordinary you really are. "It's so adorable when you leave your used nicotine patches stuck to the antique furniture." "I love the way your poppy-seed-size imagination allows you to eat the same thing for lunch every day."

In the beginning, we finally prioritize the right things in life, calling in sick to work so we can have sex all day, maxing out credit cards for hotels and lingerie, forgoing food and sleep, dumbly clutching at each other, smelling of armpit and come. It's exactly this initial tornado of mystery and hormonal connection that feels like a door cracked open to the real truth of life.

Of course, this googly-eyed behavior pisses off the hordes of people in long-term relationships who can barely remember their own euphoric beginnings. When we were first dating, I brought my ex to dinner to meet some good friends who'd been a couple for nearly ten years. I'm sure we were being disgusting during dinner, publicly groping and staring ridiculously into each other's eyes. "Remember when *we* were in the honeymoon phase?" my friend said to her lover with a tinge of contempt.

I immediately felt defensive: "This isn't the honeymoon phase. This is *real*." Everyone's had that feeling, right? Watching new lovers claw at each other while you sit mired in the domestic dreck of your own relationship. "We could be making out right now if we *wanted*. We're *choosing* to argue over who bought the wrong-sized bags for the vacuum cleaner."

I have a friend who always jokes about how Costco is trying to kill her relationship. "Every day," she says, "I feel as if I have a choice: I can say something sexy or ask if we need to buy Bounce from Costco." While I don't contend that domesticity and passion are polar opposites, I do believe that living with a partner can put a damper on things. The straight world knows this syndrome as the chokehold of domesticity. The lesbian world calls it the clitoridectomy of domesticity.

My ex-wife and I didn't move in together until we'd been dating for nearly two years, a pretty long time for lesbians. It's those first, lust-filled months that get people thinking that it would be a good idea to shack up. You're lying in bed with your brand-new lover and it feels so good to be there and maybe someone suggests breakfast, but you can barely make breakfast, let alone eat it, because you're so busy making out.

"We should live together."

"If we live together, then we could never eat breakfast again."

"I want to sleep next to you all the time."

"How can I bear to be without you, even for a night?"

Number one on my list of things to avoid in my next relationship: "Never live with a girlfriend again." There's a statistic that says every cigarette shaves seven minutes off a person's life. That's kind of how I feel about domesticity: Every discussion about who left the toothpaste cap off shaves seven minutes off the relationship.

* * *

For my first real date with E., I fly to Indiana and spend five days in her bed. My entire memory of the trip is being in her dark bedroom with the curtains drawn, listening to the rain and having amazing sex. On one of our rare trips out of the house, she stopped at a grocery store to buy some bread. I established the grocery store boundary right away. "I'll wait in the car. I've seen what grocery stores can do to lesbians." She looked at me confused until I said, pointing, "That there is the clitoridectomy of domesticity."

So I sat on the curb and smoked while she went in. Then we went back to her house and had sex in the kitchen while she made sandwiches. We gobbled them whole, like people in cartoons where you can see the outline of the sandwich sliding down the character's throat. Then we got back into bed.

During my first week with E., I secretly start making lists about our relationship. Dates we want to take each other on. Places we want to visit together. I invite E. to Thailand. She invites me to China. As I compile my list of foreign countries to visit with E., I think of how irritated my ex used to be with my reluctance to travel. What is it about a new lover that makes us willing, even eager, to do all the things we refused to do with our old lovers?

During those first days together I also tell E. that I want to take her on a date to the Madonna Inn, this ostentatious pink hotel across from Hearst Castle that has mesmerized me from the time I first saw it as a child. They have a caveman room you have to reserve a year in advance. I tell E. this in her dark bedroom. Outside, birds are singing.

"What kind of birds are those?" I ask.

"Morning birds," she says semiguiltily. Our sex marathon has turned night into morning again.

"Tell me the list of my downfalls again," E. says. Her downfalls are all the things about her that make me weak— the mole on her cheek, the beautiful swirl of pubic hair, her two crooked front teeth.

*   *   *

In a twist of pure fate both E. and I relocate to San Francisco a few months after our sex marathon in Indiana, E. for a new job; me to house-sit for friends. The first weekend E. and I both live in the same city, she makes me a peach pie because she remembers me telling her it was my favorite. After the first Friday, each subsequent Friday is dubbed "Pieday," in which E. stays home and bakes me a new kind of pie for the week. "I love to watch you eat pie," E. says. "I love how happy it makes you. If you ever need one midweek, let me know," she says, when I send her a thank-you note reporting that, sadly, I'd eaten the last piece of the strawberry rhubarb.

E., for her part, loves all gummy candy, except the yellow ones. She tells me this early on, and after that I buy her a menagerie of gummy animals—always looking for ones I've never seen before. One day we stop at a gas station and I jump out and buy her gummy worms at the convenience store inside. I pick out the yellow ones and eat them, knowing that I'm betraying myself by eating her gummy seconds instead of figuring out my own gummy firsts. As I return to the car, I make a mental note of my tendency to not investigate the kind of candy *I* like. Fun Dip, I decide. Almond Joy. Feeling triumphant, I eat another yellow gummy worm and unzip E.'s pants as she starts up the engine.

I buy E. all the gummy candy I can find. Gummy rats, gummy pizza, gummy octopi. Halloween turns out to be a gummy jackpot: Drugstores start stocking gummy body parts—severed feet, noses, and ears that E. and I both agree look like gummy vaginas. We decide that at some point in the future, we will build a gummy curio cabinet and label each gummy candy with little pins and a pretend Latin name, *Gummus octopussus*. I wonder if this grand vision for a gummy curio cabinet could emerge only at the beginning of a relationship. I wonder if what E. and I have will last long enough for us to actually build the curio cabinet. I rack my brain for ways to keep what we have as new as possible.

We hold out for four or five months before going into a grocery store together. One night, after a date, I offer to drive her to the supermarket since she doesn't have a car; once there, I realize I need a few things. "I have to go in, too," I say sheepishly, while we're still in the parking lot. "I can walk behind you. We can pretend we don't know each other."

"No," E. tells me. "We're adults. We can handle this." And I agree because, after all, we are still having round-the-clock sex. I slap E.'s ass all the way across the parking lot, pausing superstitiously before the automatic doors. Then we grab hands firmly and cross the threshold.

Once inside, standing before the can openers trying to figure out the difference between an $11 model and a $15 one, I realized how cocky I'd been to think our sexual chemistry would protect us from banal grocery store banter. "Can you believe this can opener costs fifteen dollars?" I say to E., outraged. "Why would any can opener cost fifteen dollars?" As soon as the words are out of my mouth, I want to take them back. Complaining about the price of can openers isn't sexy, and I need to hold on to the illusion that our amazing sexual chemistry makes us superior to the rest of the world. When I spend time with E., I feel as if I'm on vacation, the kind of vacation where people are relaxed and content, not the kind where you sit around the hotel room crying because one of you feels unwanted sexually and the other feels pressured.

After my can opener faux pas, E. and I mill around the grocery store trying to make a sport out of the expedition. "Should we get the big mayonnaise or the little mayonnaise?" E. says in her best dumb-boyfriend voice.

"I dunno. The big mayonnaise is bigger," I reply in my best dumb-boyfriend voice.

When we are safely back in the car, we promise each other we'll never go into a grocery store together again.

*   *   *

My friends, who all love E., hint around, wanting to know my long-term plans. "She's great," I say, "but I've just gotten out of a relationship." Besides, she's the only one I've crossed off my "People I Want to Fuck" list. But when a friend calls with a recommendation for that list—"M. has wanted to fuck you for, like, two years," she tells me—I hedge.

"M.'s cute," I say. I don't say that it makes me feel guilty even to think about having sex with someone else because I wouldn't want to hurt E. Already, I feel the lie of my casual tone when I talk about her with my friends. My heart is in deeper than I want it to be.

One time I happen to tell E. I love baseball and she says she wants to buy me tickets to a game. "Where do you like to sit?" she asks.

"I like to be somewhere where I can catch a foul ball," I say. To me, this means the cheap right-field bleachers. The day we go to the game, she walks in front of me with the tickets, leading us down to our seats. We keep passing more and more rows of people as we get closer to the field. She'd told me our seats were on the lower level, but I didn't know how low until she stops and turns into the second row. There's a row of people in front of us and then the grass field. When I see how close we are, I feel like crying. *These tickets must have cost a fortune,* I think. But it doesn't feel ostentatious. It feels like love, I think—real kindness.

"I'll buy you as many hot dogs as you want," E. says happily, even though she's a vegetarian.

I find myself extremely quiet in the face of E.'s kindness. I eat hot dogs, nachos, and a sno-cone. After the game, we walk twenty blocks back to her house. When we get there, we lay down for a nap to try to sleep off the junk food. Our sleepiness evaporates quickly like gasoline on a sidewalk, and our naptime turns into a sex marathon. *It won't always be this way,* I think. *One day, we'll lie down to take a nap and...nap.*

On another date, I pick E. up with a cooler full of her favorite snacks along with bags of gummy sharks. *Gummus sharkus.* She asks me where I'm taking her and I tell her it's a surprise. We drive along the California coastline for eleven hours, stopping in rest areas along the way to make out.

When we're half an hour away from the Madonna Inn, I tell E. that's where we are going. She gasps and says, "That's one of the dates you told me you were going to take me on." Then she gets quiet in the same way I got quiet when I saw our second-row seats at the baseball game.

Our room turns out to have a seven-foot bathtub and a wall-sized rock fireplace. For a moment, when I'm lying in the seven-foot tub, I try to remember exactly when I stopped having the energy to elaborately woo my ex this way. I try to block out the sadness of my lost ex while E. swims gummy sharks up my naked body before popping them into my mouth. More than anything, I don't want this newness to go away.

Of course, deep down, I know that at some point this lust with E. will fade. Someday, on a road trip, one of us will say to the other, "Want to pull over and have sex in that rest area?" and one of us won't want to. For now, though, we're having fun, getting high off each other, pushing each other up against walls to make out, planning daring, impractical journeys. E. also acknowledges that lust, inevitably, fades with time. "Nothing lasts forever," she says. "I'm just grateful we have this time together now."

"Yep, everything ends someday," I respond, trying to sound light, wondering if my words are as painful for her to hear as they are for me to say.

Beginnings are beautiful. And when the beginning moves to the middle or the end, the once-euphoric couple wonders what went wrong and how they could have possibly lost their beginning. It's preposterous, really, to expect to sustain the oxytocin and faulty, giddy decision making. It's like being angry at the sun for setting at the end of a beautiful day.

Sex with a (Much) Younger Man

ELIZABETH COHEN

I saw him. He saw me. We made assumptions.

His assumption: I was much younger than I actually was.

My assumption: He was much older than he actually was.

It wasn't until a few weeks and many orgasms later that we actually discovered the errors in our assumptions. And by then it was too late. We were in love.

I met my husband, Cameron, in a small southwestern town ten years ago, in the middle of a very hot summer. I was living there for about a year, working on a book. He was the community's most visible artist, with a second-floor storefront studio. He was also totally hot, with a square chin, strong nose, and green eyes that would turn blue if he was wearing a blue shirt, a phenomenon of remarkable chameleon-like matching.

I was in the second half of my thirties, biological clock in full tick. I'd envisioned myself with a brood of kids by that time, an outcome that was seeming more and more unlikely. Instead, I had birthed a couple of books and a portfolio of magazine articles that had once made me proud but now had begun to seem sort of sad. Cameron was more than a crush, he seemed a solution.

When he and I first saw each other, at a party, the attraction was instant and real, and felt, to me at least, like a low-grade electric shock. I shivered; it was as if a sudden breeze had lifted goose bumps on my back—I can still remember this vividly. Cameron walked across the room and whispered, as if we already knew each other: "Let's leave here."

What fun we had over the next year. We explored the backcountry, went rock scrambling, and slept under the stars with our rescue dog, Phoebe, who, we were certain, was part coyote. She had a way of howling at the moon that was wild and wonderful, that encapsulated all our feelings about the life we were living: wild and hungry, full of adventure, song, and lots and lots of sex.

Reader, despite his age, I married him.

Now I am going to tell you his age. Try not to gasp.

He was twenty-one when we married. I was thirty-seven. When we met, he was twenty, not even of legal drinking age. I was—do the math—a full sixteen years older. Certifiable cradle robbery.

When I found out his age, I was sort of stunned, then sort of embarrassed. I could be his mother, literally. In fact, his mother is only one year older than I.

Yet other people didn't seem to notice, or at least they didn't let on that they did. We didn't actually look that different in age. My friends and family who knew about the difference expressed their initial shock and, in some cases, disapproval. I downplayed it; I was happy, wasn't that all that mattered? I told my girlfriends the sex was unbelievable. That usually shut them up.

Here is how the sex was: Unprecedented. Delicious. Funny. Silly. Slow. Fast. Morning. Midday. Midnight. Cramped (single bed in my apartment). Spread out (futon on the floor in his studio). Outdoorsy (during hikes). Scrumptious (by the fireplace). And above all, so nice and comfortable and cozy and safe.

I remember one night our hips met like two pieces of a puzzle. I imagined us as landmasses that had separated through continental drift, reuniting, perfectly matched. His two-day-old artist's I-could-give-a-shit beard scrubbed my cheek, and, surprised by the sudden sharp sensation of him inside me, I temporarily lost my breath.

Back then, we used to read to each other by candlelight and feed each other. I remember one time how he cut pieces off a mango and rubbed them over me before we ate them. "How does that feel?" he asked.

"Perfect," I answered.

That was how our sex was, in the beginning.

I'd had many lovers. I was in my mid-thirties, after all. There was a guy I'll call Dan, my first, when I was sixteen, who was tender and gentle. There was Dave, a college beau, who asked if he could tie me up, whip me, and use various props during sex. I had a tryst with a writer who would go on to chronicle his sexual addiction, including an episode of doggy sex (and I don't mean doggy-style sex). None of these experiences, good or bad, compared to sex with my young husband, who had the most steady erotic appetite combined perfectly with sweetness. He never tired of me or of making love, no matter what we had been doing. We always took time out for a sensual moment.

I thought I'd found the ideal recipe for a sexual relationship. I told women I'd meet: "I have the secret. Go for a younger man!"

The younger man's libido is perfectly matched with the older woman's. The younger man will love you without jadedness or ennui or nostalgia for his former loves, because he hasn't had many. The younger man is still excited about sex, still new at it. He'll be awed by your sexual ideas, which an older man might find tiresome and clichéd.

Yes, I found it. Or so I thought.

Because then what happened is what happens to so many women. I got pregnant, at age thirty-nine, and pregnancy changed me.

We had by then moved to New York City. Our wild dog, Phoebe, had run away. We had left our adobe apartment in the Southwest and taken up residence in a Soviet-block-style apartment in Stuyvesant Town. While Cameron stayed home and painted, I worked for a daily newspaper under an abusive editor. We were broke and I didn't feel well much of the time. Plus, I was scared. We'd already lost a pregnancy the year before, when I was in my sixth month and as big as a house. Cameron was away, and though I had a friend stay with me night and day for a week, I'd never felt so alone.

I wanted this baby to live.

Sex was affected by all of this, as in for the first time in my life, I didn't want it.

"Do you know how long it's been?" my husband angrily shouted at me one afternoon, and for a minute or two I tried to figure out what he was talking about: *Since we met? Since we married? Oh. Sex?* It had been sixteen days!

That was when I realized that men often note and anno-tate every sexual encounter, with asterisks (she was on her stomach, I took her in the shower), while women hold on to a hazy impression of the event (the sun was shining on my arm, he was slow, it was nice). At least, that is how it was with us. Cameron was counting.

I was in my first trimester, a time when many couples still do it, he pointed out. But I was exhausted and freaked out, a hormone stew. One day I wanted ice cream, the next carrot soup. Sex, I didn't want. "Please get me some Indian food," I begged him one evening after work.

"Get it yourself," he answered. By this point we hadn't done it in twenty-three days, he informed me, and I could for-age for curry on my own, thank you very much. Tears squeezed out of my eyes as I stomped out of the apartment, trying to get as far away from his words as I could. Morning, midday, or weekend sex? I wanted no part of it. That thing that had worked so well for us before had begun to falter. When my husband turned to me at night, I mostly turned away. I was tired. He was not. Plain and simple.

Yet for the most part when we weren't fighting about sex, we still got along. He was still beautiful to me. We were happy when we could be, when we could focus on other parts of life. We had our favorite cybercafé and diner. He played chess on the weekends in the park. I started a novel.

Once in a while, we had an occasional fling on the living room rug, but by the middle of my second trimester I was get-ting bigger, and the bigger I became, the less interested I was.

My water broke on a cold morning in mid-October and we walked the four blocks from our apartment to the hospi-tal. I was annoyed when Cameron let me go in alone while he stopped at Starbucks for a coffee. Sure, technically I was hours from delivery, but it seemed symbolic of the growing distance between us that I should enter the hospital by myself.

I felt alone, too. Sex had been our bond and closeness. We'd gone from having a great sex life to having no sex life, a huge distance, and it felt as if there was no map to trace our way back again.

Two days later we came home with a baby daughter and the sense that we should be happy, but instead we were angry and sad. "Why did you have to end sex?" he asked me.

"Why can't you understand that sex was hard during my pregnancy?" I shot back.

"We quit doing it long before that," he said.

As I struggled to absorb these words, it hit me that he was right. Even before I was pregnant, sex was winding down. Losing our first baby had left me in a state of postmiscarriage depression, which pretty much snuffed out my libido. Come to think of it, the fact that we'd conceived at all was pretty remarkable and lucky.

Two weeks later, I went back to work, still tired and increasingly angry, not just at Cameron but at other things as well. How could it be that I had no more maternity leave than that? Besotted by love for our infant daughter, I cried on the subway all the way to work and had to pump my breasts in a stall in the public bathroom at my office, where one day a coworker confronted me and said it was offensive to her. She could hear the pump, she said. She said she "knew what I was up to in there," as if I were plotting to blow up the building or having sex with the janitor.

Meanwhile, Cameron had it easy, at least as I saw it. He was painting and caring for Ava and working a couple of nights a week as a manager at a theater. Once he stayed out all night and came home drunk, which was very uncharacteristic of him.

Where had he been? Why didn't he call? Our fight ended up waking the baby. My anger at myself and my decisions and work situation spilled over into the marriage. I was jealous that my artist husband was home with the baby while I traipsed to the office without her. I hated the work, hated the schedule, hated my life. I felt a physical longing for our daughter that had replaced my longing for him.

And he knew it.

"Can we go lie down sometime," he asked me, "in another room?"

"I want to," I said, "but let me finish nursing her." It hit us both then that I was using our daughter as an excuse not to be intimate. Why I did this I do not fully understand. I think the residual anger from our fights and the situation I found myself in—tired all the time, feeling used up—was an anti-aphrodisiac. If I were a man, I wouldn't be able to get it up. I went over and stood by him and ran my hand down the back of his neck. He pushed it aside and walked into another room.

Soon we began driving upstate on weekends. It was like we were trying to drive to another life, to somehow save ourselves. In each town, we visited real estate offices and paged through newspaper ads, walking through houses and listening to the sound of our shoes against the floor, as if thinking, *Would this house save us? Could it?*

It wasn't until we hit Binghamton, New York, that we found a place we could afford on a reporter's salary. The baby was getting a bit bigger, and on these trips Cameron and I felt closer. We actually embraced and kissed, and one night in a hotel room, we did it the wrong way across the bed, and then again later, he entered me from behind. The baby was sleeping in her car seat, she had begun to snore, and it made us laugh. Maybe moving was the solution.

I had met an editor at the local paper who was enthusiastic about me and I was hired. We bought an old farmhouse that we both liked, with wooden beams that reminded us of the houses out west, when things had been new between us. We packed up our life and moved on.

For a time, as we hoped, geography saved us. The air was different upstate. There seemed to be more of it, along with more birds. At first, the solitude had an arousing effect. We made love on all sorts of surfaces: floors, counters, tables, and of course our bed. But the baby was sleeping in there with us most nights so I could nurse, and that, in time, separated us again.

Again we began to argue. Again he started counting. It had been eight days, fourteen days, and finally nineteen days since we had had sex. I was manipulating him, he said.

"I am just tired," I said.

I had a new job. Cameron was doing the child care. When I came home, they'd be napping together on the couch or playing on the floor. He was good with her, and frankly, again, I was jealous. Why hadn't I arranged a life where I could stay home with her? I would walk through the mall, glancing at the stay-at-home mommies in sweats with their strollers, just passing the time, and feel envy roil over me.

"Why are you always mad at me?" my husband asked one day.

"I'm jealous of your life," I confessed.

"You're different from the person I married," he said. "I liked you better before."

The truth was out. We were falling apart; we no longer

even liked each other much. Then a new stress was added: My seventy-eight-year-old father, who would be diagnosed with Alzheimer's disease, came to live with us in our farmhouse. It was the proverbial straw that broke the marriage's back. Cameron did not want to do all it took to care for him along with the baby, and have a practically sexless marriage to boot.

So, soon after my father arrived, overwhelmed with the amount of work and growing tension in the house, Cameron left. We'd been fighting terribly, not just about my father's care but about the household chores, the baby's activities, the meals he prepared. He felt I didn't appreciate all he was doing. I felt he wasn't doing enough. He felt as if his life had morphed into an endless list of caregiving chores. In the end, we decided to separate, with him going back to the Southwest, leaving me with our baby and my dad. It was winter. Do I have to describe how hard it was? Imagine diapering two generations. Imagine working and caring for them both.

I aged.

We planned to divorce around that time. The marriage seemed simply impossible. But then, about nine months later, he called and told me how much he missed us and asked if he could come back. I realized I'd missed him, too. There was nothing to gain by staying angry or bitter, I reasoned. Plus, I didn't want our daughter to grow up without a father, which was beginning to seem like a very real possibility.

For a while, the sex was hot again and then when things got hard and I grew tired, it would fall away, like a cloak, revealing the truth of our disparities. We were very different ages, at different places in life. Plus, my father's illness was breaking my heart. My husband had not even known his father. We could not understand each other, and the thing that had once saved us—the sensuality that had bridged our gaps—seemed hard to find again. In the years that followed, my husband and I separated and reunited several times, first over my father, then over a younger woman he met. Another time, we separated over no particular incident at all except the damage that had been done.

In the process, anger annihilated my sex drive almost completely. Cameron was angry about my anger. Our bodies felt like strangers' whenever we would try to come together. We had no more children.

One day I realized I had begun to hate him. His paint-stained pants, his cigarette-stained thumbs, the teetering stack of books next to his side of the bed—all the things that had once attracted me to him now conspired against my heart. In our house of dirty laundry and dishes, his free-spirit attitude had begun to translate into laziness. Whatever it was that inspired him to have an *A* (for anarchist) tattooed on one arm, which once had seemed so daring to me, now seemed silly. He left soiled clothes on the floor, dirty cups in the sink. Who did he imagine would pick up after him?

Me, of course. And the thought of that made me boil.

Our daughter was in first grade when I found my sexuality again. We saw a therapist who told us to try. "If you had genuine passion once, you can always get it back," she said. There were other reasons, among them that our child was in school full-time and I didn't have to worry so much about her care. I didn't feel so broken about not being with her. She was growing up, after all. So Cameron and I would fight, then make up. It became a sort of pattern. As I entered my mid-forties, anger became an aphrodisiac for me: I'd boil away until I would melt into a place we shared again, away from dirty socks, dishes, anarchy, and art. Strangely, unpredictably, we found our way back to that place of pure honeyed pleasure that had been our beginning. Once he even commented on it: "Let's fight so we can have make-up sex," he said.

It seemed to me an entirely good idea. So we fought about the dishes. (Why should I be the only one who does them?) We fought about whether or not he was sexist. (Sexist men expect women to do everything—and still be ready for sex at any given moment.) We fought over whether the car needed new tires. Then we fell into bed and did the wild thing. Once our daughter's school called and asked who was picking her up. We had completely forgotten her.

By this time my young husband was twenty-nine, not so young anymore. And I had somehow hit a midlife burst of sexual desire. My breasts, which had seemed foreign and unsexual to me after breast-feeding, felt sexy again. My vagina remembered its former incarnation as a sexual orifice, not a baby-producing one. We had several years of sexual contentment, or at least I did; he was still counting. But I had begun to count as well. When a couple of sexless days went by, I'd begin to yearn for his easy rhythms, his scent on my skin.

Then everything stopped. At thirty-one, my husband of ten years, with whom I had buried two parents, birthed a child, and weathered affairs and separations, suffered a catastrophic heart attack.

It was so unexpected, so out of left field, so plain weird, that neither one of us knew what to make of it. We had seen illness and suffering, but nothing the likes of this.

And it affected us differently. Of course, I was sad and scared. Cameron was rightly terrified. I sat beside him in the hospital with his chest still raw and bleeding through the gauze from his open-heart surgery, praying for his life. So many tubes entered and exited his body it made me imagine a convention of snakes. Above him, a wall of blinking, beeping machines traced all the ways in which he could live or die.

He teetered along in that state for weeks. In adjacent rooms patients came and went, in a few cases to their graves. As I touched his hand a whole new sensation came over me: I was in love. This had nothing to do with lust or anger or sadness or anything I had known before. It was something else. Not exclusive of sex, but not limited to it. If what we had before was broken, now it seemed to be scarred but healing, and healing with a new tenderness, like a place that has been terribly hurt but splinted back together.

This was my daughter's father. My partner. My friend. His fingers seemed suddenly perfect in shape, his eyebrows perfectly etched half moons, his eyes so green they glowed. Even the stitched-up red gash in his chest seemed somehow, I don't know, precious and even darling. Call me crazy.

Cameron survived his heart attack but not as the same man I'd married. He came home frail, thirty pounds thinner, with a basket of pills that included blood thinners such as Coumadin, a drug that made it pretty much impossible for him to achieve an erection. He had a defibrillator installed in his chest that could shock him if his heart beat irregularly, not a fun thought.

You probably think this would make a good place to end this essay. It's a logical conclusion. How can I continue to write about sex with a man who cannot have sex? In fact, my husband's heart attack marked a beginning for us. After he returned from the hospital, we were so happy to have him home that every day seemed as if it should be celebrated. Each moment deserved a party, each kiss seemed as if it should be followed by a sexual encounter.

Our daughter would peek in sometimes in the middle of the night to make sure he was still there. She would graze up against him sometimes in the kitchen, as if to test and see if it was really him or a dream; flesh or imagination.

In bed, we needed some new way to express our love and the new flame of desire that had sprung up between us, like a single candle in a dark room, so we became creative, rediscovering our hands, our mouths, our tongues, our fingers. Once it was him on top, me on bottom, or vice versa. Now it was both of us any which way, spooning, changing, trying things.

The very first time we had sex after he got home had been scary. "Do you want to be on top?" I had asked timidly. "Not really," he said; the gigantic scar down his chest would throb in that position, and it just wouldn't work at all. We settled on side by side, with lots of embracing and kissing and sucking and touching, until finally we were able to both come at once in a way that seemed pretty surprising and didn't actually involve intercourse. It was fun. I was imagining us doing it in secret on the back of a truck somewhere, hidden from other people, an exciting fantasy. But what I think I was really hiding from was that biggest bogeyman of all, death. We were having sex even though by all accounts my younger-than-I-ever-should-have-married husband should have been in his grave. Take that, Mr. Death.

"You are alive," I said.

"I am," he said.

It was like we were both noticing it, really, at that moment, for the first time. That he could live. That we could love. That he could still make paintings. That our daughter still had a father and a mother who loved her father. That we were still a family.

I married a much younger man. And for a time, our sex was electrifying. But these days, I feel as if I am the younger one. I am the stronger one.

You might wonder what has kept us together through so much strife and suffering. You might wonder how we could live with our wounds, both literal and figurative. The answer is that I am so grateful for life. So grateful for sex. Our bodies are learning a new language. Beside me, he moves and I notice each second of it, to the right, the left, up, down, sideways. Next to him I feel my chest rise to meet his, the tiny beads of sweat that we can produce together. We come and then we say thank you. Once sex was merely an activity. Now, for us, it seems like a blessing.

ABOUT THE CONTRIBUTORS

Abiola Abrams is the author of the novel *Dare*, a BET on-camera personality, an independent filmmaker, and host of *The Best Shorts*, an indie film showcase. Her writing has appeared in Eve Ensler's anthology *A Memory, a Monologue, a Rant, and a Prayer* and in *Dirty Words: A Literary Anthology of Sex*. She lives in New York City.

Pari Chang is a former litigator whose personal essays have appeared in the *New York Times*, *Self*, *Glamour*, and *The Bark*. She lives in Manhattan with her family.

Susan Cheever is the author of thirteen books, including her newest, *Desire: Where Sex Meets Addiction*. She lives in New York City.

Elizabeth Cohen is a poet, columnist, reporter, and author of two nonfiction books and two books of poetry. Her book *The Family on Beartown Road* was a *New York Times* Notable Book in 2003. Her essays and articles have appeared in the *New York Times Magazine*, *Newsweek*, and *Glamour*. She lives with her husband and their daughter, Ava, in a farmhouse in upstate New York.

Stephanie Dolgoff is the former health and features director at *Self* magazine. She has written for the *New York Times, O, the Oprah Magazine, Glamour, Redbook,* and *Cosmopolitan.* She lives in New York City with her husband and two daughters.

M. P. Dunleavey writes the "Cost of Living" column for the *New York Times* and is the creator of the award-winning "Women in Red" personal finance series on MSN Money. Her first book, *Money Can Buy Happiness,* won a 2007 Books for a Better Life Award. She lives with her husband and son in upstate New York.

Hope Edelman is the author of four nonfiction books, including the bestsellers *Motherless Daughters* and *Motherless Mothers.* Her articles, essays, and reviews have appeared in numerous publications and have been included in several anthologies, including *The Bitch in the House, Toddler,* and *Blindsided by a Diaper.* She lives in Topanga Canyon, California, with her husband and two daughters.

Valerie Frankel is the author of fourteen novels, including *The Accidental Virgin, The Girlfriend Curse, I Take This Man,* and five nonfiction titles, including her memoir, *Thin Is the New Happy.* She writes for many national magazines and lives in Brooklyn with her husband and two daughters.

Lori Gottlieb wrote the national bestseller *Stick Figure: A Diary of My Former Self,* named an American Library Association Best Book of 2001. A regular commentator for NPR's *All Things Considered,* Gottlieb has also contributed to the *New York Times,* the *Los Angeles Times,* the *Atlantic*

Monthly, *Time*, *People*, *Elle*, *Glamour*, and *Slate*. She is the coauthor of *Inside the Cult of Kibu* and *I Love You, Nice to Meet You*. She lives with her son in Los Angeles.

Jane Juska is the author of the memoirs *A Round-Heeled Woman* and *Unaccompanied Women*. She taught English for forty years in high school, college, and prison. Her work has appeared in magazines and anthologies, and she is currently writing a novel. She lives in Berkeley, California.

Deanna Kizis is a screenwriter and the author of two novels, *How to Meet Cute Boys* and *Finishing Touches*. She writes for *Elle*, *Harper's Bazaar*, *Self*, *Glamour*, and *Entertainment Weekly*, among other publications. She lives with her husband, two dogs, and a cat in Los Angeles.

Jenny Lee is a television comedy writer whose credits include ABC's *Samantha Who?* and ABC's *In Case of Emergency*. She is the author of three collections of humor essays: *Skinny Bitching: A Thirty-Something Woman Mouths Off About Age, Angst, Pregnancy Pressure, and the Dieting Battles You'll Never Win*; *What Wendell Wants: How to Tell if You're Obsessed with Your Dog*; and *I Do. I Did. Now What?! Life After the Wedding Dress*. She lives in Los Angeles.

Ali Liebegott is the author of the Lambda Award–winning books *The IHOP Papers* and *The Beautifully Worthless*. She lives in San Francisco and is working on an illustrated novel entitled *The Crumb People*.

Meredith Maran is the author of several nonfiction books and an award-winning journalist who writes for *Salon*, *Playboy*,

More, *Self*, *Real Simple*, and the *San Francisco Chronicle*. She lives in Oakland, California, with her wife-to-be.

Anna Marrian has written essays, articles, and reviews for *Newsweek*, *The Observer*, the *Village Voice*, *Jane*, *Glamour*, the *New York Post*, and *Modern Bride*. She is the recipient of a Hertog Fellowship, teaches creative writing at Hunter College, and is currently at work on a memoir.

Brett Paesel is the author of *Mommies Who Drink: Sex, Drugs, and Other Distant Memories of an Ordinary Mom*. She has developed television shows for HBO, Fox, WB, Comedy Central, and Lifetime. She lives with her husband and two sons in Los Angeles.

Suzanne Paola (Susanne Antonetta) is the author of four books of poetry and two books of nonfiction, including *Body Toxic: An Environmental Memoir*, which was a 2001 *New York Times* Notable Book and won an American Book Award that same year. Her most recent book, *A Mind Apart: Travels Through a Neurodiverse World*, received the NAMI/Ken Johnson Award for achievement in handling the topic of mental illness. She lives in Bellingham, Washington.

Bella Pollen is the author of four novels: *Blue Movies*, *B Love*, *Hunting Unicorns*, and *Midnight Cactus*. She has written for the *Times* of London, the *Sunday Telegraph*, *Vogue*, and the *Spectator*. She lives in Notting Hill Gate, London, with her husband and four children.

Julie Powell is the author of the bestselling memoir *Julie & Julia: My Year of Cooking Dangerously*. She is the recipient of two James Beard awards and the 2006 Quill Book Award for Debut Author of the Year, and has contributed to *Bon Appetit, Food & Wine*, the *New York Times Magazine*, and *Archaeology* magazine. She lives in Queens, New York.

Susan Shapiro, a Manhattan-based writing teacher, has written for the *New York Times*, the *Washington Post*, and the *Los Angeles Times*. She is the author of *Five Men Who Broke My Heart, Lighting Up, Secrets of a Fix-up Fanatic*, and *Only as Good as Your Word*. She lives in Greenwich Village with her husband, a TV/film writer.

Abby Sher is the author of *Kissing Snowflakes*, a young adult novel, and will publish a memoir in the spring of 2009. Her work appears in *Modern Love: Tales of Love and Obsession*, and she has also written for the *New York Times*, the *Los Angeles Times, Self, Jane*, and *Redbook*. She has written and performed for the Second City in Chicago, the Magnet Theater in New York City, and several international arts festivals. She lives in Brooklyn, New York, with her husband.

Lauren Slater is a psychologist and the author of six books, including *Welcome to My Country, Prozac Diary, Lying: A Metaphorical Memoir*, and *Opening Skinner's Box: Great Psychological Experiments of the 20th Century*. She was guest editor of *Best American Essays, 2006*. She is a contributing editor to *Elle* magazine and writes for the *New York Times*, the *Missouri Review, Self*, and other publications. She lives in Massachusetts and New Hampshire with her husband and two children.

Susanna Sonnenberg is the author of the memoir *Her Last Death*, which was a 2008 *New York Times* and *Los Angeles*

Times bestseller. Her work has appeared in *O, the Oprah Magazine*, *Elle*, *Self*, and the anthology *About What Was Lost*. She lives with her husband and two sons in Montana.

Martha Southgate's most recent novels are *Third Girl from the Left* and *The Fall of Rome*. She has written for many magazines and newspapers, including the *New York Times Book Review*. She is the recipient of a 2002 New York Foundation for the Arts grant and has received fellowships from the MacDowell Colony and the Bread Loaf Writers Conference. She lives in Brooklyn with her husband and two children.

Betsy Stephens has written for *Cosmopolitan*, *Fitness*, *Ladies' Home Journal*, and the *Wall Street Journal*. She coauthored the book *100 Jobs in Technology* and was a contributing writer for *100 Jobs in the Environment*. She lives in New Jersey with her husband, Dean; son, Pete; and daughter, Piper.

Cheryl Strayed's debut novel, *Torch*, was a finalist for the Great Lakes Book Award and was selected by the *Oregonian* as one of the top ten books of 2006. Strayed's personal essays have appeared in the *New York Times Magazine*, the *Washington Post Magazine*, *Allure*, *Self*, and the *Sun*, among others, and have been selected twice for inclusion in *The Best American Essays*. She lives in Portland, Oregon, with her husband and their two children.

ABOUT THE EDITOR

Paula Derrow is the articles director at *Self* magazine and teaches writing workshops for MediaBistro.com. She has worked for more than twenty years at a variety of magazines and other media, including *Glamour*, *Harper's Bazaar*, and Lifetime Television. She lives in New York City.